Simulation Games

in Learning

Edited by SARANE S. BOOCOCK

and E. O. SCHILD

With a preface by JAMES S. COLEMAN

SAGE PUBLICATIONS, INC. / Beverly Hills, Calif.

For information address:

SAGE PUBLICATIONS, INC.
275 South Beverly Drive
Beverly Hills, California 90212

Second Printing

Printed in the United States of America

Library of Congress Catalog Card No. 68-21913

Standard Book Number 8039-1002-9

to

PAUL

and

YAIR

who think that learning is great fun

CONTENTS ■

5

Preface

JAMES S. COLEMAN

■ The fascination of games is a curious matter. It must arise in part from the arbitrary setting aside of the vaguely defined but complex and deadly serious rules which govern everyday life, and substitution of a set of explicit and simple rules whose consequences vanish when the game is over. But if I were to attempt to explain this fascination in general terms I should never succeed. I will instead introspect, and ask what it is that fascinates me, not as a player in a game but rather as a sociologist in constructing them. For in this there is certainly something to be explained. Why should self-respecting sociologists, who could be working in research directions that would gain far more recognition from colleagues, instead toy with games in a field — educational sociology — that has long languished in the cellar of the discipline?

Let us even take as given, for the sake of argument, that games have remarkable potentials for learning — that they could transform the techniques by which children learn in schools and thus transform children that schools presently leave untouched or mildly "educated." Important as such effects are, they are no reason for the sociologist to excite himself about games, no reason to leave his other work for the fascination of constructing and testing games. The sociologist is not, after all, educator; his task instead is to study, and hope to better understand, society and social organization.

What is it then that fascinates me and the other students of social organization whose chapters constitute this book? What makes us abandon the proper behavior of sociologists and fix instead on games that may induce learning in children?

To come to an answer requires first a closer look at the very notion of games and the peculiar relation they bear to social life. A game — nearly any game, not merely those termed "simulation games" — constitutes a kind of caricature of social life. It is a mag-

7

nification of some aspect of social interaction, excluding all else, tearing this aspect of social interaction from its social context and giving it a special context of its own. Even those games that are farthest from those described in this issue exemplify this. A boxing or wrestling match abstracts from its context the direct physical violence that resides in social life and recreates this violence under a set of explicit rules. When I was a boy in the midwest cornhusking contests abstracted one activity from the life of farmers, established a set of rules, and gave this activity a temporary but central position for the participants.

This unique relation of games to life can be seen even better in other ways. The informal games of young children appear to be crucial means for learning about life and experimenting with life. One of the most perceptive students of the social and intellectual development of young children, Jean Piaget, has observed this development in the simple games children play, such as the game of marbles. It appears that for children, games are more than a caricature of life; they are an introduction to life — an introduction to the idea of rules, which are imposed on all alike, an introduction to the idea of playing under different sets of rules, that is, the idea of different roles, an introduction to the idea of aiding another person and of knowing that one can expect aid from another, an introduction to the idea of working toward a collective goal and investing one's self in a collectivity larger than himself. It appears that games serve, for the young child, all these functions as an introduction to life.

Still another aspect of this special linkage between games and life is provided by a recent development in psychiatry — a turn from the emphasis on traumatic events in the patient's life, on oedipal complexes and mysterious fixations, toward an emphasis on the often destructive behavior strategies that adults use toward others. I refer principally to the book *Games People Play*, by Eric Berne. While Berne's use of the term "games" to describe these strategies extend the meaning beyond that used in these pages, the very use of the term indicates the close liaison between explicit games and the behavior people engage in as part of everyday life.

All these illustrations are intended to convey the intimate connections between games and social life. If there is such an intimate relation, and a few sociologists are wagering their professional lives that there is, then games themselves in all their forms become of great potential interest for the sociologist. It may be that he, just as the young child, can gain insight into the functioning of social life through the construction and use of games.

But beyond this there are certain special characteristics to the games described in this issue, and to the games that sociologists find of particular interest. Some games involve the interaction of a player with his physical environment, for example a maze or a jig-saw puzzle, or block puzzles, or a cornhusking contest, or a pole vault. These games abstract from life either certain physical skills or certain intellectual skills of inference from physical evidence. Other games such as number puzzles or crossword puzzles involve interaction with a symbolic environment, in these two instances an environment of numbers and an environment of language.

Such abstractions of activities from life hold some interest for the sociologist, but much less interest than another class of games which abstract from life some elements of social relations or social organization. Many games incorporate some aspects of such relations, but a few games incorporate enough such relations that a special term has been used to describe them: social simulation games. Such games pluck out of social life generally (including economic, political and business life) a circumscribed arena, and attempt to reconstruct the principal rules by which behavior in this arena is governed and the principal rewards that it holds for the participants. Such a game both in its construction and in its playing then becomes of extreme interest to the student of social organization. For from it he may learn about those problems of social relations that are his central concern. The game may provide for him that degree of abstraction from life and simplification of life that allows him to understand better certain fundamentals of social organization.

It is this, then, that makes the sociologist fascinated with a certain kind of game — the possibility of learning from this caricature of social relations about those social relations themselves.

But the question immediately arises, how possibly could a professional sociologist and a sixth or twelfth grade child learn about social life from the same game? My answer is that it is precisely appropriate that this be so. For children have too long been taught things that are "known," and have too seldom been allowed to discover for themselves the principles governing a situation. It may well be in the physical sciences that the young student and the professional scientist cannot learn from the same environment. (Yet Einstein, in a paper he wrote to explain the meandering of streams, mentioned that although the mechanical principles involved were well-known and simple in application to the problem, he had met very few physicists who understood these principles well enough to use them in the simple application. I suspect that a perceptive high school student would suffer no serious disadvantage relative to a professional physicist.) But it is certainly the case that the professional sociologist and the young student can learn from a single game.

It is also true that what is meant by learning is quite different for the sixth grader and the professional sociologist. The sixth grader is learning to incorporate this experience into his own life, learning to recognize the dominant aspects of this social environment so that he can respond appropriately to them when he meets such an environment in his own life. The professional sociologist is learning how to describe in general terms the functioning of this system of relations, learning to fit the system of relations to an abstract conceptual scheme.

This, then, is the fascination of the sociologist with social simulation games — the opportunity to learn about social organization by forming a caricature of such organization and then observing this caricature. This is supplemented by his fascination in seeing young children learn as much about such environments as he himself can know how to transmit through the construction of the game.

Acknowledgements

■ Much of the stimulus to present design of and research on simulation games was given by James S. Coleman, whose own work has deeply permeated and shaped the whole field. His contribution to this book is even more direct. He co-edited with us two issues of the *American Behavioral Scientist,* from which this volume grew, and he participated in planning both its structure and much of its content. It is only because he is spending this academic year in England and because he objects so strongly to taking credit for joint work unless he contributes an equal amount of time, that his name appears on this page rather than on the cover.

Beyond his specific contributions we owe a great intellectual debt to his ideas, and our own work has been strongly influenced by his perspectives. In a very real sense this book is as much his as ours.

To the Carnegie Corporation we owe more than the traditional thanks for providing the financial support for our work on simulation games. First, they saw the possibilities of the technique at a time when most educators and social scientists considered the notion of games as learning devices not only impractical but also somewhat absurd. They have since continued and increased their support. Second, having once approved our general research proposal, they gave us virtually complete freedom to carry on our research in whatever directions seemed most fruitful — without calls for regular reports, strict budgetary accounting, or other justifications of our actions. This final point deserves special emphasis, because this seems refreshingly atypical, and because we believe that this attitude has been a contributing factor to the great variety and amount of research activities we have been able to carry out, only part of which is reflected in this book.

Two persons at Johns Hopkins deserve our special thanks. Mrs. Audrey Suhr has, in addition to her duties as field director of the games project, given us valuable editorial assistance with the *American Behavioral Scientist* issues and with this book. We are also indebted to Miss Arlene Roane, the project secretary, who prepared virtually all of the manuscript, with incredible speed and accuracy.

S.S.B.
E.O.S.

CONTRIBUTORS

CLARK C. ABT.   Abt Associates, Inc., Cambridge, Massachusetts.

EUGENE H. BAKER.   School of Education, Northwestern University, Evanston, Illinois; and Lincolnwood Public Schools, Lincolnwood, Ill.

SARANE S. BOOCOCK.   Department of Social Relations, The Johns Hopkins University, Baltimore, Maryland.

PHILIP M. BURGESS.   Department of Political Science, The Ohio State University, Columbus, Ohio.

MARILYN CLAYTON.   Director of Instructional Research, Elementary Social Studies Program, Educational Services, Inc., Cambridge, Mass.

JAMES S. COLEMAN.   Department of Social Relations, The Johns Hopkins University, Baltimore, Maryland.

WILLIAM R. DILL.   Program Director, Education Research and Development, IBM, White Plains, New York.

DALE C. FARRAN.   Games Project Director, The North Carolina Advancement School, Winston-Salem, North Carolina.

MICHAEL INBAR.   Department of Sociology, University of Michigan, Ann Arbor, Michigan.

ERNEST KOBROW.   School of Business Administration, Tulane University, New Orleans, Louisiana.

JAMES L. McKENNEY.   Graduate School of Business Administration, Harvard University, Cambridge, Massachusetts.

JAMES A. ROBINSON.   Department of Political Science, The Ohio State University, Columbus, Ohio.

RICHARD ROSENBLOOM.   Graduate School of Business Administration, Harvard University; and Social Studies Program, Educational Services, Inc., Cambridge, Massachusetts.

E. O. SCHILD.   Department of Sociology, Hebrew University, Jerusalem, Israel.

WILLIAM H. STARBUCK.   Department of Social Relations, The Johns Hopkins University, Baltimore, Maryland.

BARBARA B. VARENHORST.   Counseling Psychologist, Gunn Senior High School, Palo Alto, California.

RICHARD L. WING.   Coordinator of Curriculum Research, Center for Educational Services and Research, BOCES, Westchester County, New York.

GERALD ZALTMAN.   Department of Social Relations, The Johns Hopkins University, Baltimore, Maryland.

Introduction

■ This is a book about an educational innovation: *games with simulated environments,* or simulation games. These games have two major uses: one, as research tools for the study of the process simulated (in particular as heuristics in theory-building); two, as teaching devices. It is with this latter function we are here concerned.

The book is a progress report on recent thinking and findings in this area. As such it is intended both for educational practitioners and for behavioral scientists. For the practitioner it is an introduction to a new and, we believe, powerful educational technology. Few observers have watched simulation gaming in the classroom without becoming excited (sometimes unduly excited) about the potential of this technique. We cannot aspire to such effect by writing about games, but the reader will find discussions of the rationale behind the technique as well as presentation of some evidence on its effects.

For the behavioral scientist the book may serve as a challenge to engage in further — and better — research in this field. In the Preface, Coleman has pointed to the peculiar fascination of games from which the sophisticated scientist and inexperienced teenager both can learn. Interest in a simulation as a research tool easily leads to interest in the impact of the simulation on the players — i.e., their learning. And as this book will clearly show: we are far from reaching the point of diminishing returns in research on learning from games.

We call simulation games an educational *innovation*. True, there is nothing new in the very use of games in the classroom. Individual teachers have long used games or game-like devices to arouse student interest and to dramatize materials. What is new about the games discussed in this book is the *combination* of the ancient technique of gaming with the relatively recent technique

13

of simulation.[1] Moreover, when games and play have been accepted as appropriate for the classroom, intention has primarily been to arouse interest and to motivate the student to further study. The games here discussed are intended to *teach*, as they are, just as a chapter in a textbook or a lecture can teach. (In this connection it is worthwhile to note that the traditional uses of games have generally been limited to the lower grades, the age of play, but the majority of the studies reported in this book refer to high school students.)

From several viewpoints it seems appropriate at the present time to offer a progress report on this new technology. Tests of existing games have produced intriguing results, and a number of individuals and groups at universities, research centers, and school systems are currently engaged in designing new games on a variety of subjects. (Some of the more important centers are described in the appendix at the end of the book.) Hundreds of schools and educational organizations have adopted one or more games or are in the process of doing so. But in spite of this proliferation and diffusion of educational games, there has until recently been little serious evaluation of their worth as teaching tools. It is testimony to the enthusiasm which a game session typically arouses in the observer — and to the schools' great need for new teaching approaches — that simulation games in many cases have been adopted with little empirical evidence or systematic theoretical rationale for their effectiveness.

Much of the evidence as well as newer theoretical considerations have not been published and are thus known only to a small "family" of games researchers. (And what has been published is spread over several journals and is not likely to catch the attention of the educational practitioner or the behavioral scientist unless he engages in a major search operation.) At the same time the demand for information which has been stimulated by actual use (and probably also by publicity in newsmagazines and on television) indicates the need for a work more comprehensive than is now available.

Furthermore, the development of future research activity is contingent on the delineation of the present frontier of knowledge. We hope that this book is — for better or for worse — such a representative description of the present state of the art.[2] Thus, this is not a definitive treatise on simulation gaming; nor are the chap-

14

ters the zenith of systematic theorizing or sophisticated research design. It *is*, we believe, a valid picture of what is known today about simulation games in learning and of the current work in this area.

For the reader who has never participated in or observed a simulation game in action and who is uncertain just what a simulation game is all about, it will be helpful to read descriptions of some games before proceeding further. While we have not devoted a separate section to game resumes (nor have we even attempted to include papers on all of the best or best-known games), descriptions of individual games are included in a number of the chapters. In Part II, the chapters by Boocock, by Schild, and by Baker, include game descriptions, as do the chapters by Inbar and by Zaltman in Part III. The chapter by Wing describes games developed for use on a computer — the only games of this sort included in this book.

Reading several game descriptions, while not a satisfactory substitute for actual game experience, will give the uninitiated some notion of what simulations are like and of the wide variety of social studies topics and problems that can be handled by this technique.

A CAPSULE HISTORY

Although the design of simulation games for classroom use is essentially a phenomenon of the last decade, the field has already passed through different stages of development. There seem to have been three distinct (if overlapping) phases.

Phase 1: acceptance on faith. During this phase, which lasted until 1962 or 1963, social scientists "discovered" gaming as a technique for the classroom,[3] and several games were developed and field tested. It was a time of great and diffuse enthusiasm for a technique, without much concern with collecting "hard" evidence to support the enthusiasm. Reports were mainly in the form of descriptions of new or proposed games and claims for what they would or could do in the schools. The spirit of the age is exemplified in a relatively comprehensive monograph on business gaming, which concluded that, "By virtue of its unique characteristics it has added considerably to teaching capability in this area," while admitting in the same paragraph that "few specific instances of

15

comprehensive statistical validation are as yet available" (Greenlaw *et al.*, 1962, p. 67).

The lack of rigorous research at this stage is not really surprising. Because the field was new and small, most researchers were concentrating upon designing games rather than evaluating them. Second, as Bruner has pointed out, lack of adequate experimentation is a characteristic of educational research generally. Finally, game sessions are so exciting to observe that the interest and involvement of players were often accepted as evidence of learning.

Phase 2: post-honeymoon. During the years 1963-1965, some researchers attempted controlled experiments with games. Generally inconclusive (or even negative) results led them to rather sobering conclusions: (a) that games are not a panacea for all educational ills; (b) that the games in their present form have serious flaws; and (c) that neither standard tests nor the relatively crude instruments designed specifically to evaluate a particular game or games are adequate or sufficient measures for the impact of games.

The most important study of this period was the evaluation of the Northwestern Inter-Nation Simulation by James Robinson and his colleagues (described in Robinson, 1965; and Anderson *et al.*, 1964). Comparing college students who played the INS with control classes who studied the same material via case studies, Robinson found few significant differences on a number of measures of interest and achievement — and not all of these differences favored the game. The study exemplifies a number of assumptions and problems of this phase. For example, the basic hypothesis (that the simulation would be more effective than the case studies on all the criteria investigated) was not only unrealistic but also — in the absence of any systematic theorizing — did not specify what distinguished the game from other teaching methods (and thus what specific results might be expected from the INS).

Experimentation with the first game developed at Johns Hopkins, a simulation of a national Presidential election campaign, was more encouraging and produced a number of clues as to the nature of game effects, but many of the findings were not consistent, not statistically significant, or otherwise difficult to interpret (Boocock, 1963).

The unsettling results of early experimentation could lead to at least two different attitudes toward the technique. One is to maintain the working hypothesis that games do teach — but that we do not know why and how. As a result we do not know what to look for in research on games. The following appraisal, of management gaming, illustrates this attitude: "We know little about the effectiveness of management games as an instrument of instruction. Indeed, we do not even know for sure how to distinguish a good game from a bad one" (Thorelli and Graves, 1964, p. 25). The conclusion is then to continue research in the hope of arriving at more adequate theorizing as well as research designs.

A second reaction is to retreat with respect to the original hypothesis. While games cannot teach in the way we once believed, they can produce certain limited effects, especially in the area of motivation. The most thorough statement of this view is found in a paper by Cherryholmes (1966), which summarizes and synthesizes a number of reports. Cherryholmes concludes that games do motivate, but that there is not any substantial evidence that they teach facts or problem-solving skills, or that they induce critical thinking, any more effectively than other methods of learning. It is also worth noting that one of the major ongoing research projects on simulation gaming,[4] is focusing upon the extent to which games arouse interest and change attitudes; it is, at least for the present, foregoing efforts to measure learning directly induced by the games.

Phase 3: realistic optimism. During the past year or two, the trend has been toward renewed (albeit more tempered) optimism, based upon accumulated experience with a number of games. The chapters in this volume are a representation of this new phase, which can be characterized by progress on three fronts:

(a) field testing of a number of different simulation games in a wide variety of educational settings. While it is still true that adoption of games has been concentrated in certain types of settings, we are also gaining varied enough experience so as to get some feeling for the most appropriate use of various games (or for the ways to alter a game to make it more valuable for a particular kind of student);

(b) accumulation of a pool of data on the learning effects of specific games. In several cases, a particular game has been evaluated by one or more researchers other than its designer, a necessary development if evaluation is to be free

17

of bias (for example, the chapter by Farran, in Part III, discusses tests with the Hopkins Life Career Game by persons not directly connected with the Hopkins project);

(c) revision and clarification of "theory" or claims concerning what games can do in the classroom, based upon the additional experience with games described in (a) above. It is interesting, e.g., to compare the Burgess-Robinson chapter in Part IV with the claims made by Robinson *et al*. In the evaluation of the INS cited under Phase 2.

We shall now elaborate on some of the issues on which this recent research has been focused, and on the conclusions and problems emerging from this work.

THE FUNCTION OF SIMULATION GAMES

One of the essential differences between Phase 3 and the "retreatist" reaction to Phase 2 lies in their views of the learning functions of simulation games. A natural conclusion of the post-honeymoon phase is that the sole or major function of games is to increase interest and motivation, and perhaps thereby facilitate *subsequent* learning (which presumably would take place by conventional methods). Games in themselves should not be expected to teach anything.

Ignoring for a moment the validity of this assertion (which will be challenged below), both its origins and its implications bear further examination, for it represents a view of the learning process and of children that is relatively widespread. It is tempting to term this view "inverse puritanism." By "puritanism" we here mean a belief that goes something as follows: learning is a very serious business; games are fun; therefore students cannot learn from games. Given this assumption, old-fashioned puritanism (which still dominates curriculum committees and school boards in many school districts) draws the conclusion that games, like other educational "frills," have no place in the schools. Inverse puritanism, on the other hand, asserts that schools ought to allow for play and games, because they provide morale-building relaxation from the "real" (and inherently unpleasant) business of learning. But one should not expect children to learn anything from them.

We suspect that a similar attitude is behind the greater readiness of many educators to accept games for "culturally deprived" children or "slow learners," than for bright, able students. With some exaggeration, the attitude of many teachers who work with the former is that these youngsters are unable to learn anything anyway, so the important thing is to keep them happy and out of serious trouble. Games are an appropriate technique for this purpose. Bright students (or my own kids), on the other hand, are in school to learn something, so they have no time for games.

Our own inclinations, and a good amount of the data presented in the following sections of this book, lead us to disagree with this argument. It is unquestionably true that games can generate great interest and involvement (although it is still an open question under what conditions this interest transfers to the study of related subject-matter by other methods). But we also believe that games in themselves teach, *that the players learn from their very participation in the game.* The chapters in Part I propose a number of possible learning effects of simulation games, and suggest some of the mechanisms by which such learning occurs. Proof of the learning effectiveness of games is, however, obviously an empirical question, and Part II offers empirical evidence for our assertion. The studies in Part II show that learning of various kinds — intellectual learning, learning of strategies, attitude changes which are closely related to factual learning, and so on — was a direct consequence of several simulation games.[5] (The studies in Part III go even beyond this and investigate for whom or under what conditions learning is *particularly* strong.)

As for the contention that games are appropriate for the weak but not for the strong student, it happens that games may have a special value for the culturally deprived or the slow student — but not for the reason given above (that these children are unable to learn). At the same time, however, the technique seems also to hold a particular attraction and utility for the bright student. Part IV will present some of the reasoning behind this apparently contradictory argument.

EVALUATION OF LEARNING IN SIMULATION GAMES

The issue of the learning value of simulation games is, of course, more complicated than just asserting that games teach. It is not very enlightening to know that any half-decent game will teach something to somebody; and not even the greatest enthusiast would claim that games can teach everything better to all students than any other method. An adequate understanding of a given game would involve knowing what content is taught by the game; under what conditions (including what type of players) it is most effective; and — a crucial issue for adoption and the one which caused the "retreatism" of Phase 2 — whether it teaches particular things better than alternative method(s).

We shall discuss the first questions in the subsequent section, and here turn to the thorny problem of evaluating a game relative to other methods. Ideally the research design for a comparison study would be a version of the classical experimental design in which the control group or groups would be taught the same subject matter covered in the game by one or more alternative methods (preferably including one other new or "novel" method, to control for the possible "Hawthorne effect" of the game). There are, however, numerous difficulties in executing this research design — and even a quick review of the chapters in Parts II and III of this book will show that all their research designs depart in some respects from the ideal model.

Just setting up comparable experimental and control groups is more difficult in practice than in theory. Given the structure of most schools, individual assignment to experimental and control groups is seldom practical, and matching pairs of individual students seldom possible. (The Boocock chapter in Part II describes one of the few experiments in which assignment on an individual basis was done.) Assignment by *classes* is usually the best the researcher can do, and he is lucky if he can match classes on some group measures (e.g., mean IQ or achievement scores), can have the matched classes taught by the same teacher, and can designate the classes as experimental or control by some random procedure.[6]

Controlling the behavior of the persons administering the game is another problem.

It is well known that almost any course works well in the classroom if it is taught by its inventors or by a few of their highly trained converts . . . To get a valid test of feasibility, you must turn over the program to teachers who are a fair sample of the people who would be teaching it if it were adopted on the scale for which it was intended (Moise, 1964, p. 175).

20

Doing this, of course, means lesser control over how the simulation is introduced and administered. How can a researcher be sure that two or more teachers supposedly using the "same" teaching techniques are in fact presenting materials in the same way? And even the same teacher using both techniques is liable to have some emotional investment in the success of one of the techniques.

A final problem in comparison studies concerns the nature of the activity in the control groups. Teaching the "same" content to the control group implies not only that the game designer has designated exactly what results should be obtained from the game and has designed a test to measure this accurately, but also that he can match the game with another teaching device in terms of subject matter covered, level of difficulty, clarity of instructions, and so on. The difficulty is compounded in that educational research in the past has indicated that even minor changes within a set of teaching materials can change its results.[7]

The chapters by Baker and Wing (in Part II) represent the most systematic attempts to communicate the content of the simulation to the control groups, and both studies may be interpreted as showing a higher effectiveness of games than conventional teaching methods. (Baker's research design has an additional control in that he himself taught both the experimentation and control classes — which, however, introduces other problems.) The studies reported by Boocock also represent efforts to take account of possible Hawthorne effects, although with partial success only.[8]

A final point about the interpretation of comparison studies. The Baker and Wing studies both do indicate advantages of the simulation over the conventional method. But even if the mean learning scores in experimental and control groups were equal in a given study, this would not necessarily mean that the game was not superior to the alternative method *for certain types of students*. Indeed, there is evidence that learning in simulation games is only weakly correlated with learning by conventional methods (Inbar, 1965; Cohen *et al.*, 1964). The implication would seem to be that we should search for ways in which games and other methods can be combined and integrated — so that all students are reached by one or more approaches which suit their individual learning style.

But this brings us back to the basic questions raised before — on the *differential* effect of games, with different players and under different conditions. In a sense these questions are specific reflections of the general issue: what are the mechanisms by which games induce learning and what are the parameters of these mechanisms?

THE MECHANISMS AND CONDITIONS OF LEARNING

The difficulty of this issue is derived from a unique feature of simulation games. First of all, it is clear that they constitute a new educational *technology*. New technology is usually preceded by basic scientific knowledge. This knowledge, of causal processes, of specific mechanisms and parameters, is the basis on which the technology is constructed. (Hence, also the reluctance of many scientists to work on technology; it is literally *applied* science, and does not in itself produce new knowledge.) In the present case, however, the sequence has been reversed: we have a technology which works — but we do not really know why. This is a rather unusual situation in behavioral science. The reverse is more well-known: a body of apparently well-established scientific propositions from which no effective technology has been developed. And we do, of course, have some cases of technology emerging from basic knowledge; an example in the educational context is the "programmed instruction" which is based on much research on the shaping of behavior. But the present case is rather unique.

This problem has not to any important extent been remedied by subsequent "basic science"-research of the type needed. To some degree the designers of games are themselves to blame for this situation. They (and for "they" read also "we") have been so fascinated with the possibility of really *changing* cognitions, attitudes, skills in real life, that they did not pause to undertake the particular type of experimentation needed to unravel the specific variables involved. It is a quite refreshing experience for a social scientist to be able to walk into a classroom, to initiate a certain type of interaction (i.e., start a game) and to be pretty sure what will happen. And as game designers are subject to the same laws of behavior as anybody else, they have persisted in the behavior for which they were reinforced: when designing a game they have thrown anything in that was likely to make it succeed. But in order to specify the factors which make the game succeed, the strategy should have been different. The need is for experimental designs with different versions of the games, so as to establish which factors really are important and which not. Such experimentation implies using game versions which are expected to fail (i.e., the versions without the factor hypothesized to be important). This, to construct games which are to fail, requires some self-sacrifice on part of the designer.

As a result, we have little knowledge of the mechanisms underlying the impact of the games. In the absence of detailed answers, game designing remains something of an art. And perhaps disagreements between game researchers result, in part, from the fact that (in a paraphrase of Skinner) "some designers have more luck than others" — and hence reach more rosy estimates of the impact of games.

In this situation explicit theoretical rationales for simulation games assume particular importance. It is not necessarily a question of a formally structured "theory" from which highly specific propositions can be logically deduced; in the present state of the field the researcher can be greatly helped even by informal theorizing, which provides heuristics: which phenomena are likely to be rewarding as objects of study. Following Lewin's famous dictum "There is nothing so practical as a good theory," we have included some such rationales in Part I.

Another way of attacking the basic problem of the mechanisms by which games work is to investigate the conditions which determine their effectiveness. The chapters in Part III represent the beginning of such enterprise: the study of parameters (which in comparative research designs become "variables") that might affect the perceptions, play, and learning of the players. Also the future oriented chapters of Part IV include more diffuse conjectures about the types of students who may be most affected by simulation games and about some of the factors (e.g., training of teachers) which should be taken into account when large-scale adoption of games occurs.

We believe that the available evidence, as reviewed in this volume, justifies a general claim that simulation games are not just a refreshment from "real" learning, nor a special method for handling those students from whom little learning is expected, but that games themselves have a direct impact on intellectual learning, attitudes, and strategies, so that even brief playing sessions induce measurable effects. If so, it is the type of studies presented in Part III which acquire the major importance. We already know that games work; we need more knowledge of how and why.

If we are right in this interpretation of the chapters to follow, it seems that this "progress report" indeed can report progress.

S.S.B. and E.O.S.

NOTES

1. In a sense, even games with simulated environments are not new. War games, really a type of simulated game, have been in existence for centuries, and have been used by most governments for training and prediction purposes. However, it is only since World War II that simulations have found any extended use in the social sciences, and their introduction into elementary and secondary schools is very recent.

   The aspect of simulation also distinguishes these games from some other games recently developed for classroom use (e.g., to teach mathematics, chemistry, logic). It may be that all teaching games have properties in common; in this book, however, we are only concerned with simulation.

2. We have therefore preferred not to reprint older studies. With one exception, all chapters were prepared especially for this volume or for two special issues of the *American Behavioral Scientist,* October and November, 1966 (edited by James S. Coleman and the present editors).

3. The technique was already being accepted on a large scale in the business management field. By the early 1960s, over a hundred management games were in use in business schools and executive training programs. Some of the games designed for school use borrow heavily from games in these two areas. Simulations were also being used in the field of foreign affairs. Most were for the purpose of predicting the consequences of alternative foreign policies and weapons systems, although some were adapted for training purposes.

4. Project Simile, at Western Behavioral Sciences Institute, La Jolla, California.

5. It goes without saying that assuming that intellectual learning is produced in the actual play of a game in no way conflicts with the study of the indirect, attitude-mediating, effects of games. It does, however, reflect a different view of the *major* functions of simulations — and therefore a different view of the most fruitful direction of further experimentation with games.

6. There is, of course, a large possibility of bias if assignment is not random. It is difficult, for example, to evaluate much of the early research on "progressive" education, since the children

attending such classes or schools were a self-selected group, differing from the general population of children in background, motivation, and abilities. It is likewise difficult to evaluate the results of simulation games which are tested with students who have elected a course involving simulation or have volunteered or been selected by teachers to participate in a game.

7. For example, it has been found in research on programmed instruction that simply shifting the *order* of a set of frames can produce different results with students and, conversely, that making apparently large changes in a given program often has no measurable effects (Silberman, 1962, pp. 16-17). Indeed the most consistent finding in studies comparing the relative effectiveness of different teaching methods is no significant difference — or a difference in a direction inconsistent with other similar studies (Boocock, 1966, pp. 4-18).

8. The reader interested in a more detailed discussion of the refinements of experimental design is directed to Campbell and Stanley, 1963. A sensible consideration of the practical problems involved in designing tests to measure the effectiveness of planned social change is contained in Hyman, Wright, and Hopkins, 1962, Part I.

Another way of controlling for the Hawthorne effect in games has been offered by Doris Entwisle (personal communication), who has applied aspects of placebo-effect studies from medical research to the evaluation of educational methods. Professor Entwisle has suggested an adaptation of this design, in which a control group would play a "null" game — i.e., one which did not contain the information covered in the experimental game. This would control for the Hawthorne effect *per se,* and comparison between the groups playing the experimental game and those playing the null game would indicate whether the former was producing desired learning effects apart from its attraction as a game. The research design in the Boocock chapter (in Part II) is similar to this model, in that each of the two games in a sense acts as a null game for the other when the specific content learning of the latter is being evaluated.

REFERENCES

Anderson, L. F. *et al. A Comparison of Simulation, Case Studies, and Problem Papers in Teaching Decision-Making.* Evanston: Northwestern University, 1964. (Mimeographed report.)

Boocock, Sarane S. *Effects of Election Campaign Game in Four High School Classes.* Baltimore: The Johns Hopkins University, 1963. (Mimeographed report.)

————. "Toward a Sociology of Learning: A Selective Review of Existing Literature." *Sociology of Education,* 39 (Winter, 1966), 1-45.

Campbell, Donald T. and Stanley, Julian C. "Experimental and Quasi-Experimental Designs for Research on Teaching." In Gage, N. L. (ed.), *Handbook of Research on Teaching*. Chicago: Rand McNally, 1963, 171-246.

Cherryholmes, Cleo. "Some Current Research on Effectiveness of Educational Simulations: Implications for Alternative Strategies." *American Behavioral Scientist,* 10 (October, 1966), 4-7.

Cohen, K. J., Dill, W. R., Kuehn, A. A. and Winters, P. R. *The Carnegie Management Game: An Experiment in Business Education*. Homewood, Illinois: Irwin, Inc., 1964.

Greenlaw, P. S., Herron, L. W. and Rawson, R. H. *Business Simulation*. Englewood Cliffs, New Jersey: Prentice-Hall, 1962.

Hyman, H. H., Wright, C. R. and Hopkins, T. K. *Applications of Methods of Evaluation*. Berkeley: University of Chicago Press, 1962.

Inbar, Michael. "Simulation of Social Processes: The Disaster Game." Baltimore: The Johns Hopkins University, Department of Social Relations, 1965. (Unpublished paper.)

Moise, Edwin. "The New Mathematics Program." In de Grazia, A. and Sohn, D. A. (eds.), *Revolution in Teaching*. New York: Bantam Books, 1964, 171-187.

Robinson, James A. "Simulation and Games." Columbus: Ohio State University, Department of Political Science, 1965. (Unpublished paper.)

Silberman, Harry F. "Characteristics of Some Recent Studies of Instructional Methods." In Coulson, J. E. (ed.), *Programmed Learning and Computer Based Instruction*. New York: Wiley, 1962, 13-24.

Thorelli, H. B. and Graves, R. L. *International Operations Simulation*. New York: Free Press, 1964.

Part I

THE RATIONALE

■ The two defining properties of simulation games are that they are *simulations* and that they are *games*. Coleman's and Boocock's chapters, respectively, discuss these two features. Coleman analyzes the ways in which social processes can be simulated in a game form and reviews some of the assumptions and problems encountered by the designer. Boocock reviews the approaches to games *as such* found in the literature and outlines the trend toward increased emphasis on the educational potential of games.

Abt directly considers the educational meaning of simulation games and argues strongly for their place in the school curriculum. Clayton and Rosenbloom qualify the claims: games are not appropriate for all the goals suggested; they propose that games are particularly suited to teach strategies and understanding of structure. A similar view is presented by Schild: a game highlights the structure of relations between roles (rather than empathy with roles); moreover, whatever the content of the game, it presents some features underlying interaction in general and may aid in developing interpersonal skills.

All of these chapters are "rationales" for the use of games in the sense that they suggest that games can profitably be utilized in an educational context. But the perspectives are very different — as is the extent to which generalized claims on the effectiveness

27

are made. Of particular interest is the implicit emphasis in several of the chapters on *specification* of what games can teach: What kind of sociological theory can effectively be simulated? What kind of ideas can be transmitted in the classrroom by games? What kind of behavior is evoked in the game?

None of the authors attempt to present a systematic theoretical answer to these questions. And the scarcity of empirical data also makes such formalization premature. But the perspectives in these essays are sufficient to outline the issues — and suggest the lines of attack for future research.

Social Processes and Social Simulation Games

JAMES S. COLEMAN

■ Games are of interest to a social psychologist or sociologist for at least two reasons. First, because a game is a kind of play upon life in general, it induces, in a restricted and well-defined context, the same kinds of motivations and behavior that occur in the broader contexts of life where we play for keeps. Indeed, it is hard to say whether games are a kind of play upon life or life is an amalgamation and extension of the games we learn to play as children. The book by Eric Berne, *Games People Play,* describing some socially destructive behavior as games, gives persuasive argument that in fact the latter might be the case. And the perceptive observations by Jean Piaget of the importance of simple games like marbles for young children as early forms of a social order with its rules and norms strengthen this view.

The second source of interest is the peculiar properties games have as contexts for learning. There are apparently certain aspects of games that especially facilitate learning, such as their ability to focus attention, their requirement for action rather than merely passive observation, their abstraction of simple elements from the complex confusion of reality, and the intrinsic rewards they hold for mastery. By the combination of these properties that games provide, they show remarkable consequences as devices for learning.

Both these topics are dealt with in other chapters in this volume. I want here to examine how a particular kind of game, a

29

"social simulation game," can provide still another source of interest to the social scientist. A social simulation game, as I shall use the term here, is a game in which certain social processes are explicity mirrored in the structure and functioning of the game. The game is a kind of abstraction of these social processes, making explicit certain of them that are ordinarily implicit in our everyday behavior. These games raise several questions: What is the way a simulation game characteristically mirrors social processes? What are the kinds of social processes most easily simulated in a game? What is the relation of construction and use of a game to, on the one hand observation, and on the other hand social theory? These are the questions I want to address in this chapter. I will use specific examples from games developed by the Hopkins group as illustrations of the most important points.[1]

THE ROLE OF THE SOCIAL ENVIRONMENT

A social simulation game always consists of a player or players acting in a social environment. By its very definition, it is concerned principally with that part of an individuals' environment that consists of other people, groups, and organizations. How does it incorporate that environment into its structure?

There are ordinarily two solutions, either or both of which are used in any specific game. One is to let each player in the game act as a portion of the social environment of each other player. The rules of the game establish the obligations upon each role, and the players, each acting within the rules governing his role, interact with one another. The resulting configuration constitutes a social subsystem, and each players' environment consists of that subsystem, excluding himself.

Examples of this solution occur in most of the Hopkins games. In the Parent-Child Game, there are two subsystems: one is the parent and child, and the other is the community of parents and children. Each parent's principal interaction is with his child, but he has interaction also with the other players in the roles of parents in the game. And each child's principal interaction is with his parent, but he interacts as well with other players in the roles of children. The Legislature portion of the Democracy Game consists of players in a single subsystem. Each player is a legislator, and interactions are with other players in their roles as legislators.

A second way in which the social environment is embodied in a social simulation game is in the rules themselves. The rules may contain contingent responses of the environment, representing the actions of persons who are not players, but nevertheless relevant to the individual's action. A game using this solution can in fact be a one-player game, in which the whole of this player's environment, represented by the game, is incorporated in the rules.

An example of this solution is the Life Career Game. In this game, the sole player begins as a young person, making decisions about his everyday activities and implicitly his future. The responses to these decisions occur through the environmental response rules, which represent the responses of: teachers in school, school admissions officers, potential employers, and potential marriage partners. But none of these roles is represented by a player in the game. The probable responses of persons in such roles to various actions of a player are embodied in the environmental response rules, and the actual responses are determined by these rules in conjunction with a chance mechanism. The player in the game plays for a score, and the only relation to other players is through a comparison of scores.

Most games use a combination of these two solutions. A portion of the environment is represented by other players, and a portion by the environmental response rules. An example is the game of Legislature. Players receive cards representing the interests of their constituents, and their score in the game consists of votes given by the hypothetical constituents, according to the environmental response rules which make these votes contingent upon the legislator's furthering of the constituents' interests. In some games also, alternative versions have a part of the environment as players in one version and as environmental response rules in another. For example, the complete game of Democracy includes a citizen's action meeting in which the players are constituents who determine collectively the votes they will give to their legislator contingent upon his action. This moves the behavior of the constituents from the rules into the area of play.

The embodiment of the social environment in the rules requires more empirical knowledge of the responses of the organizations or individuals than does the solution that represents them by players. For the players respond on the basis of their own goals and role constraints, and the game constructor need not know what these responses will be. In contrast, if the responses are part of the rules, the game constructor must know in advance the responses contingent upon each possible action of the players.

The representation of environment by players, on the other hand, requires greater theoretical acumen. For if the players' responses, and thus the system of behavior, are to mirror the phenomenon in question, each player's goals and role constraints must be accurately embodied in the rules. For example, in the Life Career Game, if the role of college admissions officer were to be represented by an actual player, the goals of the officer, together with his role constraints, must be approximately correctly given in the rules, if his selection of candidates is to correspond reasonably well to reality.

The decision to represent a given portion of the environment in either of these ways depends in part upon the mechanics of the game. In some cases, there will be too many players if a given portion of the environment is represented by players; thus it must be represented by the rules. In other cases, such as the Life Career Game, the player moves from one environment to another, so that each environment is only temporarily a part of the game.

Finally, it should be noted that every game selects only certain portions of the social environment to be included in either way. Some portions are left out, often because they introduce social processes other than the ones being simulated. For example, in the game of Legislature, interest groups acting as political pressure groups are explicitly excluded, because of the additional processes this would introduce, obscuring the one being simulated.

TYPES OF RULES

In the discussion above one type of rule was repeatedly mentioned, and described as "environmental response rules." This is only one of several types of rules that are necessary in social simulation games, and it is useful to indicate briefly the several types. This will give some better idea of the elements of which a social simulation game is composed. It is often stated that the rules of a game are like the "rules of the game" in real life, that is, the normative and legal constraints upon behavior. This, however, corresponds only to one type of rule necessary in any game.

The most pervasive type of rule in every game is the *procedural rule*. Procedural rules describe how the game is put into play, and the general order in which play proceeds. In a social simulation game, the procedural rules must follow roughly the order of activities in the phenomenon being studied. Sometimes, the procedural rules explicitly incorporate assumptions about the social processes involved. In the Parent-Child Game, for example, each round of play between parent and child consists of a sequence of four activities: first, discussion between parent and child in an attempt to reach agreement about the child's behavior; second, orders given by the parents in those areas where no agreemeant was reached; third, behavior decisions on the part of the child; fourth, decisions of the parent whether to supervise the child's behavior and possibly punish for disobedience. This sequence of activities explicitly embodies assumptions about family functioning. In some cultures, a different set of procedural rules would be necessary, for example, eliminating the first step. Or a more theoretically sophisticated version of the game would leave the sequence of activities undetermined, to be selected by the behavior of the players.

A subtype of procedural rule, found in all games, may be called the *mediation rule*. This is the set of rules specifying how an impasse in play is resolved, or a conflict of paths resolved. In basketball, there is an impasse when players from opposing sides are wrestling over the ball, the referee then calls a jump-ball. In social simulation games, mediation rules are necessary whenever two or more players conflict, and neither has the formal authority or the power to get his way. Mediation in the Community Response Game is necessary when two players attempt, each in ignorance of the other's action, to operate the same agency. A more important type of mediation is necessary in the Economic System Game, when workers and employer cannot agree on a wage. This impasse, if allowed to continue, would disrupt the game, just as similar impasses would disrupt the real economy if not subjected to mediation or arbitration.

A second type of rule, closely related to the first, is the *behavior constraint*. These rules correspond to the role obligations found in real life, and specify what the player must do and what he cannot do. They are often stated along with the procedural rules, but they are analytically distinct, for they represent the role specifications for each type of player. For example, in the Community

Response Game, each player in a community role is constrained to use only ten units of "energy" in each time period; and if he decides to operate a community agency, he must devote a specified number of energy units to this activity.

A third type of rule is the rule specifying the *goal* and means of goal achievement of each type of player. In every game, all players have goals, and the rules specify both what the goals are and how the goals are reached. In a social simulation game, the goals must correspond roughly to the goals that individuals in the given role have in real life. Often, the correct specification of a goal is an important aspect of the theory embodied in the game. For example, in the Community Response Game, each player's goal is to "reduce his anxiety" as quickly as possible. This, together with the specification in the rules of the amount of anxiety he receives from uncertainty about family, from non-performance of community role, etc., constitutes a theory about behavior under conditions of disaster. Or in the Consumer Game, each consumer's goal is to gain the maximum amount of satisfaction. This, together with the schedule of satisfaction received from each type of goods purchased, is based upon the economists' theory about consumer behavior. Insofar as the theory underlying goal specification is correct and the behavior constraints are correct, the behavior of the player should correspond to the behavior observed by persons in that role in real life. If the behavior of the player deviates greatly, it is very likely because the theory about goals of persons in that role is defective.

A fourth type of rule, referred to in the earlier section, is the *environmental response rule*. These rules specify how the environment would behave if it were present as part of the game. In the game of baseball, some fields with a portion of the outfield blocked off have a "ground rule double," for balls hit into that area. This rule is based on the probable outcome of play if the interference with play had not existed.

In all simulation games, the environmental response rules are more important. Since a simulation game is an abstraction from reality, the environmental response rules give the probable response of that part of the environment that is not incorporated in the actions of the players. In a social simulation game, most of the environmental response rules give the probable response of persons, groups, or organizations not represented by players. Examples are those in the Life Career and other games, as discussed in the preceding section.

There is finally one type of rule in all games as well as real life, which may be called *police rules,* giving the consequences to a player of breaking one of the game's rules. These rules sometimes specify merely a reversion to a previous state (corresponding to "restitutive law" in society), sometimes specify a punishment to the player who has broken the rules (corresponding to "repressive law" in societies). The principal function of the referee in games (besides applying mediation rules) is to note when rules are broken and apply the designated corrective action.

Ordinarily, the breaking of procedural rules leads merely to restitutive action, while the breaking of behavior constraint rules leads more often to repressive action, or punishment of the offending player. In many social simulation games, as in many parlor games, the breaking of a rule is corrected by the moral force of the other players, and their power to stop the game by refusing to play. In a larger game with more players and more differentiated areas of action, police rules are more necessary, as is a referee or policeman to note the delinquency.

THE ROLE OF BEHAVIOR THEORY

A game used as a social simulation is based upon certain assumptions, explicit or implicit, about behavior. The similarity of the assumptions from one game to another suggests, as further analysis confirms, that social simulation games have a special kinship to a certain type of behavior theory. In addition, each game designed as a social simulation implies a quite specific theory about behavior in the area of life being simulated. These specific theoretical elements are principally manifested in the goal-specification rules, but also may form part of the behavior constraints, procedure rules, and environmental response rules. Examples of this relation between rules and theory are evident in the preceding discussion; more examples and a closer examination will be given below. First, however, it is useful to examine the general affinities of games to one type of behavior theory.

In every game, each competing unit has a goal specified by the rules, and means by which he achieves this goal. If the competing unit is a team, then all players on this team share the same goal, and have individual goals only insofar as they contribute to the team goal. If it is a player, then he has an individual goal. Even in the former case, individuals as persons (not as players) may have individual goals besides the team goal given by the rules — for example, to excel within one's own team. These goals, however, are not part of the explicit structure of the game, but arise because of the rewards they bring outside the game itself.

Whether the competing unit is an individual or a team, the game functions because each individual pursues his own goal. Thus, a social simulation game must necessarily begin with a set of individuals carrying out purposive behavior toward a goal. It is hardly conceivable, then, that the theoretical framework implied by a social simulation game be anything other than a purposive behavior theory. This means a definite theoretical stance on several issues: On the issue in social theory of expressing the assumptions of the theory at the level of the individual or at the level of the collectivity or social system, the use of games implies taking the former, individualist position. On the issue of purposive theory vs. positivist theory (where behavior is described as a lawful response to an environmental stimulus), the use of games implies the purposive orientation. On the issue of purposive, goal-oriented behavior vs. expressive theory (where the individual act is an expression of some inner tension without regard to a goal), the use of games again implies the purposive orientation. On the issue of behavior determined by personality or other historical causes not currently present vs. behavior determined by the constraints and demands of the present (and possibly expected future) situation, the use of games implies the latter, the theory of present- and future-governed behavior. On the issue of purposive, goal-oriented behavior vs. behavior governed wholly by normative expectations and obligations (as, for example, occurs in some organization theory, where the individual's interests play no role, and he is predicted to behave simply in accord with organizational rules), the use of games implies the former, goal-oriented position. The use of games takes as its starting-point the self-interested individual (except in the case where the competing unit is a team), and requires that any non-self-interested behavior (e.g., altruistic behavior, or collectivity-orientation) emerge from pursuit of his goals, as means to those individual ends. For this reason, social simulation games that use a collectivity, such as a family, as a team to form a competing unit, are not as theoretically complete as are those games in which the individual player is the competing unit. To specify a collectivity as a competing unit prevents simulation of those processes that induce the individual to realize his goals through investing his efforts in a collectivity's action. It may well be, of course, that for a given social simulation, one wishes to take those processes as given, in order to simulate others. For example, in the Consumer Game, the goals of the finance officer of the department store are given as the profitability goals of the department store itself. Similarly, players acting as the consumers are given satisfaction points for purchases corresponding to the satisfaction of both husband and wife together, not corresponding to the satisfaction of one alone. For the purpose of this simulation, the question of how the department store manager induces the finance officer to act in the store's interest, or how the other family members induce the consumer to act in the family's interest, are not taken as problematic.

To state the theoretical position implied by the use of social simulation games does not answer all the theoretical questions that arise. Any given game makes certain specific assumptions about goals. For example, in the Life Career Game, the question arises whether the satisfaction points that constitute the game's goal should be given at each time period, so that the player's score is his cumulative satisfaction over the period of play representing a number of years, or whether points should depend only on his final position at the end of the game (say at age twenty-five). This question becomes almost a philosophical one; but it must be resolved to appropriately motivate the player. Again, in the Life Career Game, it is assumed that the individual represented by the player can derive satisfaction from several different areas of life, and that his behavior will depend in part upon the relative importance he attaches to these areas (e.g., family, self-development, financial success, etc.). Consequently, one decision in the game is a weighting of these areas by the player, in essence determining his own goals.

In the first level of the game of Legislature, each legislator is assumed to be motivated solely to stay in office; and it is assumed that the sole factor affecting his tenure is his success in passing those bills of most interest to his constituents. Neither of these assumptions corresponds directly to reality, though both factors are present in concrete legislatures. In order to simulate this process, all other elements are suppressed, and the single process abstracted from reality. The resulting simulation hardly mirrors reality, but instead mirrors only one component of it. In the second level of the game, a second source of motivation is assumed for the legislator; his own position, taken prior to knowledge of his constituents' interests, on each bill. Winning depends both on re-election by his constituents and on his voting in accord with his own beliefs. This introduces merely one more element into the simulation, which remains far from the reality of actual legislatures, but is instead merely an abstraction of certain important processes from them. In the Community Response Game, the appropriate balance between orientation to self-interests and to those of the community is important, yet difficult to obtain. In part, this is obtained by a balance between the anxiety elicited by failure to solve individual problems and failure to aid in solution of the community problems. But upon further reflection, it appeared that in addition to mere anxiety reduction in a disaster, individuals are to some degree motivated by their conception of the regard in which they will be held by their neighbors, among whom they must live in the future. Consequently, among the three players who have accomplished the greatest anxiety reduction, the players vote for the one who has contributed most to the community, as the overall winner of the game.

Altogether, specification of the goal for each type of player in a game is the principal means by which theoretical assumptions are introduced into the game. If incorrect goals are introduced, then the behavior of the players will deviate from the behavior that it is intended to simulate, because the players are incorrectly motivated. In most simulations, the goals introduced are only partial goals, because the game, like a social theory, is an abstraction from reality, and should contain only those motivating elements that produce the aspect of behavior of the processes being simulated.

In addition to the goals of the game, the procedure rules and the behavior constraints are also partly determined by theoretical assumptions. In the Parent-Child Game, the procedural steps used in the game are, as indicated earlier, an expression of assumptions about the activities that occur in the determination of adolescents' behavior. In every game, certain of the behavioral constraint rules correspond to role obligations of the individual being simulated.

Sometimes, these are directly observable in the situation being simulated; sometimes they are not. In the Parent-Child Game, it is assumed that the adolescent is free to behave as he wishes, subject to possible parental punishment. But in reality, this is so only in some areas, such as staying out at night. In doing homework, or other activities carried out at home, the parents' supervision may come not merely after the behavior, but during the activity itself, to insure its completion.

THE KINDS OF PROCESSES SIMULATED
AND THE MEANS OF DOING SO

It is difficult and perhaps unwise to make any general statements about what social processes most easily lend themselves to game simulation, and what is the appropriate means to mirror them. For, obviously, judgments about these matters derive from what has been done in very limited experience. Consequently, what I shall attempt here is to make some generalizations about the types of processes the Hopkins group have so far found it possible to simulate in games, and the kinds of devices members of this group have used in so doing. This may then give some insight into one general style in the development of social simulation games.

First, it is striking that in nearly all the Hopkins games, the player's goal achievement is measured by his achievement of "satisfaction" points, or some variation thereof. In the Community Response Game, it is the complement of this — reduction of "anxiety points." In the High School Game, it is units of "self-esteem" that the player tries to gain. Only in the Legislature Game is there any real deviation from this approach, for the legislator attempts to gain votes from constituents.

Even here, however, if the game were made more complex through introducing other sources of motivation for the legislator, one way of integrating these various sources of motivation to provide a single measure of goal achievement would be to calibrate all the objective measures of achievement (such as re-election, chairmanship on committees, voting in accord with prestated beliefs, etc.) onto a single scale of satisfaction. In fact, it appears likely that this is the source of the widespread use in these games of "satisfaction units" as measures of goal achievement: as the one

39

common denominator against which otherwise incommensurable objective achievements can be scaled.

In relating these objective achievements to subjective satisfaction, two quite different approaches have been used: to fix in advance, as part of the goal achievement rules, the conversion ratios between each kind of objective achievement and subjective satisfaction; and to allow the player himself to fix these ratios. Most of the games use the fixed-conversion approach, but in nearly all the games, a more advanced form can be developed in which the player himself sets these (subject to constraints that prevent him from gaining advantage in later play by strategically set conversion ratios). In a second-level form of the Life Career Game, the player decides the relative importance of each of four areas of life activity, thus fixing his own conversion ratios for satisfaction. In a form of the Community Response Game, used experimentally, each player was allowed to distribute his initial anxiety points among the different sources of anxiety in a way that corresponded to the relative anxiety he believed he would feel in each area. Similar variations have been developed in the Parent-Child Game, the High School Game, and the Democracy Game. In all but one of these the setting was based upon the player's own preconceived estimates of the satisfaction involved. But in one game, the High School Game, the conversion ratio was determined by the player as a result of his experience in the game: he decided what proportion of his "attention" he should pay to esteem he received from other students and what proportion to esteem from parents. This relative attention then becomes the weighting factor in converting esteem from others to self-esteem. This approach, also used in the Life Career Game, is the most theoretically advanced of the approaches discussed above, for it introduces as one of the processes being simulated the selection and modification of goals contingent upon the consequence of the player's actions.

Exchange processes and means of their simulation: In sociology and social psychology, the recent theoretical developments most akin to this utilitarian, purposive approach used in games depend greatly upon the idea of exchange. This is evident in the work of its principal exponents, Thibaut and Kelley, Homans, and Blau. These theoretical developments, the idea of exchange of intangibles such as deference, acceptance, autonomy, aid, and similar quantities, constitute the foundation of the approach. Each party to the exchange engages in it because of a gain that he expects to experience from it. Thus, the question of how social simulation games express the processes of exchange of such intangibles naturally arises.

In the Legislature Game, there are two types of exchange, simulated in quite different ways. One is the exchange between legislators of votes, or control of issues. This exchange is not incorporated in the rules of the game, but arises from the motivations induced by the players' goals, together with the fact that no constraints *against* such exchange exist. The exchange is not expressed by a tangible or physical exchange (as it would be, for example, if pieces of paper representing votes were physically exchanged). This has certain consequences for the functioning of the system: the exchanges are merely "promises to pay" a vote or unit of control of an issue, and the promise may not be honored; nor is the exchanged quantity easily negotiable by the receiving party.

A second type of exchange in this game is the fundamental exchange of representative democracy: continued support of the legislator by constituents, in exchange for the legislator's pursuit and realization of the constituent's interest in legislation. This exchange is simulated through the environmental response rules: the legislator's score is dependent on cards he receives showing the interests of his (hypothetical) constituents.

These two examples from the game of Legislature illustrate that a social exchange process may be mirrored in games either by an exchange between two players, or by an exchange between a player and the non-player social environment, according to the environmental response rules. Both of these cases present certain complications, and each will be examined in turn. For exchange between players, the most fundamental point, though it appears obvious, must be made: the exchange must be motivated for both parties. The exchange must contribute to both players' goals. In the Legislature game, for example, an exchange of control occurs between legislators not because it is prescribed by the rules, for the rules make no mention of such an exchange. It occurs because it is to the interest of each to concentrate his power on those issues that will contribute most to his re-election or defeat. As a consequence, the exchange occurs only when two legislators see a mutually advantageous exchange of control.

Exchange between players can be either between persons in

the same role, such as legislators in the Legislature Game, or between persons in different roles, as parent and child in the Parent-Child Game, consumer and finance officer in the Consumer Game, worker and manufacturer in the Economic System Game. When exchange is between persons in the same role, as two legislators, only one motivation need be supplied by the theory on which the game is based, for it serves both players. When the exchange is between persons in different roles, two different motivations must be supplied from a more complex theoretical base. For example, in the two-stage form of the Democracy Game, each citizen-constituent is attempting to maximize his satisfaction from the collectivity's legislation. He does this through exercising his power in a collective decision (a community action meeting) that determines the legislation that the representative-legislator must obtain in exchange for the constituency's support in re-electing him. Thus, for this exchange to take place, two different sources of its motivation must be inherent in the goal achievement rules: the representative-legislator must have control of some actions (in this case, legislation) that contribute to the citizen-constituent's goal achievement; and the citizen-constituent must have control of some actions (in this case, votes for re-election) that contribute to the representative-legislator's goal achievement.

In the Parent-Child Game, the parent and child negotiate over each of five areas of the child's behavior, and the implicit starting-point is that each has partial control over this behavior. Thus, in the negotiation, there is an exchange of control, with each being motivated to gain control of those activities most important to him (i.e., those areas where the child's behavior affects his level of satisfaction more), in return giving up control over those activities of less importance to him. Obviously, it is only in those families where different activities have different relative importance to the child and parent that a mutually profitable exchange can take place.

The initial structure of control in this game is probably not in accord with reality (although the deviation may not greatly affect the functioning of the game). It seems rather that the adolescent has full control over some actions, the parent has full control over others, and for some, both parties have a veto power. However, if the initial structure were changed in this way, the basic commodity exchanged, control over the child's activities, would remain as it is.

There is a more subtle process that develops over time in this game, akin to exchange, but somewhat different. If the parent supervises the child's actual behavior, in a later stage of the game, and punishes the child for deviations from previous agreements, then both parent and child stand to lose in "family happiness." Thus, it is to the long-term advantage of the parent to make an investment of trust in the child, if the child generally honors this trust. (If the child does not, the parent loses satisfaction.) Similarly, it is to the child's long-term advantage to honor the trust, though he may make short-term gains in satisfaction from behaving in ways that give him most satisfaction, regardless of previous agreements. (This investment may also be described as an exchange, with the parent giving up the activity of supervision and punishment in return for the child's giving up immediate gratifications. However, because the returns to the parent are long-term, it appears more useful to describe it as an investment of trust.)

Whenever, as in the exchange between legislators or the agreement between parent and child, there is no exchange of a physical commodity, but merely a promise to perform, the exchange can be considered an investment of trust by the party whose return is most delayed (e.g., in the case of legislators, the legislator whose issue of interest, on which a vote is promised to him, comes up for vote after he himself has delivered his promise). It is seldom, in areas of social behavior, just as in areas of economic activity, that two activities on which an exchange is made occur simultaneously. Thus, it is almost always true that one party must make an investment of trust. In economic exchange, one of the principal functions of money is to facilitate exchange by transferring this trust from the person engaged in exchange to a central authority, whose "promise to pay" will be accepted by all as a trustworthy promise.

In games where the action of other persons or organizations is incorporated in the environmental response rules, such as the Life Career Game and the High School Game, a different and less explicit approach to exchange exists. The player acts, and the environment responds with either rewards or punishments, depending upon his action. As indicated earlier, the environmental response rules need not show how this response contributes to the goals of the person or organization whose response is simulated. In the High School Game, the esteem from parents to the adolescent for his achievements is given by environmental response rules representing the parents, according to a schedule that corresponds roughly to empirical reality. It does not show how the exchange of esteem for achievement contributes to the parents' goal achievement, for since the parent is not a player, he need not be motivated to engage in the exchange. It is evident from this example and similar ones that the theoretical foundations of the game must become increasingly rich as the social environment is moved out of the environmental response rules and into the play by actual players.

The exchange of control over actions: It appears that exchange processes generally, in social simulation games and in reality, including economic exchange, can be usefully conceptualized as exchange of control over actions. Because of the interdependence of which society consists, actions taken by one person or collectivity have consequences for others as well. When these consequences for another are great enough, he will seek to influence the action, and often his most efficacious means of doing so is through offering control over another action in return. In economic exchange, where the exchange is ordinarily conceived as "exchange of desirable commodities," or exchange of a commodity for a promise to pay, in the form of money, the present framework would view the exchange as exchange of control over disposal of the commodity. This view accords with that of one of the most perceptive students of the nature of economic exchange, John R. Commons, who insisted that "exchange of goods" is not a fruitful way of describing economic exchange. Commons says, in describing exchange of economic goods, "Each owner alienates his ownership, and each owner acquires another ownership. Prices are paid, not for physical objects, but for ownership of those objects."[2]

In some cases, the control that is exchanged is full control over an individual action. In other cases, it is partial control over a collective action. Both processes are mirrored in the games described above. Apart from this distinction, there appear to be several other important structural differences in exchange processes, all of which have been exemplified above. One of these is the distinction between actual transfer of control and a promise to carry out the action under the other's direction. The former occurs in exchange of control over economic goods, while the latter is more frequent in social exchanges, which are ordinarily described as exchange of "intangibles." The so-called intangibles that are exchanged, such as deference, aid, acceptance, are in fact performance of actions in accord with the wishes of the recipient. A third distinction between exchanges are those in which both actions occur simultaneously, and those, far more numerous, in which one action occurs after the other, requiring an investment of trust by one player. Although the processes of trust investment do occur in the games described here, none of these games simulate extensive investments of trust, such as those that occur when a group allows its activity to be determined by a leader, or the investments which an organization manager makes in subordinates when giving them control over portions of the organization. Investments of trust such as these give rise to important social phenomena which can be simulated in games like the ones described above.

A final distinction in the structure of exchange processes is between those that involve only two parties and those that involve three or more. It may well be the case that player A has control over and action affecting B, B has control over an action affecting C, and C has control over an action affecting A, allowing a mutually profitable three-party exchange to occur where no two-party exchange could have taken place. Infrequently, such three-player exchanges occur among legislators in the Legislature Game; but their relatively infrequent occurrence suggests some serious barriers in their way. One of these is the mere mechanical difficulty of discovering a profitable transaction and arranging it; another is the greater investment of trust, requiring each of two players to trust another to whom he may have no subsequent means of retribution. However, certain organizational structures are largely composed of exchanges involving three parties, one acting as a guarantor to one party, in much the same way as the government acts as a guarantor of the value of money exchanged in an economic transaction. For example, in a business organization, one employee performs services for another, and is not recompensed directly by the other, but by the overall management of the organization. It is likely that similar structures exist in a less economic framework.

The possibility of conceiving of all social interdependence in terms of interdependence of actions that can lead to mutually profitable exchange of control over actions suggests that all forms of social interdependence can be mirrored by social simulation games, limited only by the imagination, ingenuity, and theoretical acumen of the investigator.

Currency in the system: In economic systems, exchange ordinarily occurs through physical transfer of goods, or by physical transfer of money. In non-economic exchange, there is seldom a physical transfer (though there are exceptions, such as assignment of a proxy to another person, giving him full control over the casting of the vote). Instead, each gives the other, or promises the other, effective control over an action by undertaking to act in the other's interest, while still retaining execution of the action himself. As a consequence, perhaps the fundamental difference between economic and social exchange is that nothing changes hands in the latter case. Indeed, it could hardly be otherwise, for in most cases of social exchange, it is intrinsically the *other's* action in one's interest that is the desired result. Constituents delegate their political authority to their representative; it is his action in their interest that they expect from him. He can carry out his part of the exchange only by acting in their interest — not by giving them physical control over anything.

The critical question, then, is whether in a social simulation game it is possible, and if possible, desirable, to represent such exchanges by physical transfer of something representing the "thing" that is being exchanged. It was indicated earlier that physical transfer does make an important difference, because it allows use of the thing received for further negotiability. Apart from this question, however, it appears unlikely that in most cases anything could be transferred physically, simply because it is "acting in the other's interest" that is being offered. There are exceptions, such as votes, which could be represented as a transferable commodity; but in general, it appears that the nature of most social exchanges does not allow such a transfer.

This is not to say that no elements in social exchange can be represented by a physical transfer. In nearly all exchanges, the action of one party in satisfying his part of the exchange occurs prior to that of the other. In some of these cases, the payment for the first party's action is not in terms of a specific action in return, but in terms of a kind of "social credit," which the second person can call upon when he needs it. This credit sometimes takes the form of status or reputation, and manifests itself in a variety of ways: deference, willingness to extend trust, and payment through specific actions. It is certainly possible that this "social credit" could be symbolized by a physical transfer of some paper units of account. However, this would be of use only if it served some function: if the notes thus transferred were useful to the recipient, either as negotiable property in further exchange (like the bills of exchange in Lancashire before 1800, which were promises to pay that came to have the property of negotiability, and passed from hand to hand at face value, although they were private accounts between two parties), or as a debt for which the debtor could be held to account in the courts, i.e., in the rules of the game. Yet neither of these things is true of the social credit that is incurred in social exchange. Thus provisionally, at least, it appears questionable whether a representation of the conceptual quantities that arise in social exchange is possible even if it were desirable.

It may well be that the possibility of such representation merely waits upon the further development of ideas, to provide the basis for a scheme by which accounts are balanced, and also a unit of value in terms of which accounts may be kept. Certainly primitive systems of economic exchange have in early stages not had a unit of value, and have in many ways more nearly approximated social exchange than modern economic exchange. Yet the introduction of money as a unit of account, and strict balancing of accounts into such systems has changed their functioning, and it may well be that a simulation of social processes must not be based on a conceptual structure that consists of a tightly rational and fully accounted system. However, the idea of a conservative system, in which there is conservation of some quantity, such as energy in a physical system, is an attractive one. The issue must remain unresolved, awaiting further theoretical or game development. It may be noted, however, that if one abandons the idea of social simulation games as necessarily mirroring what *is*, he can devise games that represent innovations in social organization, just as the credit card is a recent innovation in economic systems and money is an early innovation, and as the bureaucratic organization is an early innovation in social organization.

SELECTED ISSUES IN THE CONSTRUCTION OF SIMULATION GAMES

To this point, I have described the approach taken by the Hopkins group to mirroring social processes through games. I would like now to discuss certain issues that have been resolved differently in other games.

In all the games discussed above, the players receive a score, which most often is described as "satisfaction." In some other social simulation games, however, there is no final score at all. Instead, the players are assumed to measure their satisfaction by the events of the game. Two varieties of this approach can be distinguished. In one, the objective outcomes of the game clearly constitute a measure of winning and losing. Among the games discussed above, the Legislature Game, in which each legislator receives votes for re-election rather than "satisfaction points" is closest to this. The votes are objective outcomes, and because they constitute a unidimensional measure, they can be used as a score for the game. Similarly, in the commercial game of Diplomacy, that nation which outlasts all others is the winner.

The use of such an objective criterion is an excellent measure of success in the game, so long as this single objective achievement is in fact the single objective goal of persons in those roles being mirrored by play of the game. This is most often the case in games which constitute a contest for political power or ascendancy. In such games, the final power positions constitute the outcome of the game. But more often, goals of persons in roles consist of a mixture of objective results, results of different types contributing to the person's satisfaction. When this is the case, it appears difficult to use as a measure of a player's success in the game the objective outcomes of any one of the activities that contribute to the goal. The economist's solution for a similar problem has been to devise a concept of "utility" as a way of giving subjective integration of the otherwise incommensurable objective things toward which the individual strives. Until another theoretical device accomplishing the same thing is discovered, some variant of the economist's solution is necessary.

A second variety of the no-final-score approach stems from quite different directions, from the game designer's distaste for competition, distaste for the idea of "winning" and "losing." It is a defect of social simulation games in general, whether there is an explicit winner and loser or not, that they motivate the players for success *relative* to others, while in some activities (but not all), his goal derives from the absolute level of results. For example, in the Consumer Game, although units of satisfaction accrue as a result of objective purchases, the player is motivated simply to do better than others, that it, to maximize the positive difference between

48

his satisfaction and that of others. Often, this gives behavior no different than would occur if the goal were in fact to maximize his absolute level of satisfaction; but in certain cases, such as those in which he might act to interfere with another's performance instead of implementing his own, it can be different. Yet, it is not clearly the case that in real life people strive to maximize the absolute level of achievement, rather than the relative one. The phenomenon of relative deprivation in social life attests to the fact that relative outcomes do play an important part in one's level of satisfaction.

The principal defect of the no-winner variety of the no-final-score approach is that it assumes what is hardly true: that the player can understand and internalize the goals of persons in the role he is playing in the game, and when those goals are not given to him by the rules of the game, and then evaluate his performance on the basis of these assumed goals. For if he cannot, his behavior will be aimless, that is without a goal, or will be directed toward incorrect goals, thus destroying the value of the simulation. Parenthetically, I should note that this anti-competitive view apparently is a misdirected generalization from the harm that punishment through low school grades, and punishment from adults generally, does to children. The idea of winning and losing in a game, and accepting defeat, is an early element in the socialization of a child. Children unable to accept defeat in a game are as Piaget's researches suggest, at a very early stage of socialization, approximately the four to six year age level.

A second issue that is sometimes resolved differently in social simulation games is the issue of abstract simplicity vs. realistic complexity. Some games, in the area of international relations, legislatures, business, and others, have been developed as realistic and complex configurations of processes, attempting to simulate reality as well as possible. In contrast, the games discussed above are analytic abstractions from reality of single processes or delimited combinations of them. The virtues and defects of each approach as a learning device are not known. But it appears that as aids for theory, they are relevant to different aspects of theory-construction. The simpler simulations are appropriate for detailed study of single processes or small combinations of processes. Yet, because they do not attempt to mirror the richness of reality, empirical tests against reality cannot be easily made. There is too little experience, however, to have a good assessment of the values of empirical richness and analytic abstraction in social simulation games.

THE USE OF GAMES AS INSTRUMENTS OF THEORY

The relation between purposive behavior theory and social simulation games is evident from the discussion in earlier sections. It remains here only to suggest the role that the construction and use of games can play in the development of behavior theory.

Social simulation games appear to be most useful in the intermediate stages of theory development — between verbal speculation and a formal abstract theory. For a simulation game appears to allow a way to translate a set of ideas into a system of action rather than a system of abstract concepts. The concept development is necessary (if the concept of money did not exist, it would be necessary to invent it in order for a system of economic exchange other than barter to exist), but what is necessary is not to specify "relations between concepts" in the usual way that theories are developed. Instead, it is necessary merely to embed the concept in the rules of the game.

In addition to those concepts and action principles that are part of the design of the game, additional phenomena arise which require further conceptualization, and extension of the theory. For example, in playing the Legislature Game, exchange of votes occur, though this is not in the rules; and observation of this exchange led to: (a) conceptualizing the process as one of exchange of partial control over the collective action; (b) developing the concept of a player's interest in the action as the difference between the utility for one outcome and that for the other (i.e., re-election votes under one outcome and the other); and (c) the proposition that a player will exchange control so as to maximize his control over those actions that interest him most. Again, in the Parent-Child Game, although the concept of trust and investment of trust plays no part in the rules of the game, behavior arises during the game that suggests these concepts as ways of describing it.

It might almost be said that construction of a social simulation game constitutes a path toward formal theory that is an alternative to the usual development of concepts and relations in verbally stated theory. For rather than abstracting concepts and relations from the system of action observed in reality, the construction of a game abstracts instead a *behavior process,* describing through the rules the conditions that will generate that process. Then, after construction of the game and observation of its functioning, the concepts that adequately describe this process can be created, proceeding next to the development of formal theory. An important virtue of this path is that one learns, by malfunctions of the game, the defects and omissions in his abstraction of the behavior process. As a consequence, extensive corrections to the theory can be made in making the game function, even before the conceptualization that follows play of the functioning game.

NOTES

1. Descriptions of most of the games discussed in this chapter are included in other chapters in this book: the Legislature and Life Career Games in the Boocock chapter, in Part II; the Parent-Child Game, in the chapter by Schild, Part II; the Community Response or Disaster Game, in the Appendix to the chapter by Inbar, Part III; and the Consumer Game in the Appendix to the chapter by Zaltman, Part III.

2. John R. Commons, *The Economics of Collective Action.* New York: Macmillan, 1950, p. 46.

From Luxury Item to Learning Tool

An Overview of the Theoretical Literature on Games

SARANE S. BOOCOCK

■ In spite of their antiquity and virtual universality, there is a surprisingly small theoretical literature on games. This may be partly because until rather recently, games — and play in general — were considered a kind of cultural residual or luxury item, something a culture could afford after it had taken care of its "real" needs. According to the *surplus energy* theory of games, most definitively formulated by Herbert Spencer, higher animals with "time and strength not wholly absorbed in providing for immediate needs" fill up the slack with various "unnecessary" activities, "superfluous and useless exercise of facilities," and "uncalled-for exertions" (Spencer, 1873, pp. 629-630).

The Spencerian view of games as something separate from real life can lead to two quite different attitudes toward them. On the one hand, separateness may be defined as inferiority. If games are seen as not contributing directly to the real business of a society, they can be dismissed as unworthy of serious consideration. That this essentially negative conception has not entirely disappeared from the literature is evidenced in a recent treatise on the relationships between societies and their forms of play (Caillois, 1961), in which games are defined in terms of their "nonproductivity" (of wealth or goods) and "waste" (of time, energy, and sometimes money). It is, moreover, my impression that this is the view of games still held by many educators. Such a view manifests itself in a basic suspicion of any classroom activity in which the child has "fun," since this automatically precludes his "learning something."

On the other hand, the distinction between games and real life may be seen as one of the factors explaining their unique attractiveness for most people. In what is probably the closest thing to a "classic" work on games, John Huizinga's *Homo Ludens*, first published in 1938, the author defines a game as

> a voluntary activity or occupation executed within certain fixed limits of time and place, according to rules freely accepted but absolutely binding, having its aim in itself and accompanied by a feeling of tension, joy, and consciousness that it is different from ordinary life (Huizinga, 1955, p. 28).

Unlike Spencer, however, Huizinga does not interpret the freedom of games from some of the restraints of real-life activities as implying that games do not make significant contributions to culture. On the contrary, the book is devoted to demonstrating the close relationship between play and its societal environment, by pointing to the presence of play "elements" or "principles" in all basic aspects of culture. From an examination of the nature of the play elements in a variety of cultural phenomena, ranging from law to the arts to the conduct of war, Huizinga concludes that all such phenomena are rooted or arise in the form of games, contests, and other types of play, and that "pure play is one of the main bases of civilization" (*Ibid.*, p. 5). Because he views play as having civilizing functions, he regrets what he perceives to be the dominant trend since the eighteenth century — i.e., "that the play-element in culture has been on the wane" (*Ibid.*, p. 206).

GAMES AS SIMULATIONS

Other post-Spencerian analysts have tried to explain just what it is about games that makes them so appealing, including the phenomenon, typical of so many games, that although players know that the outcome will not affect what happens to them outside the game ("it's only a game"), their actual behavior in the game does not reflect this knowledge. As the economist Frank Knight put it, "the concrete objective — capturing our opponents' pieces, carrying a ball across a mark, or whatever it may be — is a matter of accident, but to achieve it is for the moment the end and aim of being" (Knight, 1921, p. 53).[1]

A possible explanation of this phenomenon which, like the argument of *Homo Ludens,* is based upon a conception of games as integrally related to the society in which they are developed and played, is offered in Georg Simmel's essay on sociability. According to Simmel, the games that people play over and over again are those which mirror important real-life situations or problems, so that in playing a game a person can in some sense "practice" real life — without having to pay real-life consequences for his actions. Simmel concludes that the game is a sociologically interesting form of activity, not only because it is "played in society (as its external medium), but that, with its help, people actually 'play' society" (Simmel, 1950, p. 50). The reason why people play a game as if it were a matter of life and death is that it is in fact a model or simulation of real life.[2]

Akin to Simmel's conceptualization is Groos's "practice theory," a kind of biological functionalism of play. Groos sees play as "an instinctive activity, existing for the purposes of practice or exercise, with serious intent," and so important to the development of humans and other higher animals that nature sets aside a special portion of the life cycle (childhood) for it (Groos, 1898, p. 35). Moreover, the various physical and mental activities of specific games are crude prototypes of later adult activities. Groos's theory has been criticized on many counts — because of its implication that every play activity is matched with a subsequent real-life activity; because its assignment of play to a particular phase of life fails to account for adult play; and so on. The rigidities of Groos's system should not, however, overshadow the importance of the practice notion. And while Groos's and Simmel's formulations differ considerably (the former focusing upon the *activity,* the latter upon the social *situation* within which the activity is performed), both attach importance to the notion of acting out, in a situation somewhat removed from reality, some of the problems that one must subsequently cope with in real life. This is an important characteristic of simulation games and one which will be discussed in greater detail later in this chapter.

55

DEWEY AND THE EDUCATIONAL
FUNCTIONS OF GAMING

The weight of theoretical argument seems to be ranged against the Spencerian notion of games as a wasteful, unnecessary type of activity with no meaningful function in the larger society. Defense of games culminates in the work of John Dewey, who examines their functions for society in general and the educational system in particular. Dewey discusses play and games at so many points in his work that it is difficult to present a fair synthesis in a chapter of this length, but three contributions seem especially relevant here.

First, Dewey goes back to some of the earlier ideas about games, synthesizing them into a more general theory of games as learning tools, and at the same time refuting earlier implications that play is essentially non-functional. In *Human Nature and Conduct* (1922), while he agrees with Spencer in seeing play as taking care of energy not used up in work, as "required to take care of the margin that exists between the total stock of impulses that demand outlet and the amount expended in regular action" (*Ibid.*, p. 160), Dewey goes beyond Spencer in that he sees play as having positive functions in itself. Indeed, he goes so far as to assign a positive *moral* value to games. He speaks of the "failure of regular occupations to engage the full scope of impulses and instincts in an elastically balanced way," and claims that play and games not only fill a basic human need for make-believe activity, but also provide "fresh and deeper meanings to the usual activities of life." The moral value of play activities also lies in the fact that, "Relief from continuous moral activity — in the conventional sense of moral — is itself a moral necessity" (*Ibid.*, pp. 160-162).

A second contribution of Dewey's work concerns his basic assumption that games are to be considered an integral part of the school curriculum, not simply as "relief from the tedium and strain of 'regular' school work" (Dewey, 1928, p. 228). Moreover, play and "work" are not really so antithetical to one another as is commonly assumed, since both are "active" occupations, and since the necessity for the student's active involvement in his own learning process, as opposed to "teaching by pouring in, learning by passive absorption," is at the core of Dewey's pedagogical philosophy. In fact, the major difference between work and play, as he sees it, is that play is its own end (i.e., participation in a game is a reward in itself), while work has ulterior ends and rewards external to itself — which would indicate an educational advantage of the former over the latter, at least in terms of motivation (*Ibid.*, p. 237; also Dewey, 1916, p. 46).

Finally, not only do Dewey's analyses of play and games *per se* form an important link in the argument developed in this paper, but Dewey's general educational philosophy contains most of the premises upon which the simulation games being designed at Johns Hopkins and elsewhere are built. It has been said that the educational innovations of the 1960s represent a second and more accurate, translation of the principles of educational progressivism into classroom practices, and the development of simulation games would certainly support such an argument. The core principles of the technique — e.g., the active and simultaneous participation of all students in an educational game, with the teacher in the role of aid rather than judge; the internal rather than external locus of rewards, and thus motivation, in a game; and the linking of the student to the outside world through the simulated environment, which, by "reproducing the conditions of real life" within the classroom allows him to practice taking the kinds of roles and making the kinds of decisions he will face in his own later life — can all be traced to one or another of Dewey's works.

GAMES IN SOCIALIZATION

Acceptance of the argument that there is a functional relationship between a society and its games can lead one in many different directions. One consists of attempts to classify and compare societies, cross-culturally and historically, in terms of their taste in games. The most ambitious work of this type is Caillois' *Man, Play, and Games* (1961). This study begins with a critique of *Homo Ludens*, in which Caillois claims that by limiting his attention to a kind of vague "creative quality of the play principle in the domain of culture," Huizinga neglects to take into account the great variety of types of play and games (Caillois, pp. 4ff). The author goes on to present a kind of property space of game characteristics (on which particular games can be located), and then classifies societies in terms of their dominant positions on the property space. Thus, e.g., the play activities of ancient China fall mainly into the category Caillois calls "competition," while those of imperial Rome would be classified in the "chance" category. This approach is subject to the dangers of over-generalization characteristic of any scheme which attempts to sum up a national character in terms of one or a few cultural manifestations. That it can be carried to silly extremes is indicated in one of the generalizations made in another recent work of this sort: "A mirror of national character can be found, for example, in the easy-going, long-drawn-out, conservative, and individualistic English game on the one hand, and the high-strung, tense, changing, and success-seeking American game on the other" (Mitchell and Mason, 1948, p. 23).

Another approach, which is related to the cross-cultural approach but which leads more directly into the type of games that are the subject of this book, is to focus upon the developmental or *socialization* functions of games. The way in which this happens is discussed in George Herbert Mead's work on the development of the social "self" (Mead, 1934). According to Mead, the child can be said to have a self only when he has gone through a process by which he learns to view himself first through the eyes of a variety of individual "others," and finally through the eyes of these others as a whole or system (the "generalized other"). For the child, games are an important mechanism in this process. Using baseball as an example, Mead shows how a child goes through the steps of learning the various positions in the field. A fully socialized player has a picture in his head of what *everyone else on the team* will do in a given situation and what *they as a team will expect him to do.* "Each one of his acts is determined by his assumption of the action of the others who are playing the game. What he does is controlled by his being everyone else on that team, at least so far as those attitudes affect his own particular response" (*Ibid.*, p. 154).

The *role-playing* aspect of games assumes considerable importance in Mead's conceptualization. For Mead, games socialize largely by virtue of giving players experience in a number of important social roles, both on the individual and group levels. A few additional comments on role-playing seem in order here, because, while one of the attractions of games is the way in which they allow players to act out roles or parts of roles which they have not yet experienced in real life, it should still be understood that role-playing has its own theoretical history and is not the same thing as playing a game.

The type of role-playing characteristic of simulation games owes much to the technique of psychodrama, as developed during the 1930s by Moreno and his followers. From his research in training schools for delinquent girls, Moreno concluded that the experiences of girls in this small, limited social world did not prepare them for many of the situations they would face outside the institution. Starting with simple simulated situations, in which subjects acted out their own personal problems, role-playing sessions were extended in scope and complexity to "give the members of the group a chance to act in a variety of functions and roles and enable them to release and shape their interests" (Moreno, 1953, p. 533). As Moreno pointed out, one advantage of role play over real-life experience (and this would seem to be an advantage of simulations in general) is their relative "safety," (a characteristic which Simmel's essay had also suggested). Subjects can test out alternative decisions, can analyze the consequences of their actions with a certain detachment, and can make mistakes without having to pay the real-life consequences — all opportunities which life itself seldom permits.

The atmosphere in many of the games discussed in this book resembles that of psychodrama in that players tend to get heavily involved in their game roles. In fact, for many, the role-playing — and the subsequent feelings of familiarity and empathy they gain with respect to their roles — is the most rewarding aspect of the game experience (see, e.g., Boocock, 1966, Chapter 6). Thus, it is important to make clear that in most of these games skillful role-play is not essential to *winning the game*. On the contrary, too much concentration on the fine points of one's game role may divert attention from the kind of rational, rigorous analysis of the simulated situation which is usually necessary to planning intelligent game strategies.

GAMES AND CHILD DEVELOPMENT

Working from an assumption of the socialization functions of games similar to Mead's, scholars interested in development patterns of childhood have also attempted to relate the kinds of games children play to the stages of their physical and mental development. For example, the play activity preferences of children at a number of different age levels have been classified, holding constant such characteristics as sex, race, IQ, and residence (see, e.g., Lehman and Witty, 1927). The key figure in this area is Jean Piaget, who conceptualizes development in terms of a sequence of phases or stages, each with its own modes of thought, behavior, and experience. (The number and names of the phases vary from one of Piaget's books to another, perhaps partly a reflection of his long and prolific research career, beginning with his first publications on learning in the 1920s and continuing to the present. However, the basic notion of regular, definable, sequential development, with each level of development finding its roots in a previous phase and continuing into the next one, holds throughout his published work.)

Piaget's research method consists mainly of observing and interviewing small groups of children (including his own), and his imaginative interviews with Swiss children on the "rules of the game" of various kinds of play activities make some of the most fascinating reading in the annals of research on children. Essentially what he demonstrates is how the characteristic games of each age level — or the way in which a single game, such as marbles, is played at different ages — are congruent with the child's intellectual development and view of the world at that particular stage. The general trend is from spontaneous, non-social play and manipulation of objects (for example, the very young child, given a handful of marbles, will simply push them about, drop and throw them, put them into and take them out of other objects, and so on, with no observable structure to his play), to the pre-adolescent's intense interest in rules *per se*, including mastery of their finer details, interest in their underlying "moral" principles, and attempts at "codification" of related rules (Piaget, 1948, Chapter I).

Unlike Mead, Piaget is essentially a *cognitive* theorist, focusing upon the intellectual life of the child. He tends to analyze a particular kind of behavior (e.g., how a child acts in some game or play activity) as *leading* to, and as a *manifestation* of, the attainment of some intellectual level. Thus, whether he is examining the *ludic*, "self-satisfying" repetitious play of the "sensory-motor phase," (roughly to age two), or the highly structured "collective" games of the "concrete operation phase" (roughly ages nine to eleven or twelve), games are analyzed in terms of their position on the child's continuum of intellectual development (*Ibid.*, see also Piaget, 1962, Part 2). Piaget's focus upon intellectual development is emphasized here not only because it leads into the next stage in the theoretical literature on games, but also because it serves as a reply to those who see "fun and games" and intellectual learning as mutually exclusive activities. On the contrary, Piaget's data provide convincing support for the view that games play an essential part in the evolution of intelligence.

GAMES FOR LEARNING

Viewing the literature on games in its historical sequence then suggests a gradual process of *recognition* of the potential learning functions of games: from the initial recognition of their inherent attractiveness, and their ability to capture interest and commitment; to recognition of the way in which favorite games mirror their surrounding environment or society; to recognition of the socialization functions of games; and finally to recognition of the way in which certain types of games are particularly appropriate at particular stages in children's development.

A logical next step in the sequence outlined above would be in a sense to reverse the process, i.e., to design and use specific games to produce desired learning and/or socialization. This kind of purposive application of the positive, attractive features of games to pedagogical problems is implied at a number of points in Dewey's work, but it was not specified until the initiation, in the 1960s, of several research projects on games for classroom use. In 1961, James Coleman concluded *The Adolescent Society,* a study of ten midwestern high schools, with recommendations for the development of academic games, organized like interscholastic athletics. According to Coleman, bringing this kind of activity into the classroom could serve not only as an effective means of communicating certain intellectual materials, but also as a means of channeling the efforts of able students into intellectual areas, which now suffer in competition with sports, cheerleading, and other activities highly valued by the young. Projects at Abt Associates, the Western Behavioral Sciences Institute, and Northwestern University are similar in purpose to the work of Coleman and his colleagues at Johns Hopkins, and are all based upon the principle that games can be designed to teach specific intellectual and social skills.

This philosophy is nicely expressed in a fictional work published in the same year that the Hopkins project began. *Island,* Aldous Huxley's 1962 version of Utopia, describes the society of Pala, as seen through the eyes of Will Farnaby, a cynical British newsman who visits the island and who serves as a kind of devil's advocate for Huxley's ideas. In the following passage, Farnaby is visiting the local school and is receiving an explanation of Pala's educational policy from the Under Secretary of Education (Mr. Menon) and the principal of the school (Mrs. Narayan):

"From about five onwards practically any intelligent child can learn practically anything, provided always that you present it to him in the right way. Logic and structure in the form of games and puzzles. The children play and, incredibly quickly, they catch the point. After which you can go on to practical applications ... Or consider another field where one can use games to implant an understanding of basic principles. All scientific thinking is in terms of probability. The old eternal verities are merely a high degree of likeliness; the immutable laws of nature are just statistical averages. How does one get these profoundly unobvious notions into children's heads? By playing roulette with them, by spinning coins and drawing lots. By teaching them all kinds of games with cards and boards and dice."

"Evolutionary Snakes and Ladders — that's the most popular game with the little ones," said Mrs. Narayan. "Another great favorite is Mendelian Happy Families."

"And a little later," Mr. Menon added, "we introduce them to a rather complicated game played by four people with a pack of sixty specially designed cards divided into three suits. Psychological bridge, we call it. Chance deals you your hand, but the way you play it is a matter of skill, bluff, and cooperation with your partner."

NOTES

1. There are, of course, situations in which one's performance in games does affect one's real-life standing. In certain upper class groups, a minimum level of competence in sports such as tennis or golf is, like good manners, a prerequisite for social acceptibility. Likewise, the leaders of slum gangs often gain and hold their positions in part because of their skill at the sports and games valued by the group. Doc in Whyte's *Street Corner Society* (1943) is an example. Knight's point, however, is that *in addition to* any real effects of a person's game performance

upon his other social activities, games have an attraction such that people play as if their lives depended upon the outcome, even when they do not.

2. Some clarification of terminology may be useful. While some writers use the terms "simulation" and "gaming" interchangeably (e.g., Robinson, 1965), they are differentiated here because they do come out of two different theoretical traditions. What is new about the teaching device discussed in this book is that it *combines* two different techniques: the game structure, with rules of play, a method of determining a winner or winners, etc.; and the simulated environment with its creation of key elements of the outside or future world within the classroom so that the student must make decisions and act *as if* he were actually operating in this environment.

Simulation in the broad sense of reproducing or imitating certain features of an object or process is not a new idea. Probably the first widespread use of simulation principles was in the construction of physical models for testing parts of large objects before building the real things — e.g., testing models of ship hulls in tanks, or airframes in wind tunnels. While simulations of this sort are actual physical models of the object being developed, the important thing is not that the model *look* like the real object, but that its components *respond* in the same way as in real life. (For a good discussion of the general concept of simulation, see Dawson, 1962.)

For the social scientist, simulation has typically involved the construction of an operating model which is a *symbolic* rather than a physical representation of some individual or group process. Unlike the survey technique, in which the researcher collects data on the variables he is interested in, the simulation technique requires him to assign values to his variables. "Running" the simulation then involves tracing out the results of a given set of parameters, probably making adjustments in one or another of them in successive runs. The growth of simulation as a technique in the social sciences is thus largely a product of the past decade, paralleling the development of mathematical models and the use of high speed computers by social scientists. Also, since the model is only as good as the accuracy of its parameters, it is not surprising that the most sophisticated simulations to date are of social processes that social scientists know quite a bit about. These include models of: voting behavior, designed by Waldorf and Coleman (1961); international relations, designed by Guetzkow and his associates at Northwestern University (1963); birth and marriage rates, and other demographic behavior, designed by Orcutt *et al.* (1961); and high school clique formation and behavior, designed by Coleman (1962).

REFERENCES

Boocock, Sarane S. *The Effects of Games with Simulated Environments upon Student Learning.* Baltimore: The Johns Hopkins University, Department of Social Relations, 1966. (Unpublished Ph.D. dissertation.)

Caillois, Roger. *Man, Play, and Games.* New York: Free Press, 1961.

Coleman, James S. *The Adolescent Society.* New York: Free Press, 1961.

—————. "Analysis of Social Structures and Simulation of Social Processes with Electronic Computers." In Guetzkow, Harold S. (ed.), *Simulation in Social Science.* Englewood Cliffs, New Jersey: Prentice-Hall, 1962, 61-67.

Dawson, R. E. "Simulation in the Social Sciences." In Guetzkow, Harold S. (ed.), *Simulation in Social Science.* Englewood Cliffs, New Jersey: Prentice-Hall, 1962, 1-15.

Dewey, John. *Democracy and Education.* New York: Macmillan, 1928.

—————. *Human Nature and Conduct.* New York: Henry Holt, 1922.

—————. *The School and Society.* Chicago: University of Chicago Press, 1916.

Groos, Karl. *The Play of Animals.* New York: D. Appleton, 1898.

Guetzkow, Harold *et al. Simulation in International Relations.* Englewood Cliffs, New Jersey: Prentice-Hall, 1963.

Huizinga, Johan. *Homo Ludens.* Boston: Beacon Press, 1955.

Huxley, Aldous. *Island.* New York: Harper, 1962.

Knight, Frank H. *Risk, Uncertainty and Profit.* Boston: Houghton Mifflin Co., 1921.

Lehman, Harvey and Witty, Paul A. *The Psychology of Play Activities.* New York: A. S. Barnes, 1927.

Mead, George H. *Mind, Self and Society.* Chicago: University of Chicago Press, 1934.

Mitchell, E. D. and Mason, B. S. *The Theory of Play.* New York: A. S. Barnes, 1948.

Moreno, J. L. *Who Shall Survive?* Beacon, New York: Beacon House, 1953.

Orcutt, Guy *et al. Microanalysis of Socioeconomic Systems: A Simulation Study.* New York: Harper, 1961.

Piaget, Jean. *The Moral Judgment of the Child.* Glencoe, Ill.: Free Press, 1948.

—————. *Play, Dreams and Imitation in Childhood.* New York: W. W. Horton and Co., 1962.

Robinson, James A. "Simulation and Games." Columbus, Ohio: Ohio State University, Department of Political Science, 1965. (Unpublished paper.)

Simmel, Georg. "Sociability: An Example of Pure, or Formal Sociology." In Wolff, Kurt (ed.), *The Sociology of Georg Simmel.* Glencoe, Ill.: Free Press, 1950.

Spencer, Herbert. *The Principles of Psychology,* Vol. II. New York: D. Appleton, 1873.

Waldorf, Frank and Coleman, James S. "Study of a Voting System with Computer Techniques." Baltimore: The Johns Hopkins University, Department of Social Relations, 1961. (Unpublished paper.)

Whyte, William F. *Street Corner Society.* Chicago: University of Chicago Press, 1943.

Games For Learning

CLARK C. ABT

SOME PROBLEMS OF TEACHING SOCIAL STUDIES IN ELEMENTARY AND SECONDARY SCHOOLS

■ Social studies, as they are taught in most secondary schools today, generally consist of geography, history, "civics," and sometimes economics. From the aspects of analytic precision and comprehensive scope, these subjects are closer to the humanities (if indeed history is not considered such) than they are to the sciences. There are no elegantly simple rules of behavior in social studies, because they deal with animate individuals in societies, rather than with the inanimate material objects of mathematics, physics, and chemistry. There usually are no formulae to be remembered, no theoretical calculations to be made, and no experiments to be executed and observed in secondary school social studies classes.

If learning is based on experience and drawing analogies to previous experiences, it seems clear why the effective teaching of social studies is most difficult when only conventional techniques are used. In English, mathematics, physics, and chemistry, there are frequent situations where the child can learn by doing, such as listening and talking, reading and writing, problem solving, and experimenting. Similar situations are not usually available to the teaching of social studies because there are no opportunities for students to make history, write history, solve problems of global geography and economics, or experiment with forms of civic organization.

EDITORS' NOTE: This paper is reprinted by permission of the author and of Educational Services Incorporated.

In conventional secondary school social studies, the students may not learn as much or as deeply as in other subjects, because they cannot readily learn to be surprised at things without having some experience of how they ought to be. They cannot learn that they have made mistakes unless they can make mistakes — and making a mistake in history means making a wrong decision, not failing to remember a date.

It is the argument of this chapter that heuristic games constitute a technique that improves student understanding of social studies, by means of the well-established devices of conditioning through doing and analogizing to the students' previous experiences.

SIMILARITIES AMONG FORMAL GAMES AND SOCIAL STUDIES TOPICS

Games are most familiar as amusements and sports, but they are not necessarily only amusing or even sporting. For the professional athlete or gambler, games are a completely serious matter. For the players of political games, such as "I Will Not Be A Candidate" and "Consensus Building," they can be matters of political life and death. For the players of corporate games such as "My Ambitions Are All For The Firm" and "Expanding Markets," they can be matters of a company's life and death. For the players of romantic games such as "If I Ignore You Maybe You'll Notice Me" (also known as "Hard To Get") and "Hidden Depths," they can be matters of emotional life and death. For the players of marriage games such as "You Made Me Do It" and "I Can't Understand You," they can be matters of a marriage's life and death. For the players of crime games such as "Getting Even" and "Then They'll Respect Me," they can be matters of personal life and death. And for the players of political-military war games such as "Getting In The First Strike" (also known as "Defensive Preemption") and "My Last Offer" (also known as "Controlling The Escalation"), they may be matters of a nation's life and death. In sum, many games are very serious indeed.[1]

Why are these groups of events games? Why are careers sometimes called the "advertising game," or the "teaching game"? Why are certain types of personal behavior called "that old game"? These are games because they all contain the basic elements of games. A trial of abilities is a test. When more than one person is

tested and the results are compared, we have a contest. A game
may be defined as any contest (play) among adversaries (players)
operating under constraints (rules) for an objective (winning,
victory or payoff). Mathematical game theory defines games in
terms of the number of independent players, the degree of competition and cooperation among them, the amount of information
they have about their adversaries, and whether the game is de-
terministic or probabilistic.

Whether games are defined as contests played according to
rules with power resources, skill, and luck; or as mathematical
exercises,[2] they always have the characteristics of *reciprocal actions
and reactions* among at least partly *independent entities* having
different objectives.

In "I Will Not Be A Candidate," for example, the reporter acts
by asking questions of the potential candidate intended to exact
a commitment from him to the role of candidate. The reporter's
objectives may be both professional and political: the achievement
of a "scoop," and the "flushing out" of disavowed intent. The potential candidate reacts with various forms of the statement, "I
will not be a candidate," strongly implying, however, that he is
certainly considering becoming a candidate and would like to be
asked the question again. The potential candidate's objectives are
to continue to be asked if he will run so as to gain publicity by
building up suspense, while at the same time avoiding the loss of
political bargaining power incurred by a premature declaration
of intent.

This is a partly cooperative game (a game with a non-zero
sum), but it also has partly competitive objectives for the two
players.[3] They can both lose if the reporter stops asking too soon
or the candidate announces too late, and they can both win if the
reporter asks just long enough for the candidate to announce his
candidacy. The reporter "wins" most if he can trick the candidate
into announcing slightly prematurely, when the news values of
novelty and significance are maximized. The candidate may then
lose a little of his preferred timing for the announcement. The
candidate "wins" most if he can get the reporter to keep asking,
but announces only when it best suits his political purposes. By
that time the announcement may not come wholly as a surprise,
and the reporter will have lost some of his "scoop."

Games such as this are examples of informal games, because

their rules are implicit rather than explicit. Formal games, on the other hand, have at least some explicit rules, although there are usually additional implicit rules involved. Formal games may be classified according to three major types: *Showdown* games, in which each player exhibits his best physical or mental performance and luck without interference from any other player, and the results are compared; *Strategy* games, in which opposed players interfere with each others' exhibited performances; and *Combination* games incorporating strategic exchanges preliminary to showdowns. In each of these categories, the substance of the game may consist of various combinations of skill, chance, realism, and fantasy.

Examples of formal *showdown* games are poker, craps, treasure hunts, charades, most races, and golf. (Informal showdown games are "Getting Even" or competitive secret bidding on jobs.) Examples of formal *strategy* games are bridge, chess, checkers, ghosts, boxing, and wrestling. (An informal strategy game is "Hard To Get.") Examples of formal combinations of strategy and showdown (racing) games are football and hockey.

Among animals, most games are of the informal strategic type, although the mating displays of birds are showdowns. Many games may have originated as youthful efforts to imitate adult activities, or as religious rites preceding military struggles (invoking the gods controlling "chance"). It is in the examination of game origins that we return full circle to the relation between formal games and social studies.

The ancient priests who first formulated the predecessors of some familiar games of skill and luck sought a symbolic isomorphism between some critical elements of large scale historical developments such as wars and social conflicts, and their religious ceremonies. If their magical skills could demonstrate power over the ceremonial analog of the dread historical crisis, then it would seem to many seekers after certainty that these same magical skills might control — or propitiate — the real world crisis. Many of these serious religious rituals are still played today by primitive peoples. They resemble games in their formal simulation or modeling of larger processes, but differ from games in the asymmetry of power among the players (men and gods) and the greater certainty of a formal outcome.

Another kind of relatively primitive people — children — also seek comprehension of and power over larger-scale adult activities by playing mimetic games or role plays such as "Doll House" and "Soldier."[4] Children incorporate and organize much perceived adult behavior by playing the role of adults, and games seem to be one of the fundamental means by which children learn about the larger world outside. What could be more natural, then, than to continue the play-learning process in the schools? It would exploit a behavioral mode toward which children are already strongly motivated, and by the use of which they have repeatedly demonstrated impressive learning performances.

Given the desirability of teaching with games, is it feasible? Specifically, is there enough similarity between social studies topics and games that can be played effectively in high school classrooms? We think so. Consider the following table of social studies topics, and how they can be decomposed into play elements that are common to formal games.

In addition to the sometimes surprising similarities between the structure and dynamics of social studies topics and formal games, there are the well known similarities between group military conflicts and the classical "war games" of chess, checkers, go, etc. These similarities are not accidental; the games were probably originated by military practitioners for their part-amusement, part-training. Variations of these games of military strategy share many common elements with those social studies topics dealing with military or military-like conflicts, such as wars, revolutions, insurgencies, price wars, industrial and class conflicts, elections, etc. These similarities have been found sufficiently valid to have provided generations of military careerists with diversion and perhaps some indirect instruction in such basic military principles as the offensive, concentration of forces, mobility, reconnaissance, etc.

Although there are many similarities between familiar formal games and elements of social science topics, there are also some important differences. Most games provide for a uniformity of initial player resources — in real life it is seldom so. Most games have fixed uniform rules clearly known by the players. In real life, the rules of the "games" are continually (although often slowly) modified by the players, and there is often a game over the nature of the rules themselves (sometimes called "Legislature" or "Supreme Court"). Real life "rules," or constraints on behavior, are often tacit rather than explicit, and sometimes not even completely known to the players.

69

TABLE 1

| Subject | Social Studies | | | Elements Common to Social Studies and to Games | Formal Games | |
	Topic	Players	Objectives	Typical Resources	Example	Type
History	Civil War	Loyalists vs. Rebels in Civil War	Gain support of neutrals	Coercion and persuasion		Strategy
		High, low vs. middle in High-low poker	Gain support of opposite	Sequence and betting	High-low poker (2 winners)	Showdown
	Colonization	Colonizers vs. Colonizers	Control colonial region	Power, decision, speed		
		Climbers vs. Climbers	Control "mountain"	Power, decision, speed	King of the Mountain	Showdown
	Raw Materials Production	Producer vs. Producer	Capture market	Location closest to market		
		Player vs. Player	Capture ball	Closest to ball	Soccer	Strategy
Geography	Trade Routes	Civilization vs. Geography	Get closest to market	Mobility		
		Players vs. Position	Get closest to objective	Movement	Shuffleboard	Showdown

Category	Activity	Parties	Object	Means	Sport example	Type
Civics	Legislative Processes	Elected reps. vs. Elected reps.	Vote or kill legislation in spite of blocks	Numbers, organization and timing		
		Players	Score goals, deny opponents goals	Mobility, specialization, coop-eration	Basketball, Football	Strategy
	Elections	Candidates vs. Candidates	Win	Outdis-tancing opponents		
		Racers vs. Racers	Win	Run faster	Races	Showdown
	Union-Management Collective Bargaining	Union vs. Management	Increased share of profits	Strike-lockout		
Economics		Teams	Goals	Massed power	Rugby	Strategy
	Competitive Investment	Investors vs. Investors	Profit	Capital, calculation		
		Players	'Play' profit	Capital, calculation	Monopoly	Showdown

Perhaps the greatest difference between traditional formal games and real life "games" is that the formal games are mostly pure competitions — that is, they usually have only one winner, and all the winner's adversaries are losers. Most formal games thus most closely resemble the bitterly competitive power struggles of wars, revolutions, and intense political and economic combats. Obviously most political, economic, and social processes are at least partly cooperative, and many are almost wholly cooperative. In cooperative processes, all the "players" (participants) "win," although perhaps in different degrees. Formal games rarely simulate this common aspect of our experience, being usually oriented toward conflict. Only to the extent that the loser of a formal game who cooperates in playing "wins" the pleasure of playing, do formal games also represent the mutual benefits of cooperative activities.

Some recently developed formal parlor games have introduced cooperative activities specifically intended to simulate partly cooperative historical activities such as international alliance-forming. Cooperation, of course, exists in formal card games such as bridge, but it is abstract and does not refer to a specific historical situation. Recently a number of educational games have been designed that involve realistically cooperative behavior. Some of these are described later in this chapter.

AN ELEMENTARY THEORY OF EDUCATIONAL GAME DESIGN

The design of educational games is different from that of games designed primarily for entertainment, although their forms may be similar. An educational game's objective is to educate, not to entertain. Entertainment becomes an instrumental value, rather than the design objective. In entertainment games it is just the opposite; for achieving the maximum of entertainment, the players must be "educated" in the game's possibilities.

The following educational game design procedure constitutes a kind of elementary theory, much of which remains to be verified by observation of experimental games. It consists generally of a *system analysis* of the substantive problem, process, or situation to be taught; the design of a *logical or mathematical model* that is a simplified manipulable analog of the process or problem to be taught; the *design of a human player simulation* of the model;

and the *refinement* of both the original system analysis and abstract model through repeated test plays of the game.

System Analysis: The educational objectives of the game are specified in terms of substantive scope, structural comprehension, factual detail, and relationship to other educational material. The educational objectives are used to limit the situation or process to be analyzed in time, geographic area, and functional scope and detail. This time-area-function-bounded "problem space" is then subjected to a system analysis. The system analysis generally consists of identifying all the major decision-making entities, their material and information inputs and outputs, and the resources and information exchanged by these decision-making elements. Typical decision-making entities are government institutions, political leaders, and participating publics in political history models; individual hunters, families, and tribal leaders in anthropological models; and producers, consumers, entrepreneurs, and traders in economic models.

A sequential analysis is then made to determine the sequence and rate of flow of information and resources among the decision-making entities that have been identified. The flow of information and resources in most political, economic, social, and natural systems is usually largely cyclical. If it is completely cyclical, we have what is called a "closed" or "conservative" system or cycle, in which the total amount of whatever flows through it is a constant quantity, more of it in one place resulting in less of it in another. Over a short period of time, material or resource flow is usually in the form of a closed cycle because it is mostly the distribution rather than the total quantity that changes. The flow of information is more complex, since it is not "consumed" so much as it is withheld, lost, modified, or distorted. The sequential analysis determines the information and resource inputs to and outputs from each of the decision-making entities.

Analytic Model: A decision-analysis is now made of the decision-making entities, to determine what operations they perform on their information and resource inputs in order to produce their respective outputs. It is much easier to identify the alternative decision "rules" or criteria for the decision-making entities after their inputs and outputs have been specified over a range of typical conditions. For example, to determine the probable criteria used by a cabinet in making its political decisions, it helps to know

73

what it decided to do in response to what kind of information and with what available resources in a number of situations. A decision-analysis usually identifies the relatively stable criteria or motives of decision-making entities by dividing them into absolute values and instrumental values (those helpful in achieving the absolute values). Thus, for King Charles in 1640, the royal prerogative was a stable absolute value pursued in all his decisions, while loyalty to his Lord Lieutenant, Strafford, was more of a negotiable instrumental value.

The decision analysis determines which "problems" are perceived in which way by the decision-making entities. "Problems" may be defined as discrepancies between the ideal state of the world perceived by the decision-making entity according to its values, and the perceived actual state. This problem recognition is followed by a problem-solving response, which may range from denial that the problem exists to the decision to allocate and engage various political, social, economic, or military resources to correct the discrepancy between ideal and reality. The criteria for recognition of a problem usually include its saliency for the decision-making entities' values. The criteria for the allocation and engagement of resources to correct problems usually include expectations of the relative cost, risk, and effectiveness of alternative responses.

In sum, the system analysis identifies the major actors in a process, their interactions, and their decision rules in responding to each others' actions.

Simulation Design: Given the model of decision-making entities, their interrelations, and their individual decision rules developed by the system analysis, it remains to translate this analytical model into a human player simulation or "game" which can communicate the results and implications of the analysis to the student. To communicate effectively with the student, the model must be translated into a social drama that involves the student's interest and enables him to experiment actively with the consequences of various "moves," or changes in the system under study. This remains the case whether the "system" is a psychosocial one, as in the conventional drama, a sociopolitical one as in most historical crises, or a socioeconomic one as in most situations of technological innovations and social change.

The technique used to maximize student motivation for participating in the simulation, and thus learning the analytic model, is to turn it into a game. The game combines elements of dramatic conflict, curiosity over the outcome of uncertain events and direct emotional expression through role playing. The game may be viewed as a dramatization of an analytic model of the situation to be studied, enacted by the students themselves in the roles of the decision-makers. To achieve an effective balance between analytical "truth" and dramatic communication, some degree of simplification is needed to form the basic "plot" of this sociodrama or game. Choices must be made about which subplots, characters, and events most lucidly dramatize the material to be conveyed. These choices will be influenced by the school situation constraints on time, space, student number and student capacity. Classroom time and student capacity for abstraction are the most common limiting factors.

The game teams, player objectives, allowable activities, win/lose criteria, and rules are then developed to achieve a maximum of learning in the participating student/player. The game design involves compromises or "tradeoffs" between the competing objectives of comprehensive realism vs. simplification for the sake of playability (a form of experimental manipulability). If a very comprehensive analytical model is simulated, it will either take many hours to play or, if played within a classroom hour, be very confusing to the student. On the other hand, if the model is greatly simplified, it may result in superficial student comprehension of the problem situation. The optimum degree of game detail from the aspect of "truth" and unlimited learning time conflicts with the optimum degree of student comprehension in the time available. This is no different from the conventional teaching problem. What does seem to be different in game learning is the greater information-comprehending capacity of the student in an active role. Nevertheless, shorter games require more simplification and risk some distortion, exactly like shorter lectures.

Refinement: Once designed, educational games are refined by a series of test plays, in which various clumsinesses and distortions are identified and corrected. It is a form of repetitive "tuning."

In "tuning" the game parameters, various design tradeoff decisions must be made. (A "tradeoff" is a situation in which two or more characteristics interact competitively, and their optimum mix must be determined to assign them their relative weight in the process.) Some of the most important educational game design tradeoffs are listed below:

Realism (at the cost of ease of playing)	vs.	Simplification (at the cost of intellectual validity)
Concentration (at the cost of topical coverage)	vs.	Comprehensiveness (at the cost of detail and realism)
Melodramatic Motivation (at the cost of calm analysis)	vs.	Analytical "Calm" (at the cost of reduced emotional involvement and reduced motivation)

In deciding how to resolve these and other game design trade-offs, it is necessary to remember that educational games must operate within fairly rigid temporal, spatial, and behavioral constraints. In educational games designed for secondary schools, it must usually be assumed that a given game must be played by from twenty to thirty students in one large room for a maximum of fifty minutes at a time, and that physical violence or loud outbursts must be avoided. (E.g., personal physical combat situations cannot be used even though they might be educational.)

There are equally important educational requirements that must be met by educational games with the available players, time, space, and behavior, *better* than by conventional teaching, to justify educational gaming. The design criterion for an educational game should be cost-effectiveness or educational efficiency superior to alternative techniques for the particular subject to be taught. For example, if the history syllabus calls for a classroom hour to be devoted to the American Constitutional Convention, then a game can be justified only if it gives the students a deeper understanding of what happened than they can obtain from conventional teaching in that same hour, or if the game can put across an equally good understanding of the topic in less time. To the extent that educational games incur equipment expenditures, these must also be justified by correspondingly superior teaching effectiveness.

TYPES OF EDUCATIONAL GAMES

Educational games may be classified according to whether they emphasize skill, chance, reality, or fantasy; as well as according to whether they are strategic or showdown games.

In games of skill the outcome depends on the capabilities of the players, as in chess, tennis, or some types of business. Games of skill reward achievement, encourage individual responsibility and initiative, and discourage laziness. However, games of skill have the possible educational disadvantage of discouraging slow learners, dramatizing student inequalities, and feeding the conceit of the skillful.

In games of chance the outcome is independent of player capabilities, as in dice, roulette, and pure financial speculation. Games of chance have the educational advantages of dramatizing the limitations of effort and skill, humbling the overachievers and encouraging the underachievers. (It is no accident that they are the most popular types of games among slum populations, most of whom are probably underachievers.) On the other hand, games of chance minimize personal responsibility, effort, and skill, and may encourage magical thinking and passivity.

Games of reality are essentially models or simulations of non-play, real world operations, as in the theater, fiction, military maneuvers and such games as Monopoly and Diplomacy. They offer the greatest educational potential for student comprehension of structural relationships, the problems, motives, and methods of others, and for vicarious experiences of possibilities beyond the student's direct experience. Games of reality exploit the child's and adolescent's love of adult reality, achieving very high student motivation. A possible danger of reality games is the learning of spurious analogies and an overrating of the predictability of events.

Finally, games of fantasy which many persons would not call games at all, while admitting that they do involve play, release the player from conventional perceptions and inhibitions, as in dancing and skiing. There is emotional refreshment and stimulation of the imagination, but low cognitive content.

Most intentionally educational games are reality games of the strategic (rather than showdown) type. This is a matter of emphasis on the simulation of the reality to be learned, rather than

77

the exclusion of skill, chance, and fantasy. With experience, reality games tend to become skill games as the players gain information through experimental manipulation of the game variables. The chance elements used to simulate detailed processes of uncertain or irrelevant mechanism in reality games also tend to become subject to skillful play, at least to the extent of statistical effectiveness.

ADVANTAGES AND LIMITATIONS
OF EDUCATIONAL GAMES

Self-directed learning in games occurs in three, usually successive, phases as a result of active participation and intense involvement of the student:

1. Learning *facts* expressed in the game context and dynamics;
2. Learning *processes* simulated by the game;
3. Learning the relative costs and benefits, risks and potential rewards of *alternative strategies* of decision-making.

Because these three levels of game learning can occur simultaneously in multi-player teams, individual games accommodate a very broad range of student ages and achievement levels. (For example, reading levels ranging from grade 4 to grade 9 have successfully played in the same game.) The slower students also learn from the faster ones, sometimes better than from teachers. Both slow and rapid learners can share social interactions in the game while learning from it at quite different levels. Culturally deprived students respond relatively better to game teaching than to less dynamic, more expository methods. For this and other reasons, games may be able to test the comprehension and solution of complex problems better than purely verbal tests, as well as offering highly motivated self-directed learning.

To summarize, the games method of education at its best includes the following characteristics: A combination of the systems sciences and the dramatic arts — the systems approach for analysis, drama for involvement and motivation. Emphasis is placed on developing analytic approaches and organizing concepts transferable to other problems identified by the students themselves. Intuitive thinking is encouraged, as well as analysis by use of analogy, testing of limiting conditions, and visual expression of solutions. Learning is made entertaining and relevant to the student's life experiences. There is no "talking down" to students — realistic, adult materials are used. Learning is achieved by exploratory problem-solving simulations (games) involving role play, with self-directed student participation. Communications and negotiations skills are developed by team activities. A cross-disciplinary, concrete experiential view of problems is expressed dramatically and abstraction capabilities are built on multiple sensory experiences.

Educational games use the *student's* way of viewing things. They present *concrete* problems in a simplified but dramatic form that mediates between abstraction and confusion, between dry theory and multi-variable reality. For *elementary* school children, educational games translate the child's primarily concrete, intuitive thinking into a sequence of dramatized possibilities that expands his awareness of hypothetical alternatives and fundamental relations. The child deeply involved in the concrete activity of educational gaming becomes aware of formal relationships by direct experimental manipulation. Pleasurable rewards for manipulating formal relationships effectively are fed back immediately in the form of game success. Elementary school children tend to focus on only one aspect of a phenomenon at a time, greatly limiting their ability to comprehend phenomena with even a few interactions among elements. Games present simultaneously progressing multiple interactions that can first be examined one at a time, and then gradually together with increasing comprehensibility.

Educational games often use probabilistic mechanisms to simulate subordinate causal sequences too complex or uncertainly understood to be replicated directly. The natural interest of the children playing the games in these decisive probabilistic mechanisms leads to their learning to understand simple probability from a series of direct experiences. Awareness of probability, together with game pressures to make decisions under conditions of uncertainty, leads children to develop logical strategies taking account of both probabilities and costs. This is the essence of modern statistical decision theory and cost-effectiveness analysis. Elementary school children can learn it by playing games.

The attention span of elementary school children is stretched by educational games. Games generate potent motivation due to the expectation of pleasure children associate with them, and because of their inherent dramatic interest deriving from action, conflict, and uncertainty of outcome. Sustaining motivation is provided by the responses of the other players in the game to the actions of the student player. The student feels himself a cause of events, rather than a merely passive spectator.

The student player gains a growing sense of structure among the game variables, with a correspondingly growing sense of structure of the subject simulated by the game. This can expand the student's attention span and intellectual confidence. The more densely packed a game is with such structure (up to a surprisingly high degree of apparent confusion), the longer the learning episode than can be tolerated by the student without fatigue or loss of interest. The longer and more concentrated the learning episode, the greater the student's understanding and confidence in the intellectual satisfactions of subsequent episodes.

One of the main problems for *secondary school* students is their sense of the relevance of what they are learning to their future expectations. Motivation must be sustained beyond the transient rewards of grades and college admission. Students must believe, and believe correctly, that what they learn will be important to them as adults. "Importance" should be defined broadly, to include not only useful career guidance and training, but also a sense of meaningful identity and the appreciation of general intellectual and social values. Students should have reason to believe that what they learn will help them to understand, predict, and control to a socially acceptable degree their own future environment, as well as their own actions in it.

Educational games that simulate reality can present the great problems of contemporary society on a level of specific human action that directly relates the student's decisions to the larger world. The relevance of educational games perceived by students is both substantive and methodological. Games dealing with economic, political, social, and scientific problems on the adult scale are of obvious substantive relevance to the student's future adult activities. But educational games and simulations also encourage the student to make systematic rational cost-benefit calculations in the face of uncertainty, and use intuitive heuristics.

Educational games incorporate the human aspects of analytic problem-solving. In conventional school situations, the solution to problems is taught on an abstract, impersonal basis. This neglects the interpersonal aspects of most of the decision problems faced by adults. In educational games, a player needs not only to calculate his best moves, but he also needs to persuade his teammates of the effectiveness of these moves. Student players learn loyalty and the decent limits of rivalry. The compressed competitive experience gives students a realistic foretaste of the nature of competition and negotiation, where technical success can be spoiled by social neglect or greed. Over-aggressive, uncontrolled, or apathetic behavior is punished in a non-fatal way in games, disciplining and institutionalizing behavior through peer interactions. The intellectual and the social skills needed to solve adult socioeconomic problems are developed in concert in educational games, as they must be applied in concert in adult life.

The clearest advantage of educational gaming is increased student motivation. Particularly where student motivation may be very low because of sociocultural factors, and where students find much of their curriculum irrelevant to their own life experiences, educational games can make previously uninteresting material fascinating. Although conclusions would be premature, we have noticed a certain differentially greater improvement in the poorest students when learning with games. Students with culturally impoverished home backgrounds seem to be at less of a disadvantage in educational games than they are in conventional classroom situations. The poorest children can play games, and play them well.

A yet unmeasured advantage of educational games, and one that may not exist for all social studies, is the greater understanding of the relationships in integrated historical processes that they provide. It is one thing for a student to learn some facts of mercantilism, and quite a further step for him to grasp the forces that caused its development, determined its successes and failures, and led to its decline.

Teachers implementing the educational games developed by Abt Associates have commented that they are "very exciting" and, unlike any other techniques, involve almost 100 per cent of the students. They believe that a great deal of learning occurs, but that the best use of such games is in conjunction with background reading before the games and class discussion afterwards. In short, most feel that the most effective use of educational games is achieved by a considerably less than total allocation of classroom time to gaming.

81

Some of the principal limitations on the effectiveness of educational games are the attitudes that teachers have about them. Some teachers feel that games are not "serious," or that students will not take them sufficiently seriously, thus possibly dissipating student concentration on the topic being taught. Our experience has been quite the contrary, with students becoming utterly absorbed in the game situations. The games seem to be an excellent means of sharpening concentration.

A possibly more permanent problem is the attitude some teachers have toward complexity in games. Almost all the students we have observed have been impatient to begin playing the educational games, while the rules were being patiently and repeatedly explained by the teacher. The students are quite accustomed to plunging into situations of which their understanding is uncertain or incomplete. The teachers, on the other hand, often feel constrained to understand the rules completely before they will permit the game to begin. This may be a natural extension of a teacher's felt need to maintain control of classroom behavior, and is certainly a useful and necessary attitude in conventional situations. However, in an educational game situation, a more permissive attitude may be more fruitful, wasting less time and avoiding the dissipation of student interest.

Educational games of considerable complexity can be designed so that only very simple rules must be understood to begin playing. The students may then discover additional rules and complexities in the course of the game.

A few teachers distrust educational games because they doubt their intellectual validity, or historical verisimilitude. They ask, for example, how an historical game can be truthful and valid if its outcome is uncertain, or differs from actual history. This objection is based on a misunderstanding of game objectives. It must always be clearly explained to both teachers and students that educational games are not intended exactly to reproduce some series of historical events. If they did, they would not be games, because there would be no element of uncertainty, curiosity, and surprise about the outcome. The object of the game is to involve the student in the *types* of situations, motives, practical constraints, and decisions that are the subject of study, not the specific details. The student should emerge from the game with a better understanding of what it was all about, what was possible and what was not, and why.

Of course, students could deduce incorrect conclusions from a too small number of game experiences, just as they could deduce incorrect conclusions from too small a number of case studies, or from too few lectures on a subject.

A possible and readily avoidable disadvantage of educational games arises when the above misunderstanding becomes a self-fulfilling prophecy. If the only exposure of students to an historical situation is a game, and the game outcome differs from history, then obviously the student will have learned some wrong things for whatever right reasons. This risk is readily avoided by preparatory teaching of the general aspects of the game situation, and post-game comparison and discussion of game "simulated" history and actual history.

A more serious limitation of educational games is their very attractiveness to students. It must be recognized that educational games are not a substitute for, but only an enhancing complement of, conventional study methods. Background information must still be carefully studied. Integrative syntheses and evaluative judgments must still be worked out and clearly expressed in recitation and writing. Furthermore, educational games are impractical or inappropriate for teaching some topics, as well as not especially helpful in developing some intellectual skills. Yet there is the danger that a poorly disciplined class of students will find educational material not in games relatively boring. This limitation can be overcome by carefully relating gamed and non-gamed material, so that the games are only the integrative culminations of a series of educational steps involving reading, writing and discussing.

If the students' given initial capabilities and resources in educational games were determined by their performance on examinations on background material, then they might be all the more motivated to do their conventional studies. In this sense educational games may enhance the effectiveness of conventional study exercises in which they are embedded.

NOTES

1. For other examples of serious games, see Eric Berne, *Games People Play,* 1964; and Anatol Rapoport, *Fights, Games, and Debates,* 1962.

2. See for example, Von Neumann and Morgenstern, *The Theory of Games and Economic Behavior,* 1944; J. D. Williams, *The*

Compleat Strategist, 1954; Melvin Dresher, *Games of Strategy,* 1961; Luce & Raiffa, *Games and Decisions,* 1957.

3. In mathematical game theory "zero sum" means that the arithmetic sum of the payoffs to the players is always zero — that is, if one player wins all $(+1)$, the other loses all (-1).

4. Role plays differ from games in that the former have more determined outcomes and may not be competitive.

Goals and Designs

Games in a
New Social Studies Course

MARILYN CLAYTON and
RICHARD ROSENBLOOM

■ Games are a natural medium to employ in the design of new curricula for the schools. Their characteristics are compatible, in a number of important respects, with the main spirit which infuses contemporary curriculum revision, and games offer the potential for a new and more effective kind of learning experience. But games are not a universal medium for instruction, no more so than the books and lectures whose shortcomings they might help us to offset. Hence, one should seek a balanced view of the uses of games in education. This chapter attempts to offer such a view from the perspective of our own work on the design and evaluation of games for young children.

Our experience has been with the design and evaluation of

AUTHORS' NOTE: The authors have benefitted beyond the limits of attribution from continuing discussion of this subject with numerous colleagues in the Social Studies Program at Education Services, Incorporated. We wish to acknowledge, specifically, the perspective given our thoughts by the work of Jerry Fletcher, and the impetus to our action provided by Peter B. Dow. Needless to say, the views in this chapter are our own, and do not necessarily reflect those of these individuals or of Educational Services, Incorporated.

games for a new social studies course for children in the upper elementary grades. "Man: A Course of Study," has been described by its initiator, Jerome S. Bruner, in this way:

> The content of the course is man: his nature as a species, the forces that shaped and continue to shape his humanity. Three questions recur throughout:
>
>> What is human about human beings?
>> How did they get that way?
>> Ho can they be made more so?
>
> We seek exercises and materials through which our pupils can learn wherein man is distinctive in his adaptation to the world, and wherein there is discernible continuity between him and his animal forebears. (Brunet, 1966, p. 74).

As part of the attempt to understand the nature of the human species the children look at man in two societies, which are deliberately quite foreign to their own — the Netsilik Eskimos and the Kalahari Bushmen. Simple games are one of several means planned to help the children understand the complex interweaving of environmental, technological, and social forces involved in the main activities of these societies.

Our aims are somewhat different from those of others using simulations of social systems as part of new developments in curriculum. In some cases games have been used to give students insight into situations so familiar that their characteristics are unperceived, for example, the Parent-Child Game described by E. O. Schild in this volume. A related purpose is to acquaint students with the dynamics of a situation in which they will be future participants, for example, games used in graduate business education. In both cases, the strategies learned have a direct relevance to the student's life.

American fifth graders can make no practical use of an understanding of caribou hunting strategies — the subject of one of our games. But they can benefit by experiencing one part of a foreign culture, learning about the social and physical conditions that confront an individual in this culture, seeing the inherent logic in the way he deals with his environment, perhaps gaining an understanding of his emotional life. Naturally, we hope that this can lead to increased ability to discern the structure of any culture, as well as to increased self-insight.

The lessons of our experience with games, to date, have been clear and simple. Although a game can be a powerful instrument for learning, its effectiveness depends not only on the game's context within the curriculum but also on the appropriateness of the pedagogic goals toward which it is used.

INITIAL EXPECTATIONS

To make clear why games are attractive to curriculum designers in social studies, let us begin with some axioms for learning. The 1959 National Academy of Sciences Conference on Science Curriculum defined four, having to do with aims, readiness, methods, and motives. As reported in Bruner's, *The Process of Education* (1961), the conference emphasized that the proper stuff of education was the fundamental structure — as opposed to the factual detail — of a subject. They argued that the structure of a field, comprising the ideas and themes which lie at the heart of each subject, would prove to be as simple as it is powerful. This led to an important conclusion about readiness, the often quoted dictum that any subject could be taught to anybody at any age in some honest form. The conference also drew attention to the important role of intuitive thinking in the process of learning, discussing the virtues of the shrewd guess, the tentative hypothesis, and, more generally, of inductive thinking as a way of coming to grips with the inherent structure of a field. On the subject of motives for learning, the conference acknowledged that the best stimulus for learning was that which came from the subject matter itself, from an intrinsic student interest in the material at hand.

Two related themes have achieved prominence in more recent curriculum reform efforts. These are expressed by the words "discovery" and "diversity." Materials which honestly embody the fundamental structure of a subject and which hold an intrinsic interest for the child can be a medium by which children — at any age — gradually uncover the nature of that structure for themselves through a combination of intuitive and more formal learning processes. It has become evident, furthermore, that the diversity of both students and teachers demands a diversity of materials and methods in the design of new curricula. Not all children will

87

learn equally well, or at all, from the same experience, and not all teachers can teach effectively in a single mold. Harvard's Project Physics has been successful in taking account of such diversity by providing materials of many kinds: verbal, visual, auditory, manipulative, and so on.

Finally, in theories about learning, there has been the theme of "the whole child." As A. S. Neill puts it, "textbooks do not deal with human character, or with love, or with freedom, or with self-determination. And so the system goes on, aiming only at standards of book learning — goes on separating the head from the heart" (Neill, 1960, p. 26). A curriculum should provide opportunities for emotional as well as cognitive experiences.

Seen against these aims and assumptions, educational games have evident advantages. For the curriculum developer, the very process of formulating the game model, if done well, forces attention to the inherent structure and the fundamental themes of the subject at hand. As with programmed instruction, the requisite analysis of a subject matter in terms of behavioral goals and presentation sequence benefits pedagogy. For children, games could impart information in a meaningful way because they present problem-solving situations which, when well designed, require immediate application of new facts. Games should be conducive to discovery and intuitive thinking because they provide a laboratory-type setting where independent variables can be freely manipulated to test consequences of guesses and hypotheses. The player is free not only from fact-bound reality, but also from a teacher's affectively charged feedback. Games could prove to be a powerful way to reach the child low in verbal skills. Games should aid empathetic understanding because of the opportunity they offer for role-playing. And as for motivation, children at all ages take readily to games and find them stimulating in themselves.

During 1965 and 1966 several games were designed for "Man: A Course of Study" by an organization specializing in such work. In early 1966, when these games were still under trial, their expected benefits were described by their principal designer, Clark Abt:

> Educational games use the *student's* way of viewing things. They present *concrete* problems in a simplified but dramatic form that mediates between abstraction and confusion, between dry theory and multi-variable reality. For *elementary* school

children, educational games translate the child's primarily concrete, intuitive thinking into a sequence of dramatized possibilities that expands his awareness of hypothetical alternatives and fundamental relations. The child deeply involved in the concrete activity of educational gaming becomes aware of formal relationships by direct experimental manipulation. Pleasurable rewards for manipulating formal relationships effectively are fed back immediately in the form of game success. Elementary school children tend to focus on only one aspect of a phenomenon at a time, greatly limiting their ability to comprehend phenomena with even a few interactions among elements. Games present simultaneously progressing multiple interactions that can be examined one at a time, and then gradually together with increasing comprehensibility.

· ·

The student player gains a growing sense of structure among the game variables, with a correspondingly growing sense of structure of the subject simulated by the game. This can expand the student's attention span and intellectual confidence. The more densely packed a game is with such structure (up to a surprisingly high degree of apparent confusion), the longer the learning episode that can be tolerated by the student without fatigue or loss of interest. The longer and more concentrated the learning episode, the greater the student's understanding and confidence in the intellectual satisfactions of subsequent episodes. (This passage is from the chapter by Abt in this volume, pp. 79-80.)

GAMES AS ROLE PLAY

This enthusiasm has led to overambitious design goals. The resultant games combined, and confounded, the potential of games for role-playing and strategic uses. Role-playing and strategic analysis, rather than complementing each other, turn out to be incompatible behaviors: one requires immersion and loss of perspective, the other requires stepping back and objectivity. This and a number of other problems have become evident through the classroom trial of educational games.

Consider the problems that get in the way of learning when games are used as occasions for role-play and intended to give the players empathetic insight in a culture and the meaning of its roles. One problem is that games tend to evoke much "noise," primarily because of young players' common lack of success in maintaining the appropriate psychological role. If our model of the best educational environment for analytic examination is the laboratory, with its potential for manipulation of variables and realistic feedback, it does not make sense to allow the stimulus situations and outcomes for student responses to be ones we cannot specify in advance. If in a chemistry class we wanted totally uninitiated children to learn about the properties of acid and base reactions, we would not demonstrate with chemicals which equally naive students had put together. Students interacting with each other in games do learn something about human behavior, but what they learn is how other school children respond to an unfamiliar game, not how Netsilik hunters respond to an approaching caribou herd.

A second important variable in game construction is that of "cycle length": how many times can a student test out the problem situation from beginning to end? Take the simplest case in which there is one "type" of cycle: one player faces one stimulus situation and the problem is to figure out the best strategy for dealing with it; only one student plays at a time. (The most basic case would be one in which only one response is necessary, but anything called a "game" rather than a "problem" will involve at least several responses with branching contingent outcomes.) Even in such a simple case, if the game is at all challenging, the student can discover strategy and structure only if he can replay the game cycle enough times to test out several alternatives.

Most educational games have a more complex structure and call for several players. Each one, of course, has a set of possible alternative responses, each response with a different outcome. This multiplicity of outcomes exponentially increases the number of cycles a student would have to play through in order to perceive the structure of the situation and the best strategy. Add the complication of having several personae, e.g., slaves, traders, ship owners; to perceive structure and strategy now the student has not only to play repeatedly from his own position but from that of each type of persona. And finally, as we have noted, there is the unanticipated complication of other players not knowing how to play their roles and filling the available game time with irrelevant cycles.

Of course, structure and strategy can be, and probably often are, perceived through "insight" rather than through plodding "trial and error" responses. We may not need as many cycles as

there are possible combinations of moves, but it is plainly unrealistic to expect that insight into sequences as complicated as
those noted above can occur in one, two, or three attempts.

A third problem again points up the need for specifiable outcomes and immediate feedback: just because a particular strategy
(the one *we* know is best) is permitted does not mean either that
it will occur or that it will be favored if it does, unless other strategies are made impossible by their consequences, or the best strategy has at least a noticeably superior result. If transfer is to take
place, the strategy must not only be "reinforced," but the game
situation must be replicable enough, at will, for a student to discover why the strategy was successful.

GAMES TO TEACH STRATEGY AND STRUCTURE

It therefore seems that the empathy goal is unrealistic, and we
should turn (indeed, we have turned) to games which emphasize
strategy and structure rather than role-play.

If this is the goal, a number of considerations become crucial
for game-design. Consider again the problem of "noise" in games.
It may be difficult for young players to assume not only the appropriate psychological, but also the appropriate *strategic* role. And
it is the general level of skill and understanding in the group of
players which determines the stimulus situation and feedback any
one player will receive. Children become competitive, or bored,
but anything other than the psychological model of hungry Net-
siliks cooperating with each other to catch a caribou to bring home
to their families. The experimenter learns the obvious — that attempts to make students feel lonely, religious, or hungry in a game
situation are ineffective, competitive attitudes and time-foreshort-
ening effects always become salient.

Another related difficulty is that the only kind of reward that
can be realistically built into a game situation is maximization of
some countable entity, be it money, token food, points, or stars.
This imposes a very unrealistic picture of psychological motivation
in other cultures, for example, why Bushmen hunt together. Com-
panionship is perhaps as important a factor as the large catch; some
Bushmen could do better alone but still hunt in groups. Students
may learn to cooperate in a game to show that cooperation is better than competition, but they are cooperating to maximize an out-

come of the game, rather than some inner feeling unconnected with the game.

And lastly, events of real magnitude such as death, hunger, separation are divorced from emotional consequences and can only be represented in the most artificial way. Ability to test action without consequence may be a real boon to structure and strategy perception but it is not conducive to empathetic insight into the lives of others.

CONCLUSIONS

These considerations lead to specific requirements for the design of games intended to induce understanding of a culture. We believe that the fruitful path is to choose games which emphasize strategy and structure, rather than personal roles. Moreover, if children play against "nature" rather than against other children, feedback can be specifiable and immediate (that is, the children may *compete* against each other, but *direct interaction* is with "nature"). Naturally "nature" may include human as well as physical agents, but feedback from human agents is part of the game itself, constructed for maximum realism to the situation being simulated. Such games are intended for repetitive play in short cycles by small groups of children with an entire class usually playing simultaneously on a number of set-ups. This means that procedures must be simple and readily learned because little direct supervision is possible.

The idea behind this sort of game is that it can serve as the equivalent, in the social studies, of the laboratory kit for the physical sciences, to make it possible "for the student to confront the real world . . . directly, rather than through intermediaries such as textbooks." For we believe that games, soundly conceived with an integrated curriculum design effort, can be effective, as their physical materials are, in making "highly sophisticated concepts available in delightful ways" (Educational Services, Inc., 1966, Introduction).

REFERENCES

Bruner, Jerome S. *The Process of Education*. Cambridge, Massachusetts: Harvard University Press, 1961.

————. *Toward a Theory of Instruction*. Cambridge, Massachusetts: Belknap Press, 1966.

Educational Services, Inc. *Elementary Science Study*. Cambridge, Massachusetts: Educational Services, Inc., 1966.

Neill, A. S. *Summerhill*. New York: Hart Publishing Co., 1960.

Interaction in Games

E. O. SCHILD

■ Games are very much *social* events. There may be considerable similarity between the reasoning of a player in a game of strategy and the solving of a puzzle; but the essence of a game is in interaction: you play with or against *somebody*. Your own success is contingent on other players' behaviors; in interaction games every outcome depends on other players' strategies and even in "showdown games" (Abt, in this volume, pp. 65-84); your final status is codetermined by other players' achievements.[1] Indeed, the other participants in the game provide cues (and reinforcements) for the very way in which you approach the game: to take it seriously or make fun of the whole thing, to become involved in the game itself or to behave toward the other participants as you would were you not engaged in gaming.

This is a major difference between simulation games and other recent educational innovations. These, such as programmed in struction, refer exclusively to the relationship between the individual learner and the subject to be learned. They do not, as simulation games, involve any particular form for interaction among the learners. (Note, however, that an apparently non-social device for instruction may in fact build on the establishment of appropriate social conditions prior to the instruction; thus Moore reports (1966) that the success of his "talking typewriter" to a considerable extent is dependent on the pattern of interaction between the child and the administrator.)

The social nature of learning in simulation games has been empirically demonstrated by Inbar (in this volume, Part III). He presents evidence that the response to a simulation game to a great extent is a *group effect,* and thus determined by attributes of the group (such as size), beyond the attributes of the individual learner.

I shall here discuss some characteristics of the interaction in simulation games, in order to infer what kind of effects we are likely to find in these games. By necessity (i.e., the absence of data) the discussion will be speculative and the "conclusions" are therefore to be taken as hypotheses.

MAINTAINING THE FOCUS OF INTERACTION

For a game to succeed the participants must first of all enter the role of "player." This is logically prior to the entry into the specific role defined for him in the game. (In the same way an actor must first enter the role of "actor" and subsequently the one defined in the script of the play.) Of course, the extent of involvement in the general player role is in itself affected by the events pertaining to the player's specific game role. If this game role requires routine and monotonous behavior, the player is likely to fall out of his player role and withdraw (at least psychologically) from the game; if the game role offers opportunity for intrinsically desirable activities, the player is likely to become more involved. Nevertheless, we have two distinct, albeit interdependent, roles; the general one of "player" and the specific persona in the game.

The general problem of involvement in a game as focus of interaction has been brilliantly analyzed by Goffman (1961), and I can do no better than refer the reader to that paper. Actually it does not seem to constitute a "problem" for the educational use of simulation games. Virtually all users of games report high involvement on the part of the participants. But it is important to realize that involvement in the role of "player" is not a sufficient (although presumably a necessary) condition for the appropriate entry into the specific role defined in the game — and learning is contingent on the latter. Consider as an example the game of Democracy.[2] Sometimes players get highly involved in the peripheral aspects of their roles as legislators — such as making speeches in defense of their stand on various issues. Great interest is shown, the interaction is focused on the game — but the participants do not learn much about the structure of political exchanges and about the basic mechanisms underlying collective decision-making.

94

Nevertheless, the very maintenance of the game as focus of interaction may be important for some students. Note that a cooperative effort is required in order to maintain an appropriate level of involvement. Withdrawal on the part of a player is likely to disturb the other players, both because of its direct effect on the functioning of the game and because of the violation of the consensual definition of the situation. On the other hand, withdrawal in the conventional classroom setting has no particular impact on the other students. In the game we are thus likely to find other players encouraging the withdrawer and attempting to integrate him anew in the interaction.

Let me phrase this point as a specific hypothesis: in game situations students will engage in encouragement of withdrawers more than in conventional learning situations; this phenomenon will be more pronounced, the more the game itself requires interaction (i.e., is less of a showdown game).

As a result, less withdrawal is to be expected in the game situation. It may, of course, be that the game itself evokes more intense participation, because it is "fun," more intrinsically attractive than the conventional classroom activity. But the present hypothesis affirms that even students who initially find the game no more appealing than the conventional activity should withdraw less in the game — because they would be drawn into the situation by the other players.

ROLES AND ROLE RELATIONS

If the game is successfully maintained as the focus of interaction, the content and structure of this interaction is then largely determined by the rules of the game.

I know of no better way to conceptualize this aspect of the rules but to say that they are a set of role definitions. They define for each player his goals, the resources with which he can pursue the goals and the activities which legitimately may be performed in this pursuit. Thereby the relations between roles are also specified: the nature of interdependencies, what a player may legitimately claim from others, etc.[3]

If a player is to succeed in the game he must understand not only his own role, but also other roles:[4] their goals, resources and constraints. In a sense he is forced into the position of a sociological observer: to focus his attention on the structure of role relations. (At the same time, it may be added, he cannot make do with a perception of global structure; he must develop a *"causal* imagery" of relations — in particular as pertains to the effects of his own activities.)

There is here a crucial difference between simulation gaming and role play, as this technique has been used in much Human Relations training. In both, an artificial role is prescribed for the participant, but in entirely different contexts. In role play the primary purpose is to make the player *empathize* with the goals and constraints of the role; the worker playing the role of foreman is to learn what a foreman wants, to understand his motivation and the emotions aroused in response to workers' behavior. No such empathy is needed in the game: the goals of other players are explicitly described in the rules and the motivations simple — to achieve these imposed goals and thus to succeed in the game. On the other hand, the player must understand the structure of relations: which behaviors of the workers are contingent upon which activities of the foreman, where the foreman can and cannot exert power — and how this relationship is conditioned by the strategies of other roles (e.g., whether the workers organize). The adolescent who plays child in the Parent-Child Game will not learn to understand why parents may emphasize homework or why they may impose an "unreasonably" early curfew; his parent in the games does so because the rules make him profit by this (and in respect to the concrete issues concerned the game surely deviates from the reality of many family situations — and conforms to many other). He will (if he is to succeed in the game) understand what control he has over his parents and what control they have over him; what kind of strategies will evoke repeated clashes and what kind may lead to mutual profit in spite of opposing interests. Interests and motivations are "given" in the game and are basically simple; the way to satisfy these interests is, because of the structure of interdependencies, complex. In this sense simulation games conform to the dictum of a psychological sophisticate, Simenon's Maigret: "People are simple; they cannot afford but to be simple. But the relations between people are very complicated."

A related difference between simulation gaming and role play concerns the relative emphasis on instrumental versus expressive behavior. To a considerable extent the purpose of role play is to highlight the importance of expressive behavior; that the actor chooses a course of action not because of its pay-off value in the interaction, but because its very performance is satisfying — e.g., releasing his anger. In the game such behavior is usually self-defeating: if the player wants to succeed, the only criterion for action is its effect on his score. Thus, the game focuses attention on the instrumental aspects of behavior.

Considering these characteristics of simulation gaming, it might be expected that game experience would have purely perceptual effects and not affect attitudes of evaluation toward the role assumed in the game. Nevertheless, there is empirical evidence for attitude change induced by the games (see Boocock's chapter in Part II). The mechanisms involved are not clear, particularly as the nature of the change is puzzling and apparently inconsistent.

One might speculate on the implications of dissonance theory (the pursuit of a certain strategy might, if counter-attitudinal and not particularly successful, generate dissonance and possible attitude change) (Brehm and Cohen, 1962); or that there after all is some role taking in the game and that improvisation in the role does have an attitudinal effect (Janis and King, 1954; King and Janis, 1956); or on some version of reinforcement theory. The present state of evidence on these theories of attitude change seems, however, puzzling in itself (see in particular Greenbaum, 1966).

I would venture to raise one possibility by which games under some conditions might affect attitudes. Assume that the universe of content toward which an attitude is defined consists of several subuniverses, i.e., that the object of the attitude has several aspects. The actor has an evaluation of each of these aspects, and his global attitude toward the object is some kind of sum of his evaluations of these aspects. But the evaluation of each aspect is weighted by the *salience* of this aspect relative to the others.[5] Thus, change in the global attitude may be brought about if the relative salience of subuniverses change — even if evaluations remain constant.

Note that the direction of such change in the attitude will be dependent on the evaluation of the aspect(s), the salience of which changes. Thus, suppose that a player has a more favorable attitude to a legislator's exchange of votes with other legislators than toward other aspects of the legislator's role; as vote exchange is highly salienced in the game of Democracy, we should expect the player to become more favorable toward legislators. If, on the other hand, his attitude toward exchange of votes is less favorable than toward other aspects, we should expect him to develop a less positive (more negative) attitude. The end result of the game in respect to attitudes may thus differ from player to player, even though the mechanism is the same.

I know of no evidence available to test this hypothesis; nor do I want to assert that this is indeed the only way in which games can affect attitudes. But it would seem worthwhile to obtain the relevant data.

Simulation games, I argued above, focus attention on relations and on instrumental aspects of interaction. If the hypothesis is true, attitude change is then likely if the players' evaluation of these aspects differ from their evaluation of other (e.g., expressive) aspects of the roles and process simulated.

EXPEDIENT BEHAVIOR AND EMERGING NORMS

Within the structure defined by the game, the player is free to act as he pleases. But if he is involved in the player-role, his course of action will be guided by considerations of expediency: behavior alternatives are evaluated in terms of their contribution to his success in the game. This emphasis on expedient behavior is a rather important characteristic of simulation games, and has caught the attention of some critics who have searched for values in the games.

Games are amoral. Beyond the requirement of conformity to the rules, no action has any intrinsic properties of being "good" or "bad"; the only yardstick is its effect on the player's score. In terms of the game's structure, there is nothing wrong in breaking promises in the Democracy Game or in being disobedient in the Parent-Child Game. The only criterion for behavior is the player's self-interest.

Nevertheless, in most simulation games there is an inducement to something like "ethical" behavior. In continued play additional norms of interaction, not contained in the rules, are likely to emerge. It is not expedient in the long run to break promises in Democracy, because other players will refuse to make agreements with the untrustworthy individual; and the increased predictability of the process which results when promises are kept will usually be desirable to the players (with exceptions — and hence, as in real life, with deviations from the norm). This can be a very slow process. Baldwin (1966) has shown how in a game involving trade and war between nations, about 20 hours of play were necessary to produce norms which regulated interaction. (Not by coincidence this game is called "All Against All.")

These emerging norms are surely not "values" in the sense of being given, beyond considerations of expediency. They are simply expressions of *long-range expediency* rather than short-run self-interest. They are exactly norms in Homans' sense of

> a statement made by some members of a group that a particular kind or quantity of behavior is one they find of value for the actual behavior of themselves and others, whom they specify, to conform to. The important thing is not that the behavior is conformity, but that it is valued (Homans, 1961).

The emergence of such norms in a situation characterized by the opposing interests of players, and without their being imposed by any authority with extraneous legitimation, is intriguing for the student of interaction who does not want to assume either consensus of interests or the existence of norms *deus ex machina*. They are also interesting from the viewpoint of the training functions of games. Much use of small group processes in training has been based on the assumption of a "conflict-less group" (Verba, 1961), where the members basically were in agreement and the purpose of the group experience to release this latent agreement. In simulation games the purpose is rather to have "Human Relations behavior" evoked in a situation of conflict — simply because it is expedient in the long run. Thus, the same behavioral results may be produced by entirely different premises; "the rational approach which appears to treat human beings as objects to be manipulated, often leads to identical results as the most empathic and subject-oriented approach" (Kahneman and Schild, 1966).

CONTROL OF ENVIRONMENT

In games of strategy the player has considerable control over his own success. Recent psychological research has presented impressive evidence on the importance of the actor's belief in "internal versus external control" (Rotter, 1966), i.e., the extent to which his destiny is contingent on his own behavior as opposed to luck or other arbitrary features of the environment. Coleman and Campbell *et al.* (1966) have shown such belief to be the most important predictor of achievement in school. Seeman has in a number of papers interpreted "alienation" in this way. (Seeman, 1966; Seeman, 1963).

It may be fruitful to distinguish between two components of this "control." The pay-off for an actor is jointly determined by (a) his strategy and (b) the state of the environment in which he acts; the more favorable the state of the environment, the higher the pay-off. Assume now that the environment is given, i.e., the probabilities of different states fixed. "Control" then means that different strategies for given states of the environment produce different outcomes. I shall call this form for control "Control of Outcomes"; the higher the variance over strategies of their expected values (with the given probabilities for the states of environment) — the stronger the Control of Outcomes. The actor optimizes his welfare by adapting to the given environment.

But it may also be that his strategies can influence the environment itself, i.e., that the probabilities of different states are not fixed, but a function of the actor's behavior.[6] I shall call this "Control of Environment." Note that an actor may have Environment Control without having Outcome Control: he can affect the relative probabilities of different environmental states, but once these probabilities are given, he can no more affect his pay-off. Similarly, he may, of course, have Outcome Control without Environment Control. In a sense Control of Environment refers to the actor's adapting the environment to himself.

Corresponding to these forms of control, we may distinguish between belief in control of *outcome* and in control of *environment*.[7] In general it is true that learning is influenced by the control beliefs of the learner. A learner who believes that reinforcement is independent of his actions, is less likely to select the behavior which actually is reinforced and which is to be learned. But the two types of control belief may be of different relative importance in different contexts.

In most situations of directed learning, the belief in *Outcome* Control would seem to be the important variable. These situations are typically constructed so as to require the adaptation of the learner to the teaching environment. Academic learning, from reading through differential equations as well as the development of vocational skills, builds on such adaptation. But several interpersonal skills seem rather based on belief in *Environment* Control. A recurring type of social situation is the one in which one course of action is profitable if its effects on the attitude of other actors are not taken into account — but is not profitable when it is considered that this action may make the other actors unfavorably disposed in the future, i.e., it affects not only the immediate outcome, but also the state of the social environment. A crucial element in continuous interactions (as opposed to one-shot encounters, "endgames") is the fact that P's action not only (together with O's present behavior) causes a certain outcome but also may change the probabilities of O's future behavior. A naive belief in the importance of "personality," i.e., that a given person will tend to respond in the same way to a certain stimulus independently of the definition of the situation evoked by P's previous behavior, implies a belief in low Environment Control — and does not induce success in establishing and nurturing interpersonal relations.

The behavior of a person with low belief in Environment Control is likely to be one of short-range expediency rather than long-range expediency. Other factors, too, may contribute to this (e.g., low tolerance for delay of reinforcement, Mischel, 1960; limited time perspective, Lewin, 1948). But a typical case of conflict between short-range and long-range expediency is one where a certain behavior would be expedient if the environment would remain constant; at the same time, the behavior in question changes the environment in an unfavorable direction. Only confidence in his Environment Control will induce the actor to select that behavior which actually is expedient in the long run.

To sum up, the presence or absence of control beliefs may affect behaviors which are basic to social life. These beliefs are particularly crucial, because they not only affect behavior in a given context, but also affect the capacity to *learn* and change behavior in accordance with changing situations.

Little is known about the methods to increase control beliefs. One possibility would be to let the actor experience situations which are sufficiently simple so that outcomes and environmental states are *clearly* contingent on his own behavior, and which at

101

the same time are sufficiently similar to real-life situations so that generalization is feasible. Simulation games exemplify such a possibility. The contingencies are usually clear and the fact that they are simulations of real-life situations should aid generalization.

If indeed control beliefs can be changed by repeated exposure to contingencies of the appropriate nature, there are presumably many ways other than simulation games to attain this goal. Outcome Control in particular may be demonstrated in many simple situations. But simulation games seem to be one fruitful possibility, which it would be especially worthwhile to pursue in respect to belief in Environment Control. As argued above, a simulation game highlights causal relationships — the way in which other actors' responses are contingent upon the player's actions. And because an interaction game in its very essence involves attempts to influence the behavior of others not only in a specific move, but also in their general strategy, control of environment is more salient than in many other interactions.[8]

If this is true, games are not only an occasion for interaction but may also contribute to some interpersonal skills (such as many training courses in Human Relations attempt to impart). Games *are* to some extent a paradigm of interaction in general; therefore the players not only learn by interacting — they also may learn to interact.

NOTES

1. I shall, however, only consider interaction games, not "showdown games." Moreover, the game paradigm I have in mind is that reflected in the Hopkins games such as Democracy, Community Response, Parent-Child.

2. Copyright James S. Coleman, 1965.

3. The extent to which these role definitions actually constrain, and are exclusive in constraining, behavior is an indication of the extent to which the players are involved in the structure of the game.

4. This is, of course, Mead's insight on the function of games in developing a "self" (Mead, 1934).

5. D. Kahneman suggested this notion to me several years ago. His is the credit for the idea — and mine the responsibility if its application to simulation games is invalid.

   For a more detailed argument that salience and valence in some multiplicative fashion determines the potency of behavior alternatives, see Herman and Schild (1960).

102

6. For a formal treatment and experimental study of behavior in a situation with control of a computer-environment, see Rapoport (1967).

7. Preliminary evidence indicates that these two beliefs may be but weakly correlated.

8. A detailed field experiment is presently under way at Hopkins to test this and related hypotheses on the impact of control beliefs on game behavior and of game experience on control beliefs.

REFERENCES

Baldwin, John. "All Against All: Conflict Resolution in a Simulation." Baltimore: The Johns Hopkins University, Department of Social Relations, 1966. (Unpublished paper.)

Brehm, Jack W. and Cohen, Arthur R. *Explorations in Cognitive Dissonance.* New York: Wiley, 1962.

Coleman, James S., Campbell, Ernest Q. *et al. Equality of Educational Opportunity.* Washington, D.C.: U.S. Government Printing Office, 1966.

Goffman, Erving. *Encounters.* Indianapolis, Indiana: Bobbs-Merrill, 1961.

Greenbaum, Charles W. "Effects of Situational and Personality Variables on Improvisation and Attitude Change." *Journal of Personal and Social Psychology,* 4 (1966) 260-270.

Herman, S. N. and Schild, E. O. "Ethnic Role Conflict in a Cross-Cultural Situation." *Human Relations,* 1960.

Homans, G. C. *Social Behavior: Its Elementary Forms.* New York: Harcourt, 1961.

Janis, I. L. and King, B. T. "The Influence of Role Playing on Opinion Change." *Journal of Abnormal Social Psychology,* 49 (1954), 211-218.

Kahneman, D. and Schild, E. O. "Training Agents of Social Change in Israel: Definition of Objectives and a Training Approach." *Human Organization,* 25 (1966), 72-77.

King, B. T. and Janis, I. L. "Comparison of the Effectiveness of Improvised Versus Non-Improvised Role Playing in Producing Opinion Changes." *Human Relations,* 9 (1956), 177-186.

Lewin, Kurt. "Time Perspective and Morale." In Lewin, G. (ed.), *Resolving Social Conflicts.* New York: Harper, 1948.

Mead, G. H. *Mind, Self and Society.* Chicago: University of Chicago Press, 1934.

Mischel, W. "Preference for Delayed Reinforcement and Social Responsibility." *Journal of Abnormal Social Psychology,* 62 (1961), 1-7.

Moore, Omar Khayyam. Plenary Address presented at *Meetings of the American Sociological Association*, 1966.

Rapoport, Anatol. "A Study of a Multistage Decision-Making Task with an Unknown Duration." *Human Factors*, in Press.

Rotter, J. B. "Generalized Expectancies for Internal vs. External Control of Reinforcements." *Psychological Monographs*, 80 (1966).

Seeman, Melvin. "Alienation and Social Learning in a Reformatory." *American Journal of Sociology*, 56 (1963), 270-284.

———. "Antidote to Alienation — Learning to Belong." *Transaction*, 3 (May-June, 1966), 35-39.

Verba, S. *Small Groups and Political Behavior*. Princeton, New Jersey: Princeton University Press, 1961.

Part II

THE IMPACT

■ If simulation games are to be taken at all seriously as tools for learning, it must be demonstrated that they do teach. This is the purpose of the chapters to follow.

The studies by Boocock and Schild show the variety of learning which may be obtained; they demonstrate the impact of games on factual knowledge, on attitudes and on strategies. In both cases the amount of learning is presumably an underestimate of the teaching-potential of the games, as the data refer to a *single* game session only.

Both Baker and Wing report on use of games over a longer time period, and compare their effects to learning by conventional methods. It is clear that the superiority of a specific simulation over conventional teaching does not imply that all games are more effective; similarly, negative findings in respect to specific games do not discredit the method as a whole. Our object in Part II is thus not to prove a far-reaching generalization about the favorable properties of all simulation games, but to demonstrate by specific instances the *potential* of the method.

The hastiest review of the research design of these studies shows how much they leave to be desired in regard to experimental method. One reason is to be found in the need for testing the impact of games in the *field*, rather than in a well-controlled laboratory setting. This makes it exceedingly difficult to refute a criticism that confounding variables may have been operative. Obviously, attempts to obtain a larger degree of control should be made; at the same time our own feeling is that the most fruitful attack on the problem of proof is by *replications* in different field settings.

An Experimental Study of the Learning Effects of Two Games with Simulated Environments

SARANE S. BOOCOCK

■ One of the major unresolved issues in the field of simulation gaming concerns the type and effectiveness of the learning produced. While most researchers are agreed on the power of such games to interest and motivate students, there is disagreement over whether games also teach intellectual content and skills. This chapter will evaluate the educational value of two of the learning games developed at Johns Hopkins, by an analysis of data from an experiment conducted at Berkeley, California, in the fall of 1964.

THE TWO GAMES

The first of the two games used, the Life Career Game, simulates certain features of the labor, school and marriage "markets" as they now operate in American society. Its purpose is to give students familiarity with the kinds of decisions that must be made about jobs, further education or training, family life and use of leisure, and with the probable consequences of particular decisions given the personal characteristics of the person making them.

AUTHOR'S NOTE: This paper reports some of the findings of the author's unpublished doctoral dissertation, *The Effects of Games with Simulated Environments upon Student Learning*, Department of Social Relations, The Johns Hopkins University, Baltimore, Maryland, 1966. The research was carried out under a grant from the Carnegie Corporation of New York. In addition to the grantor I wish to thank Mr. Edgar Reeves of the U.S. Department of Agriculture and Dr. R. O. Monosmith, Agricultural Extension Service, University of California, for help in the planning and administration of the experiment.

107

The Life Career Game can be played by any number of teams, each consisting of two to four players. Each team works with a profile or case history of a fictitious person (a student about the age of the players).

The game is organized into rounds or decision periods, each of which represents one year in the life of this person. During each decision period, players plan their person's schedule of activities for a typical week, allocating his time among school, studying, a job, family responsibilities, and leisure time activities. Most activities require certain investments, of time, training, money and so on (for example, a full-time job takes a certain amount of time and often has some educational or experience prerequisites as well; similarly having a child requires a considerable expenditure of time, in addition to financial expenses), and a person clearly cannot engage in all the available activities. Thus, the players' problem is to choose the combination of activities which they think will maximize their person's present satisfaction and his chances for a good life in the future. In addition, for certain activities — a job, or higher education — a person must make a formal application and be accepted. (An integral feature of the Life Career Game is that in the normal course of playing, students acquire such skills as filling out college or job application forms correctly.)

When players have made their decisions for a given year, scores are computed in four areas — education, occupation, family life, and leisure. Calculators use a set of tables and spinners — based upon U.S. Census and other national survey data — which indicate the probabilities of certain things happening in a person's life, given his personal characteristics, past experiences, and present efforts. A chance or "luck" factor is built into the game by the use of spinners and dice.

A game runs for a designated number of rounds (usually ten to twelve), and the team with the highest total score at the end of the game is the winner.

The second, the Legislative Game, is essentially a game of strategy, designed to teach the basic processes of negotiation through which collective decisions are reached on issues in which different segments of society have differing interests. Unlike the Career Game, the Legislative Game puts the student into a role that few of them have experienced and that few are likely to play as a major role in their adult lives.

The game calls for six to ten players, each acting as a legislator, and collectively acting as a legislative body deciding upon a series of public issues. Each player is dealt a set of cards which indicate his constituents' attitudes about various issues. For example, one such card reads: Federal aid to education — 70 persons against, 30 persons for. Another reads: Retaining military base in your constituency — 250 persons for, 50 persons against. By studying his whole set of cards, a player can tell how his "district" feels about the various issues, and which issues are most important to them.

After an initial round of short speeches, the game alternates between (a) informal "bargaining" sessions of two or three minutes, when players may contact any other legislators and try to gain their support on issues of the greatest importance to them; and (b) formal sessions of the legislature, during which players bring issues to the floor, discuss them according to rules of parliamentary procedure, and vote. A legislator's success — i.e., whether or not he is re-elected at the end of the game — is determined by his success in getting passed or defeated those measures his constituents most want passed or defeated.

THE DATA

Delegates to a conference of the National 4-H Clubs (about 1,200 young people ranging in age from thirteen to twenty) were randomly assigned to one of the two games. The design of the experiment is shown in Figure 1. The special virtue of the design, besides the large sample and the random assignment on an individual basis, is its control of the Hawthorne effect. Everyone was subject to the "novelty" of a game (and to the experience of the conference itself), but since each delegate played only one game each group acts as a control for the other. Thus questionnaire responses which change in the experimental group and either do not change or change in a different direction in the control group can be postulated as effects of that particular game.

Note, however, that this design does not allow measurement of the effectiveness of a game or games as a learning tool *as opposed to other learning tools,* since both experimental and control groups were exposed to games.[1] Another thing not controlled is the type of student who participated in the conference. Over eighty per cent said they were in the top half of their high school classes academically; over seventy per cent expected to graduate from college. In other words they were clearly not a representative sample of American or even California students.

A weakness of the design which does not show in Figure 1 is that the games were played in a single half-day session, with the two questionnaires administered only a few days apart. Thus the minimum effect of the games would be expected, plus a high likelihood of a test effect of the first questionnaire on the second.

FIGURE 1. Design for Test of Legislative and Career Games, Berkeley, California, September, 1964.

	before	treatment	after
Experimental group: 600 boys and girls	test 1	legislative game	test 2 test 2a
Control group: 600 boys and girls	test 1	career game*	test 2 test 2b

*for analyzing the effects of the career game this group is treated as the experimental group and the legislative game players as the control group

All participants filled out identical questionnaires before and after the games, with some additional questions afterwards pertaining to the particular game they had just played. In order to reduce the sheer number of possible dependent variables (the questionnaire contained 45 individual items about the career game, 74 about the legislative game), and to see whether certain sets of items were related to each other in a meaningful way, the technique of factor analysis was used with the entire set of items for each of the two games. The sample was broken down into four sub-groups (boys in the legislative game, boys in the career game, girls in the legislative game, girls in the career game), and since all respondents answered the same questions twice, eight separate factor analyses were made.

Where the factor loading pattern in all eight runs showed that a particular set of items clustered together in a factor, a multi-item index was constructed which was used as a dependent variable in the analysis. This was done by giving each respondent a score representing the sum of his scores on all the items comprising the factor. Changes in these composite scores in experimental and control groups will be compared in the following discussion.

In addition, a series of multi-variate analyses, holding constant simultaneously respondents' sex, reported grades in school, age and father's education, as well as the game they played, were carried out to examine differences between experimental and control groups when other factors (which might affect the dependent variable) were controlled, and to examine the effect of the game relative to these other variables. The statistical test used with the multi-variate tables is Coleman's a, which gives a measure of the "effect" of each independent variable, obtained by computing for each variable a standardized average of the difference of proportions, controlling for all other variables.[2] The full multi-variate tables are not shown in this paper, but Table A in the Appendix gives the values of a for each analysis discussed in the main text. The size of an a depends upon a number of things including the choice of cutting points for dichotomizing a variable, and interpretation of a particular value should also take into account its size relative to other a's. I have taken an a of .100 or higher to represent a strong effect, and .070 as indicative of some effect of the game, especially if it is in a series of tables with similar kinds of dependent variables and values of a. Given the single playing session which comprised players' experience with the two games at the conference, it seemed more important to point to as many potentially interesting game effects as possible, rather than requiring an artificially high value of a.

In addition to the obvious motivational effects of games which are reported by virtually all observers, simulation games seem capable of producing a variety of learning effects. The Berkeley data indicated three rather different kinds of learning, which will be described in the following three sections.

SIMULATION GAMES AS VICARIOUS EXPERIENCE

When players are asked what they themselves think they learned from a particular game the most frequent response has to do with a general *feeling* for the situation simulated. For example, a content analysis of essays written by Northwestern students who played the Inter-Nation Simulation showed that players felt the most important thing they had gained was a more vivid or "real" understanding of international problems than their textbooks conveyed, including a realization of the complexities of international relations, a better understanding of the problems and goals of nations unlike the United States, and an appreciation for the dilemmas faced by persons in decision-making roles (Guetzkow, 1963, pp. 179-184). The meaning of the vicarious experience afforded by games with simulated environments has been of interest since the beginning of the Hopkins project, and a number of the Berkeley questionnaire items dealt with this kind of learning effect.

Career Game

The great mass of material with which players are confronted seems to produce appreciation of the complexities of career decision-making, especially for those players who try to apply what they learn in the game to their own lives. As one girl wrote:

> All the possibilities that popped up in the game made me realize how difficult decisions will be when I get older.

Another learned that —

> A twenty-four hour day is not long enough to allow a girl to hold a job, be a wife, raise a family, and get an education. Something must be left out.

This point was quantified in reactions to the statement: "It's awfully hard to plan your life in advance, because there are so many things to take into account." As Table 1 indicates, there was a tendency for career game players to change toward greater agreement with this statement after playing the game, while such a pronounced change did not occur in the control groups.[3]

112

TABLE 1. Percent of Respondents Who Agree That it is Hard to Plan Your Life in Advance

	BOYS				GIRLS			
	Career Game		Legislative Game (Control)		Career Game		Legislative Game (Control)	
	before game	after game	before game	after game	before game	after game	before game	after game
	24% (238)	34% (238)	27% (225)	30%* (225)	19% (371)	30% (371)	22% (376)	21%* (376)

*difference between change of experimental and control groups significant at .05 level, 2-tailed test

TABLE 2. Summary of Scores of Dropout Image

	BOYS		GIRLS	
	career	legislative	career	legislative
Mean score, positive items, after game	1.9	1.6	2.3	2.2
% of respondents who checked more positive items after game than before	24%	21%	27%	27%
Mean score, negative items, after game	2.0	1.8	1.9	1.8
% of respondents who checked more negative items after game than before	36%	28%	29%	30%
Total Respondents	(238)	(225)	(371)	(376)

Since the conference delegates were assigned randomly, not only to the career or legislative games but also to teams and profiles within the career game, some boys had a boy's profile, others a girl's. Likewise they may or may not have been assigned to a profile whose abilities and interests, home life and other characteristics were like their own. The experiment thus allowed evaluation of the extent to which assignment to a given type of person made players more sympathetic toward that kind of person.

Questionnaire data were collected about two of the types of roles which players might encounter in the game: (1) the deviant or potential school dropout, and (2) the woman's role. Since about two-fifths of the players were assigned a profile of a potential dropout, not only can career game players as a whole be compared with other respondents in terms of their attitudes toward deviant-type adolescents, but it is also possible to compare those players who were actually assigned this role with players who played a more conformist role in the same game.

Before and after the game, respondents were asked to check on a list of twelve personal characteristics those "you think describe what a typical dropout is like." The factor analysis indicated that eight of these items clustered together in a pair of factors. One included four items that represent a positive or sympathetic attitude toward the dropout — he is confused, has problems at home and school which prevent his doing well. In essence his position is not really his fault. The other factor contains the most negative items on the list — the dropout's own personality and behavior are the source of his school difficulties.

Respondents were given scores based upon the number of items from these two factors they had checked. A recapitulation of scores in experimental and control groups is shown in Table 2. There is virtually no difference between girls in experimental and control groups, but for boys the career game seems to have had the effect of making them both more positive and more negative. That is, some boys checked more items — or saw more dimensions to the character of the dropout — as a result of the game experience.

Table 2 does not, however, tell anything about role empathy

as a result of role assignment within the game, since it has not separated those who actually took the part of a potential dropout from those assigned more conformist roles. Table 3 shows data on the image of the dropout with the variable of role assignment held constant. Boys who took the role of a potential dropout were more likely than other boys to hold a positive image of the dropout after playing the game and less likely to have a negative image or to change in this direction. On the other hand girls who played the deviant role were more likely to have high negative scores at the end of the game and to increase their score in this direction. Apparently, playing a deviant role in a simulation makes girls more severe rather than creating sympathy for this kind of person.

In Table 4, which further clarifies the nature of the game effect on role attitudes, the additional variable of role identity — whether or not the respondent said he himself was like the person he was assigned in the game — is controlled. What seems to "allow" boys who take deviant roles to feel sympathy toward their role is identity with this person. Thus boys who played a potential dropout were more likely to have a higher positive score and less likely to have a higher negative score after the game than before than boys who played a conformist role *if* they felt they were like the person they had played (28 per cent vs. 17 per cent, and 37 per cent vs. 44 per cent). On the other hand, there is a reverse trend for boys who did *not* identify with their role assignment (23 per cent vs. 35 per cent, and 35 per cent vs. 24 per cent). In other words, the experience of playing a deviant role does not create empathy with dropouts generally unless feelings of identity with the particular person are aroused. For girls, the pattern is similar to that in Table 3 with the experience of a deviant role related to *less* sympathy toward the dropout, regardless of whether there is any role identity.

The second type of role studied in connection with this game is the woman's role. Since girls have been playing and thinking about female roles all their lives it is boys who have the greatest chance to "learn" about the feminine role in the game. Our prediction was that there would be greater changes in definition of the appropriate female role — in the direction of a broader

TABLE 3. Image of Dropout by Role Assignment in Career Game

	BOYS		GIRLS	
Played potential dropout?	yes	no	yes	no
Mean score, positive items, after game	1.9	1.7	2.3	2.3
% of respondents who checked more positive items after game than before	25%	23%	27%	28%
Mean score, negative items, after game	1.9	2.2	2.1	1.8
% of respondents who checked more negative items after game than before	33%	39%	35%	22%
Total Respondents	(94)	(97)	(147)	(149)

TABLE 5. Attitude Toward Woman's Role, by Sex and Game

	BOYS				GIRLS			
	Career Game		Legislative Game (Control)		Career Game		Legislative Game (Control)	
	before	after	before	after	before	after	before	after
% of respondents who — agree that woman should do more than marry and raise a family	40	42	34	34	42	51	55	46*
change attitude in direction of agreeing that a woman should do more than marry and raise a family	19		14		18		9	
Total Respondents	(238)		(225)		(371)		(376)	

*difference between changes in experimental (career game) and control (legislative game) groups significant at .05 level, 2-tailed test or less conservative view — among boys assigned a girl's role in the game than among boys who took a boy's role.

Table 5 shows the proportions of respondents who agreed with the statement: "An intelligent girl with a good education really should do more with it than just get married and raise a family."[4] Respondents who played the career game were both more likely to favor the broader feminine role at the end of the game and to change their attitudes in the direction of the broader role than respondents of the same sex who played the legislative game.

Table 6 tests the prediction that there will be a further effect of the game on those who were specifically assigned a girl's role. The table indicates that this prediction is true for boys — i.e., boys assigned the role of a girl were more likely than other boys to agree that a girl should do more than marry and raise a family, although the difference is not statistically significant. This kind of effect does not seem to apply to girls.

A further difference is revealed when one controls, in addition, the extent to which players identified with the role to which they were assigned. As Table 7 indicates, not only are boys who take a female role more likely to endorse a fuller life for women (51 per cent vs. 41 per cent, and 41 per cent vs. 32 per cent), they are also more likely to do so if they identify with their assigned role (41 per cent vs. 32 per cent, and 51 per cent vs. 41 per cent). In fact, boys assigned one of the girls' profiles and who also say this girl is like them in some ways are as likely to endorse the fuller woman's role (51 per cent) as girls are.

Legislative Game

To get a measure of respondents' image of the legislator we asked them to circle, on a list of sixty adjectives, all which describe "what most legislators or politicians are like." Words circled by most respondents included "intelligent," "ambitious," "clever," "capable" and "alert." Words least often circled included the most negative words on the list — "cynical," "cruel," "lazy," "weak" and "cowardly" (data not shown). In other words the general image of the political role is one of positive, intelligent activism.

Concerning the question of whether the game had an effect

on role image, the words circled were about the same in control and experimental groups and before and after the games. In order to see whether there was any evidence of game effects the analysis was carried further, focusing upon the degree to which players felt positively or negatively toward the political role.

TABLE 4. Image of Dropout by Role Assignment and Identity with Role

A. Percentage of Respondents Who Had a More Sympathetic Image After the Game than Before.

		BOYS		GIRLS	
Played potential dropout?		yes	no	yes	no
Identified with role?	yes	28	17	17	27
		(46)	(63)	(30)	(92)
	no	23	35	29	30
		(48)	(34)	(115)	(57)

B. Percentage of Respondents Who Had a More Negative Image After Game than Before

		BOYS		GIRLS	
Played potential dropout?		yes	no	yes	no
Identified with role?	yes	37	44	37	21
	no	35	24	35	25

The first two factors extracted from the legislative game items consisted of a set of positive or favorable adjectives ("good," "wise," "sincere," "honest," "dependable," "helpful" and "pleasant"); and a similarly structured cluster of negative or unfavorable adjectives ("unreasonable," "insincere," "greedy," "conceited," "undependable," "dull" and "corrupt").

TABLE 6. Attitude Toward Women's Role Among Career Game Players, by Sex and Game Role Assignment

Sex of player:	BOY		GIRL	
Sex of role assignment:	boy	girl	boy	girl
% respondents who agree woman should do more than marry and raise a family	39	46	49	51
Total Respondents	(144)	(93)	(222)	(147)

TABLE 7. Percentage of Respondents Who Agree that Women Should Do More than Marry, by Sex Role, Assignment and Role Identity, After Game

Sex of player:		BOY		GIRL	
Sex of role assignment:		boy	girl	boy	girl
Identify with role?	yes	41 (97)	51 (47)	45 (97)	51 (64)
	no	32 (47)	41 (46)	52 (124)	48 (81)

TABLE 8. Comparison of Positive and Negative Image Scores Before and After Legislative Game

	BOYS		GIRLS	
	Legislative	Career (Control)	Legislative	Career (Control)
Mean # positive adjectives circled after game	1.9	2.2	1.7	1.8
% respondents who circled at least 2 more positive adjectives after game than before	11%	21%	13%	15%
Mean # negative adjectives circled after game	1.1	1.0	.8	1.0
% respondents who circled at least 2 more negative adjectives after game than before	11%	8%	6%	11%

TABLE 9. Mean Number of Correct Items Listed Relating to Job Opportunities and Marital Satisfactions, Before and After the Games

	BOYS				GIRLS			
	Career Game		Legislative Game (Control)		Career Game		Legislative Game (Control)	
Mean # of correct items on list of:	before	after	before	after	before	after	before	after
—Jobs open to non-high school graduates	2.8	2.8	3.0	2.5	4.0	4.1	4.3	3.4*
—Jobs open to college graduates	3.0	3.1	2.9	1.8*	4.5	4.4	5.0	3.5*
—Resources might use in planning for future	2.8	3.1	2.9	3.0	3.3	3.7	3.1	3.1
—Occupations I have thought of for myself	2.6	3.0	3.0	2.7	3.1	3.3	3.2	3.2
—Factors related to marital satisfaction	2.1	2.2	2.1	1.7*	2.8	2.8	2.9	2.4
Total Respondents	(238)	(238)	(225)	(225)	(371)	(371)	(376)	(376)

*difference between change in experimental (career game) group and change in control (legislature game) group significant at .05 level, 2-tailed test

Several of the words in factor one are antonyms of words in factor two. Respondents were given scores based upon the number of these words they circled before and after the game. Some comparisons of these scores are shown in Table 8. This table suggests a small negative effect of the game upon boys. Compared with boys in the control group, boys who played the legislative game tended to circle fewer positive adjectives and more negative adjectives after the game than before. For girls, what little difference there is is in the reverse direction.

In summary, the basic dimensions of students' image of the politician do not seem to be affected by their brief experience with the legislative game. What changes did occur were in the direction of a rather more negative image for boys.[5]

SIMULATION GAMES AND INTELLECTUAL LEARNING

Although the content and structure of Hopkins games vary, each is based upon a theoretical model of how some social process or institution operates, plus empirical data about the real world. Thus in the process of playing a student should begin to learn not only the rules of the game but also how the game model works, and in doing so he will also learn some factual information about the real-life phenomena simulated in the game.

Career Game

Several questions were designed to "test" players' learning of career information. Respondents were asked to describe or list information covered in some part of the game — e.g., all the jobs they could think of that a person without a high school diploma could get; all the factors they could think of that "affect a person's satisfaction with his or her marriage"; all the sources of "ideas or assistance in planning for your own future." Table 9 shows the mean scores (number of correct items given) for each of five questions of this sort. Students who played the career game did better on the average than those who played the legislative game, with several of the differences statistically significant.

In the factor analysis these five items formed the clearest cluster among the career game questions, suggesting that one skill which can be acquired from the game is a kind of general assimilation of factual information relating to career decision-making. The composite score made up of these items was used as the dependent variable in the multi-variate analysis. Computation of Coleman's *a*, as shown in Table A (Appendix), indicates that the most powerful effect on initial scores is sex (girls do better at this kind of task) and that school grades also have a strong effect. However, when one looks at the *rate of improvement* in scores during the course of the game (Table A2), the game is the only variable which has any real effect. In other words, playing the game produced a clear increase in the amount of specific career information these students possessed, although sex and general academic ability also affected performance.

Another group of test questions focused upon respondents' understanding of the "education market." These were five statements about educational institutions, opportunities and consequences designed to test knowledge which could be gained from the game. The proportion of respondents answering these questions "correctly" before and after the game are shown in Table 10. There is a general tendency in the experimental groups for higher percentages of players to answer correctly after the game than before. In the girls' control group there is almost no before-after change except on the third item, and in the boys' control group the percentages actually change in the opposite direction on three out of the five items.

That the amount of learning (the before-after differences) does not seem terribly large may be partly because a majority of respondents answered the questions correctly before playing the game. On item 4, e.g., over ninety per cent in each subgroup gave the right answer at the beginning, so there were few left to learn the relationship between education and income in the process of playing (even so the rate of learning was significantly different in experimental and control groups among the girls). It must be remembered, though, that this sample consisted of young people of above average intelligence and achievement, and it cannot be assumed that this kind of information is "common knowledge" to most students.

Although the factor analysis did not indicate any consistent clustering of these five items, they were combined to form an index with each respondent given a score representing the num-

TABLE 10. Percentages of Respondents Giving Correct Answer to Five Quiz Items, Before and After Game

% of respondents who:	BOYS				GIRLS			
	Career		Legislative (Control)		Career		Legislative (Control)	
	before	after	before	after	before	after	before	after
disagree that the chances of getting a job are about equal for high school dropout and graduate but are better for college graduate	65	70	66	69	67	73	71	73
agree that amount of education person has affects his marital satisfaction	58	66	55	50*	60	60	57	58
agree that greatest variety of course offerings usually found at state university	52	63	51	55*	45	61	48	55*
agree that income a person can expect to earn is related to how much education he has	95	94	93	86	91	96	92	92*
agree that there are many opportunities for free education even after leaving high school	64	67	60	56	56	60	61	62
Total Respondents	(238)	(238)	(225)	(225)	(371)	(371)	(376)	(376)

*difference between change in experimental and change in control group significant at .05 level, 2-tailed test

ber of questions answered correctly. In the multi-variate analysis, the learning effect of the game is clearly the strongest among the variables studied (Table A4), although judging from the size of the a's it is not as strong as for the career listing items (Table A2). Table A3 indicates little effect of any of the external factors upon performance on these items.

Thus the evidence indicates that students can acquire factual information from the career game. The quantitative findings also parallel what students themselves say they learned from the game. For example, one girl mentioned "learning about careers we had never even thought about before" (cf. Table 9, items 1 and 2). Another said, "many girls will learn, as I did, that higher education goes hand in hand with higher pay and a better job" (Table 10, item 4).

Legislative Game

This game provides an interesting test of the power of simulations to shape young people's views in a more realistic direction, since the "bargaining" and "compromising" built into the game are activities that students are typically taught to condemn. Civics and American history courses tend to cloak Congress in an idealistic aura, and the dealings of legislators with their colleagues and with lobbyists off the floor are either ignored or dismissed as something a few members of "corrupt political machines" indulge in.

A pretest of the legislative game with a group of students in Washington, D.C., had indicated that players do acquire strategic sophistication from the game. When asked to describe what they thought were the most effective strategies for doing well in the game, 70 per cent of the boys and 84 per cent of the girls mentioned either exchanging support or cooperating with other legislators, indicating that the major principle of the game model had been clearly communicated (Boocock and Coleman, 1966, pp. 227-229).

Two items designed to measure understanding of the legislative process were used in the Berkeley questionnaire. Responses are shown in Table 11, and the values of a from the multi-variate analysis are in Tables A5 and A6.

The first item: "Pressure groups are useful, effective features of representative government" was designed to test recogni-

TABLE 11. Respondents' Orientations Toward Political Processes Before and After the Legislative Game

	BOYS				GIRLS			
	Legislative Game		Career Game (Control)		Legislative Game		Career Game (Control)	
Percent of respondents who:	before %	after %	before %	after %	before %	after %	before %	after %
agree that pressure groups are useful	23	34	23	25*	17	24	13	17*
disagree that legislators should always vote convictions	24	23	17	17	23	28	25	23*
Total Respondents	(225)	(225)	(238)	(238)	(376)	(376)	(371)	(371)

*difference between changes of experimental and control groups significant at .05 level, 2-tailed test

TABLE 12. Percentage of Respondents Expressing Efficacy with Respect to Four Political Items, Before and After Game

	BOYS				GIRLS			
	Legislative		Career (Control)		Legislative		Career (Control)	
% of respondents who disagree strongly that:	before	after	before	after	before	after	before	after
individual citizens can't do much about dirty politics	47	51	45	44	50	55	45	45
letters to congressmen are waste of time	43	44	48	39*	47	48	39	40
politics too complicated for persons like me to understand	20	23	17	21	14	20	16	21
people like me have no say about what government does	41	52	39	43*	44	48	45	41*
Total Respondents	(225)	(225)	(238)	(238)	(376)	(376)	(371)	(371)

*difference between change in experimental and change in control group significant at .05 level, 2-tailed test

tion of and attitude toward the political functions played by lobbies and pressure groups (a type of political group usually viewed with suspicion by political idealists). Table 11 shows that boys and girls who played the legislative game were more likely than the other respondents to move toward agreement with this statement. Table A5 indicates a fairly strong game effect. The only other variable which seems to affect this attitude is sex — boys tend to be more "realistic," less "idealistic."

The second item: "On most issues, we should expect our representatives to vote according to their convictions, even though they may not reflect the opinions of their constituents" measures acceptance of the political fact of life that a successful political career is based upon staying in office. In the game, being re-elected is a direct consequence of satisfying one's constituents on a sufficient number of important issues. On this item there was a tendency for girls in the experimental group to move away from the idealized view of the legislator, although this change did not occur among boys. The game effect is less strong on this item (Table A6).

SIMULATION GAMES AND FEELINGS OF EFFICACY

An attitudinal concept whose implications for behavior are only beginning to be understood is a person's feeling of *efficacy* or sense of being able to understand and control the world around him. (The opposite end of the dimension is alienation, or *lack* of understanding, control and belonging in relation to one's environment.) Confidence in the efficacy of one's efforts is, of course, important for mental health generally, but the concept is of further educational interest in that this attitude sccms to be related to participation and performance in a variety of situations.

Sociological studies of political behavior, e.g., have shown that the people most likely to take an active part in politics are those with strong feelings of political "potency" or efficacy — who feel that their actions (voting, working for a political party, etc.) will have a desirable effect upon their government (Campbell, Gurin and Miller, 1954, pp. 187-194; or Knupfer, 1953). Seeman drew a similar conclusion from studies on the relationships between feelings of alienation, group member-

126

ship, and level of knowledge about public issues. In each organization studied (reformatories, hospitals, and labor unions, in the United States and Sweden), he found that the ability to learn and retain "knowledge which has some connection with control over an individual's future" was related to the efficacy dimension. "To the extent that he feels powerless to affect his future, he will not learn as well what he needs to know to affect it . . . To the degree that he *expects* to achieve his goal, he will attend to the associated learning" (Seeman, 1966, p. 39).

In the report to the U.S. Office of Education on a national survey of American elementary and secondary schools (Campbell, Coleman *et al.*, 1966), one of the most powerful predictors of school success is feeling that one's share of the rewards of the school system is not controlled by luck or other forces beyond one's control, but that one's own efforts will be rewarded. While feelings of efficacy have also been found to be related to other characteristics, such as family status and the quality of school attended, Campbell and Coleman find the relationship between efficacy indicants and school performance holds even when these other factors are held constant. The implication is that if ways can be found to imbue students with the feeling that it is possible to control their environment and that it is therefore worth making an effort to understand it, the level of student performance can be raised, regardless of the other features of the school and its student body.

Legislative Game

A third cluster which emerged from the factor analysis of legislative game items consisted of the following set of statements about politics and politicians, on which respondents were asked to indicate their agreement or disagreement:

The average citizen can't do much about "dirty" politics, so he might just as well stay out of the whole thing.

Sending letters and telegrams to congressmen is a waste of time, since they have so little influence upon legislation.

Sometimes politics and government seem so complicated that a person like me can't really understand what's going on.

People like me don't have any say about what the government does.

In other words, there does seem to be a general dimension of efficacy, incorporating several different indicants, which has meaning for these respondents.

Comparison of responses before and after the game is shown for each of the four items separately, since there are some rather interesting differences. Table 12 shows the proportions of respondents who strongly *disagree* with each of the four statements — i.e., who display a sense of efficacy with respect to that item. In the experimental groups there is an increase on all items, with a smaller change or change in the opposite direction in the control groups on all items except the "politics too complicated" one. Likewise a's in the multi-variate analyses show a relatively strong game effect on the items of dirty politics (Table A7), letters to congressmen (A8) and having a say in politics (A10); but virtually no effect on the item of politics being too complicated (A9).

The differences between Tables A9 and A10 may point to two rather different aspects of the political potency dimension. The first item refers to intellectual understanding of politics. While the percentages did change slightly in the direction predicted in both experimental groups, a similar change occurred in the control groups, suggesting that these changes may have been an effect of the *conference* (which was indeed conceived as a kind of laboratory of citizenship education, with lectures, discussions, and field trips designed to increase understanding of political processes). The second item, on the other hand, referred to whether a person's *actions* could have an effect upon government, and it is here that there is a difference between experimental and control groups. In other words, the unique contribution of the simulation experience to feelings of efficacy may be in giving young people the confidence needed to *act* upon the intellectual information they have acquired about a political or other social situation.

Career Game

While none of the career game items were designed specifically to measure players' degree of confidence about their own future careers, the item of whether or not a girl should do more than marry and raise a family, already discussed in connection with role empathy, also seems to tell something about girls'

128

perception of their own future possibilities. Table 5 showed that girls who played the career game were more likely to endorse a broader role definition for women after the game than before, while girls in the control group moved away from agreement with this statement. That this trend may reflect an increased confidence in the likelihood of a richer, fuller life for women is suggested by players' essays. For example, one girl, who wrote that the game had broadened her range of thinking about her own future, concluded:

> I think many girls would be happy to learn of all the things they can do besides being wives and mothers. Many girls who might have been resigned to being a housewife could see that if a girl in the game could get a successful job, so could they.

A final observation about the nature of feelings of efficacy is that they can apparently occur *along with* a realization of the difficulties of decision-making in complex social situations. There are several possible results of such a realization, one being that players would become pessimistic about the chances of understanding and acting effectively. The data just presented indicate that such is not the case. On the contrary, "practicing" in a simulated environment gave some players greater confidence in their ability to control social situations, at the same time that they acquired a more realistic view of what the situation was like and saw the necessity for further learning about it.

SUMMARY AND CONCLUSIONS

The career game provided the richest data on the generation of role empathy. Boys who took a feminine role or the role of a potential dropout in the game were more likely to take a liberal or sympathetic attitude toward these roles after their game experience. The effect on girls of taking a deviant role seems to operate in the opposite direction, although it is not possible to say at this point whether this is a general reaction of girls or unique to this particular group of conformist, achieving girls. Players' basic image of the political role was not changed by the legislative game, although there was a tendency for boys to have a more negative image after the game than before.

The career game also produced the most convincing evidence of factual learning. Players did better than their controls on listing items and on questions that required understanding of the general relationships between educational and other institutions. While certain kinds of students (girls, older, and high-achieving) do better at some of these tasks there is no evidence that these kinds of students learned at a faster rate in the game itself. The kind of intellectual learning that occurred in the legislative game was in the form of a tendency toward a more realistic view of the pressures on legislators which prevent their acting solely on "principle."

The legislative game data revealed a trend toward greater feelings of political efficacy. The actual changes were not large, but in view of the short-term use of the game it seems a potentially important trend.

Of course, substantial amounts of learning or changes in attitude could hardly be expected from such a brief game experience. Given the circumstances, the changes reported are rather impressive, and one would predict that longer use of the games would produce more learning. Further testing should also include a broader cross-section of students. While there was no apparent relationship between rate of learning in the game and reported general academic performance, it is not possible to tell from this atypical sample whether the really weak student could hold his own in a simulation game. (The focus of recent research at Johns Hopkins has been upon testing these and other games over longer periods of time with students representing a greater range of ability and motivation.)

As usual, the evidence examined here is far from conclusive, and it raises as many questions as it answers. The over-all impression one gets from this experiment is that a good deal of learning — and several different kinds of learning — can occur in simulation games of this sort. And the experiment supports a basic tenet of the philosophy of educational gaming — that students can have fun and learn at the same time.

APPENDIX

TABLE A.   Values of Coleman's *a* for Multi-Variate Analysis, Controlling for Game, Sex, Grades in School, Age and Father's Education

1. Percentage of Respondents with High Career Information Score (4 or More) Before Game

Effect of —	a
game	.003
sex	.243
grades	.127
age	.067
father's education	− .021

2. Percentage of Respondents with Higher Career Information Score After Game than Before

Effect of —	a
game	.168
sex	− .006
grades	− .036
age	.000
father's education	− .037

3. Percentage of Respondents with High Education Information Score (4 or More) Before Game

Effect of —	a
game	− .007
sex	.008
grades	.001
age	− .019
father's education	.025

4. Percentage of Respondents with Higher Education Information Score After Game than Before

Effect of —	a
game	.092
sex	.047
grades	.043
age	− .039
father's education	.021

5. Percentage of Respondents Who Agree More that Pressure Groups Are Useful, after Game than Before

Effect of —	a
game	.092
sex	.087
grades	− .005
age	− .007
father's education	− .008

6. Percentage of Respondents Who Disagree More that the Legislators Should Always Vote Convictions Regardless of Constituents' Wishes.

Effect of —	a
game	.076
sex	.034
grades	− .060
age	.058
father's education	.015

7. Percentage of Respondents Who Disagree More that Citizens Can't Do Anything about Politics

Effect of —	a
game	.072
sex	− .001
grades	.018
age	− .047
father's education	− .045

8. Percentage of Respondents Who Disagree More that Letters to Congressmen are Waste of Time

Effect of —	a
game	.071
sex	− .020
grades	.048
age	− .092
father's education	− .056

9. Percentage of Respondents Who Disagree More that Politics is Too Complicated

Effect of —	a
game	.004
sex	.025
grades	.032
age	− .049
father's education	− .059

10. Percentage of Respondents Who Disagree More that People Like Me Have No Say in Government

Effect of —	a
game	.076
sex	.025
grades	− .027
age	− .046
father's education	− .055

NOTES

1. The only attempt to establish this kind of control known to the author was in the evaluation of the Northwestern Inter-Nation Simulation. Here an alternative teaching method — reading and discussion of case studies covering the same subject matter — was used in control classes. For a report of this experiment see Robinson, 1965.

2. This test is described in Coleman (1964), Chapter 6.

3. A note about the form of Table 1 and other comparing changes in percentages or means in experimental and control groups. The experimental group will sometimes be the students who played the career game, as in Table 1, and sometimes the students who played the legislative game, as in Table 11.

   An asterisk (*) following a *pair* of before-after comparisons indicates that the difference between the *change* in experimental and the *change* in control group is significant at the .05 level, in a two-tailed test. That is, the test used indicates not whether the before per cent is significantly different from the after per cent in the same group, but whether the before-after *difference* in one group is significantly different from the before-after difference in the other group of the same sex. This test is used in Tables 1, 5, 9, 10, 11, and 12.

   It should also be noted that while these tables show only marginal data (for purposes of clarity), the estimate of variance in the test is based upon *individual turnover data* and thus takes into account the total amount of change within a group.

4. There has been considerable debate over what constitutes satisfactory "femininity," and what constitutes "progress" in women's opportunities, much of it highly emotional. Whatever one's opinions as to whether women's lives — and women themselves — are getting "better" or "worse," there is pretty general consensus that the major changes in their lives in recent decades are related to their increased participation in activities and roles outside the home.

5. These findings are consistent with some from a test of another Hopkins game on a political theme. In a test of a game simulating a national Presidential election campaign, in which students were also given an adjective check list, the image of the political role was similar to the one just described, and there were no large changes in the words most often circled before and after the game. On a question asking them to rate politician as a career for *themselves* on a list of twelve occupations, the proportion saying politician was one of the jobs they would most like for themselves decreased in the experimental but not in the control groups. Responses to an open-ended question asking players what they felt they had learned from the game offered an indirect interpretation of this negative trend. Among students who said that the most important thing they had gained was a feeling for the complexities of the campaign process or for "what politicians

have to go through," a number included comments to the effect that "there is a lot more to campaigning than the average person thinks about," or "it takes a lot of work to wind up with the right result." That is, the loss of enthusiasm for politics as a profession may reflect learning that a political career has less glamor and more hard work than the players had formerly realized. (This study is reported in Boocock, 1963.)

REFERENCES

Boocock, Sarane S. *Effects of Election Campaign Game in Four High School Classes.* Department of Social Relations, The Johns Hopkins University, Baltimore, Md., 1963. (Mimeographed report.)

Boocock, Sarane S. and Coleman, James S. "Games with Simulated Environments in Learning." *Sociology of Education*, 39 (Summer, 1966), 215-236.

Campbell, Angus, Gurin, Gerald and Miller, Warren E. *The Voter Decides.* Evanston, Ill.: Row, Peterson, 1954.

Campbell, Ernest, Coleman, James S. and Mood, Alexander. *Equality of Educational Opportunity.* A report to the U.S. Office of Education, 1966.

Coleman, James S. *Introduction to Mathematical Sociology.* New York: Free Press, 1964, Chapter 6.

Guetzkow, Harold *et al. Simulation in International Relations: Developments for Research and Teaching.* Englewood Cliffs: Prentice-Hall, 1963.

Knupfer, Genevieve. "Portrait of the Underdog." In Bendix, R. and Lipset, S. M. (eds.), *Class, Status and Power.* Glencoe, Ill.: Free Press, 1953, 255-263.

Robinson, James A. "Simulation and Games." Department of Political Science, Ohio State University, Columbus, Ohio, 1965. (Unpublished paper.)

Seeman, Melvin. "Antidote to Alienation — Learning to Belong." *Trans-action*, Vol. 3 (May-June, 1966), 35-39.

A Pre-Civil War Simulation for Teaching American History

EUGENE H. BAKER

■ This chapter reports some of the results of an experiment conducted during the winter of 1965-66 with eighth grade students. One half of the students participated in a simulation of the American pre-Civil War period, designed by the author; the other half were taught the same subject matter by conventional teaching techniques.

The objective was to determine whether teaching American history by a simulation could increase learning, relative to teaching by conventional methods. Specifically, the impact of a simulation experience was compared to that of conventional teaching in respect to the students' immediate learning, their retention of the material learned and their attitudes to issues pertinent to the pre-Civil War period.

THE SIMULATION[1]

This simulation reproduces the major characteristics and problems of the social, economic, and political system in our country between 1840 and 1860. Participants work through a series of problems such as fugitive slave laws, the abolitionist movement, distribution of economic prosperity, territorial expansion, and tariffs.

The four sections of our country (the north, the south, the border states and the west) are designated as nations (with pseudonyms), cooperating through a strong alliance. Each nation is assigned basic capabilities, natural and economic resources, growth potential, and population comparable to their actual status in the 1850s. These units of capability may be: invested internally in basic industries; exchanged through international trade agreements; exchanged through international treaty agreements; or used to increase military capability.

Each player is assigned a role as a national official in one of the four fictitious nations. The players comprising each nation have the responsibility for maintaining the policies of the nation they represent, and their objective is to have their nation prosper and to maintain its prestige in the game's World Council. A few students are members of the international press, and write up the events of the simulation for *The World Newspaper*.

Each class session is organized around a problem, which covers one or more of the unit topics. The four nation-groups meet privately for the first part of the period to study the problem and plan strategy. The latter part of the period consists of a meeting of the World Council, to take appropriate action by voting.

An example of a "problem" is the following (the first problem introduced in the game):

(PROBLEM NO. 1: TRANSPORTATION, ECONOMICS, SLAVERY)

The Gray Goat government would like to have a railroad running through their territory to join the Blue Bear and Black Fox governments. Gray Goat does not have the money to build the railroad; however, Blue Bear and Black Fox are interested, as is Brown Buffalo, in joining the proposed railroad venture. The money problems have been solved, except for who will manage and control the railroad. Gray Goat at this point is insisting that tenant farmers be used to build and maintain the railroad because this type of labor is cheap, and Blue Bear emphasizing in all cases that labor should be free men. Resolve.

The teacher acts as the president of the World Council. He must handle the debate during the council meeting, keep it focused on the problem at hand, and give all nations an opportunity to express themselves. In addition, the teacher must be prepared to settle disputes which may arise among the players, regarding interpretation of the rules.

Best results will be obtained if the structured simulation is not run on consecutive days. The students must have time to discuss both inside and outside the classroom, the events of the game, their significance, and the future problems to be resolved. On alternate days, simulation may be used in combination with lectures, student reports, and/or discussion of historical problem areas, or information on current available historic material both in the classroom and in the library which may assist various governments in arriving at a decision.

An effective post-game discussion will provide valuable insight into the nature of the structured simulation, and real historical events. The teacher should in these post-game discussions be alert to, and exploit, all of the strategies of the various governments.

EXPERIMENTAL METHOD

Design

The subjects were 131 eighth graders at a junior high school in Lincolnwood, Illinois. They were randomly assigned to four classes in American history. In two classes (total N: 64) the simulation method was used, and two classes (total N: 67^2) were taught by conventional methods.

The Otis Intelligence Test and the social studies section of the Stanford Achievement Test Advanced Battery (Form W) were administered to all subjects. No significant differences were found (by pair-wise t-tests) among the four classes on either test; the mean IQ for the entire group was 114.

Measurements

A test was constructed to measure knowledge of American history in the pre-Civil War period, including items similar to those in ordinary textbooks. Initially a 76-item test was constructed and subjected to a pre-test; reliability was measured[3] and the test revised. The final test included 55 items, had a coefficient of reliability of .74 and an internal item difficulty of .46.

Examples of items are:

In this section of the test, one, two, three — or none — of the answers given may be right. For each correct answer, put an x in the box marked with its number. For example, if you think answers

137

1 and 3 are correct, mark the boxes in this way: ☐ ☐ ☐
                                                     1   2   3

If none of the answers is right, leave all the boxes blank.

  a. The "fugitive slave" laws: (1) Stated that ☐ ☐
                                                     4   5

     a slave owner could recover a runaway
     slave; (2) Were not fully enforced in
     many of the northern states.

Underline the one best answer. Read each question carefully.

  37. In the period before the Civil War, New
      England generally opposed the opening of
      cheap Western lands because this would:
      (1) Deprive her of her labor supply, (2)
      Reduce the market for her goods, (3) Add
      to the power of the Southern planters, (4)
      Hurt trade with the Pacific coast.

A questionnaire was also developed to measure attitudes to centralized policy-making and appreciation of the complexities of foreign policy decisions. This questionnaire was an adaptation of the instrument developed by Cherryholmes to measure attitude change after a simulation experience.[4]

Procedure

This experiment took place in a period of fifteen teaching days, from February 14 to March 4, 1966. All four classes were taught pre-Civil War American history for the same length of time. (The fifteen days did not include the days spent in testing before the unit was taught or after it was completed.)

The two "simulation classes" participated in the simulation described above. The two "traditional classes" used the sections of a commercial textbook which covered the same content as the simulation. This textbook has been used for several years by the school in which the experiment was carried out. In the "traditional classes," the teacher presented the historical material stated in the book, each pupil read the material, discussed it briefly in class and was occasionally given some of the questions at the end of the chapter to write out or to discuss in class orally. The class plan for each day was the same: the teacher had the students go over the textbook material, after which they then discussed orally or were assigned questions to be written out.

Before and after the unit the knowledge test and the attitude survey were administered to all classes. In order to measure retention, the knowledge test was re-administered after six weeks. (The students were not told in advance that such retention test would be given.)

FINDINGS

Table 1 presents mean pre- and post-test scores (on the knowledge test) for each of the four classes in the experiment.

TABLE 1
Mean Pre- and Post-Test Scores (Knowledge Test)

Class	Pre-test	Post-test	N
Simulation Class 1	32.78	39.06	32
Simulation Class 2	31.38	39.66	32
Traditional Class 1	32.14	35.88	34
Traditional Class 2	32.15	34.00	33

It is immediately seen that both simulation classes were superior at the post-test to both classes taught by traditional methods. In order to test the statistical significance of this superiority, an analysis of variance was carried out. Table 2 presents the results of this analysis.

TABLE 2
Analysis of Variance of Post-Test Scores

Source of Variance	Degrees of Freedom	Sum of Squares	Mean Square	F	P
Experimental Treatment	1	19.52	19.52	17.25	$p < .01$
Classes	1	0.42	0.42	0.37	n.s.
Interaction	1	1.53	1.53	1.35	n.s.
Error	127	143.76	1.13		

It is seen that the difference between the results of the simulation and those of the traditional methods is significant.[5] It thus seems that the superiority of simulation as a teaching method is confirmed.

Table 3 presents mean scores of the four classes on the retention test, and Table 4 the corresponding analysis of variance.

TABLE 3

Mean Scores on Retention Test (And Post-Test)

Class	Retention-test	(Post-test)
Simulation Class 1	35.00	(39.06)
Simulation Class 2	38.50	(39.66)
Traditional Class 1	35.26	(35.88)
Traditional Class 2	33.58	(34.00)

TABLE 4

Analysis of Variance on Retention Test

Source of Variance	Degrees of Freedom	Sum of Squares	Mean Square	F	P
Experimental Treatment	1	5.43	5.43	4.01	$p < .05$
Class	1	0.82	0.82	0.60	n.s.
Interaction	1	6.73	6.73	4.97	$p < .05$
Error	127	172.96	1.35		

It is noticeable that a greater loss of retention was experienced in the simulation condition than in the traditional condition. The simulation students do remain superior to their peers who learned by traditional methods (now at the .05 significance level), but their superiority has decreased. In particular, loss of retention was strong in Simulation Class 1, so that the interaction of Treatment and Class now becomes significant.

It is difficult to interpret this unexpected finding. One possibility would be that simulation learning indeed is retained less than learning by traditional methods. This, however, does not explain the strong interaction effect: Simulation Class 2 does not experience a comparable loss of retention. It would then seem necessary to look for an explanation in events pertaining to Simulation Class 1, rather than to the simulation group in general.

The relatively low mean retention in Simulation Class 1 might be due to a *few* students with a great loss of retention. In other words, it might hold that the relative frequency of students who retained learning was about the same in all classes, but that in Simulation Class 1 those students (or some of those students) who did forget something, for some reason forgot more than did their counterparts in other classes. In order to investigate this possibility, the number of students in each class who retained all learning (i.e., whose retention score was bigger than or equal to their post scores) was counted. The results are presented in Table 5.

TABLE 5

Number and Proportion of Students with Retention Scores At Least Equal to Post Scores

Class	Number	Proportion
Simulation Class 1	12	.38
Simulation Class 2	19	.59
Traditional Class 1	20	.59
Traditional Class 2	16	.48

It remains true that there was less retention in Simulation Class 1, while the results in Simulation Class 2 are as good or better than the results in the classes taught by the traditional method. No explanation for the phenomenon can be offered here.

The issue thus remains open. Nevertheless, it is worthwhile to recall that in spite of this problem the total retention score in the simulation condition is superior to that in the traditional condition.

In summary it may then be concluded on the basis of the data here presented, that the simulation was a more effective teaching device than traditional methods.

We turn now to the results of the attitude survey. The hypothesis here was that students in the simulation classes would develop a more favorable attitude to centralized and efficient policy-making procedures, appreciating more the complexities of the pre-Civil War problems. No such change was expected for the students taught by traditional methods. Table 6 presents the relevant data.

TABLE 6

Mean Attitude Scores, Pre- and Post-Test

Class	Pre-test	Post-test	t	P
Simulation Class 1	27.65	29.16	2.74	<.01
Simulation Class 2	28.43	29.81	3.06	<.01
Traditional Class 1	28.44	28.50	0.13	n.s.
Traditional Class 2	29.66	29.84	0.45	n.s.

The data support the hypothesis: the expected change took place in both simulation classes; no change was found in the traditional classes.

CONCLUSION

The sum total of the evidence presented in this paper, on learning and on attitude change, seems rather clear: the traditional method of teaching American history to the above average child in junior high school may not be the most effective way. The simulation technique, which represents a break from currently accepted classroom procedures, is a potentially more efficient means of communicating historical facts, concepts, and attitudes to children at this age level.

NOTES

1. Copyright, Eugene H. Baker, 1966. The Teachers' Guide, Participants' Manual and sample tests can be obtained from the author.

2. The unequal N's derive from the elimination of a few pupils who missed more than five class sessions because of illness.

3. Cyril Hayt, "Test Reliability Estimated by Analysis of Variance," *Psychometrica,* VI, (June, 1941), 153-160.

4. Cleo Cherryholmes, "Developments in Simulation of International Relations in High School Teaching," *Phi Delta Kappan,* January, 1965, 227-231.

5. A similar analysis of variance was carried out for the pre-test scores. No F-ratio was higher than 0.63 — the F for the "experimental treatment" was 0.01.

The Shaping of Strategies

E. O. SCHILD

■ Games may induce learning in at least two distinct ways. One, by generating a high level of motivation and interest and by focusing the attention of the player, (Boocock and Coleman, 1966); in this way the learning of facts or beliefs presented to the player should be facilitated. Two, by establishing a series of contingencies, where reinforcement — success in the game — is contingent upon specific behaviors ("good play"); in this way strategies and skills conducive to winning the game should be learned.

These two teaching-properties of games are clearly related. Only if sufficient motivation to win is generated will success in the game be an effective reinforcer. At the same time these two ways of learning will produce different contents of learning. When the game is seen as a series of contingencies, the expected learning is simply that of strategies and other behaviors directly relevant to success. Only if the game also has *generally* motivating properties may we expect the players to learn other contents, facts, insights associated with the game.

It seems that the more elementary learning is that pertaining to strategies and skills of winning. Whatever the intricacies of the psychology of learning, a basic law of behavior would

AUTHOR'S NOTE: The work here reported was financed by a grant from the Carnegie Corporation for the study of games with simulated environments. I am greatly indebted to my friends and colleagues at Johns Hopkins who introduced me to simulation games and shaped my own strategies in this field. In particular I owe thanks to Sarane S. Boocock for her many insights on games and education — and for improving the present chapter.

143

appear to be that "behavior is controlled by its consequences" (Skinner, 1953), and the core of a game is to establish certain consequences (winning or losing) as contingent upon certain behavior (the play of the participant). It is then somewhat surprising that studies of learning in games have not paid particular attention to this facet of learning. The variables by which "learning" has been measured have typically been unrelated to behaviors needed for winning; rather, it has been expected that the players learn several other contents, even if these are not necessary for successful play. It may indeed be so;[1] but this would seem to be a higher-order learning, dependent on *additional* properties of the game beyond its basic structure. It is characteristic that the somewhat pessimistic review of evaluation-studies by Cherryholmes (1966) does not refer at all to the learning of strategies, although this may be the most immediate learning involved in the playing of games.

In fact, the use of games as a research *tool* has focused on the strategies selected by players. In some studies a complex social situation is simulated and the players' behavior observed in order to derive hypotheses for the real-life situation (e.g., Kinley, 1966). In other cases a simple (rather, deceptively simple) game is used as an experimental situation, where strategy-choice are the data from which basic psychological propositions may be generated. This has been the approach of the research tradition represented in Rapoport and Chammah (1965).

These two uses of games, as educational devices and as research tools, converge in the issue of *changing* strategies. Systematic change of strategies is a "finding" in itself — as a description of human behavior in the experimental setting or as an indication of certain characteristics of the real-life situation simulated. But a systematic change of strategies is also *learning,* and thus of immediate concern for the educationally oriented student of games.

The present chapter is concerned with such learning of strategies. Taking one specific game, I shall show what the optimal strategies in this game are and then present evidence that the behavior of the players over repeated plays approximates these strategies; that is, that the behavior is indeed "shaped" by the reinforcement contingencies of the game. Subsequently, I shall inquire into some implications of these findings, both for the educational applications of games and for the use of game-simulations in sociological research.

THE PARENT-CHILD GAME[2]

The game simulates one aspect of the interaction between a parent and an adolescent son or daughter, that aspect having to do with the adolescent's behavior.

The game is played in pairs, with one member of each pair playing "parent" and the other playing "child." Several pairs play at the same time and competition is among the "parents" and among the "children," so that two winners, a parent-winner and a child-winner, may be selected. Thus the members of a pair do not compete against each other, although the structure of the game, as elaborated below, does impose conflicting interests on them.

The game concerns the child's behavior on five "issues" — how much homework he does, how frequently he dates, how late he returns home, how much help he gives around the house and his appearance (dress, make-up, hair-cut etc.). For each issue the child has four alternative behaviors,[3] each of which, if selected by the child, gives a certain score to the parent and a score to the child. Scores are constructed so that a behavior giving a high score to the parent will give a low score to the child and vice versa.

In the beginning of each round parent and child try to reach agreement on how the child should behave on each issue. For issues on which no agreement is reached within five minutes, the parent gives an "order" to the child how to behave. The child then "behaves" by selecting, for each issue, a card on which the behavior he desires is printed. (Such a card may read, e.g., "I am home at ten o'clock" or "I am home at twelve o'clock.")

The rules of the game permit the child to violate any agreement and disobey any order. The child puts the behavior-cards he selected on the table, face down. The parent may now, within certain constraints, "supervise" the child's behavior on some — usually not all — issues, by flipping the cards over and thus learning the child's behavior on a particular issue. If the child is caught violating an agreement or disobeying an order, the parent may "punish" him by subtracting a certain number of points from the child's score.

The parent's score in the round is determined exclusively by the child's actual behavior (i.e., his choice of cards), independently of agreements or orders. The child's score is derived from his actual behavior, minus punishments if any.

One more feature of the game should be stressed: the scores differ from issue to issue, both for parent and for child. While the *mean* score over the four alternative behaviors is the same for all issues, the *variance* differs: for some issues the difference in scores between alternative behaviors is larger than for other issues.[4] Thus issues with larger variance are more important in determining the total score of the player than the issues of smaller variance. This relative importance of the issue to each player is determined by a random draw of a "score card" indicating the importance of each issue to him at the beginning of each round.

LEARNING TO EXCHANGE

From this brief description of the game several principles of good play can be pointed out. The fact that different issues have different importances to child and to parent indicates how any agreements between the two should be made so both may maximize their scores. On issues of relatively high importance to the child and of relatively low importance to the parent, the agreement should be more favorable to the child than on issues which are of relatively low importance to the child and of relatively high importance to the parent. This is, of course, an elementary principle of exchange: each side giving up what is relatively unimportant to it in return for what is relatively important. Note that this principle does not imply whether the agreements as a whole tend to favor the child or the parent; but if agreements are made on a set of issues, it implies which issues should be decided *relatively* more favorably to the child and which relatively more favorably to the parent.

Since agreements following this principle improve the scores of *both* parent and child it is rational strategy to pursue this line of action. The question then is whether this strategy of exchange was indeed learned by the players.

The game was played by four groups of subjects. One group was a senior class in an all-Negro high school; the second was a selected group of students from the same school, chosen by teachers for the explicit purpose of playing games; the third and fourth groups consisted of undergraduates at The Johns Hopkins University. The groups consisted of 24, 16, 28 and 18 students respectively. As will be seen, the major argument for the validity of the findings is in their consistency from group to group; in other words, replicability, not sampling properties, is the basis for generalizations made from the data.

For each round of the game the extent of good strategy, i.e., rational exchange, can be measured as follows. For each pair of players, each issue is classified in one of three ordered categories: (a) high importance to parent and low importance to child; (b) high importance to both or low importance to both; (c) low importance to parent and high importance to child. Similarly, the issues can be ordered by the agreement made (if any) in terms of the extent to which the agreement is favorable to the parent. Rational exchange now implies, and is implied by, a high positive association of the two orderings. The measure of association used was gamma.

By computing the gammas for each round the development of rational exchange can now be traced. The data are presented in Table 1. About six weeks after the initial game with the

TABLE 1: Gammas by Rounds
(Four Groups of Subjects)

	High School Class	Selected Students	Under-graduates I	Under-graduates II
Round 1	−.12	.10	.06	.34
Round 2	.26	.25	.27	.48
Round 3	.65	.62	.67	.80

TABLE 2: Gammas by Rounds
(Selected Students—Second Session)

(3rd round of first session)	.62
Second session, Round 1	.58
Second session, Round 2	.78
Second session, Round 3	.85

"selected student," six pairs replayed the game. The gammas are presented in Table 2.

The general trend is the same in all replications. Surprisingly enough, even the absolute values of the gammas for the second and third rounds are highly similar for three of the groups. (The higher values for the fourth group will be discussed below.) The data thus demonstrate the emergence of rational exchange. In all groups the play improved from round to round, and this improvement continued for the players who replayed the game. It seems justified to conclude that the behavior of the players was shaped by the structure of the game.

STRATEGIES OF AGREEMENT AND OBEDIENCE

The structure of the game gives both players in a pair great power to damage the other player. The child can, by consistently being "delinquent" (i.e., by always choosing the behavior-alternative favorable to himself), keep the parent's score down to minimum. At the same time the parent can keep the child's score down by issuing strict orders and by being punitive. Such a situation is fertile ground for "strategic moves" of commitments and counter-commitments, with the attendant risk of mutual destruction, (Schelling, 1960).

Against a weak player who can be intimidated, it may be good strategy for the child to be delinquent or for the parent to be strict and punitive. But for two reasonably good players, the only way to success is to establish some kind of *modus vivendi*. Such a *modus vivendi* must be based on mutual yielding: the parent must agree to some behavior-alternatives desired by the child, in return for the child's obedience on some issues where the outcome is in the parent's favor.

To give such concessions is then good strategy, provided the other player reciprocates. The rules of the game do not completely define the contingencies here, since these are partly dependent upon the behavior of one's partner. If the partner does not reinforce a given concession or concessions by reciprocating, concessions cannot be prescribed as rational behavior. Thus if strategies are learned by the contingencies of the game, we shall expect to find an association between changes in the two players' behavior. In pairs where the parent accepted agreements or gave orders less favorable to himself, the child should show increased obedience (even if it still is profitable for him to disobey on some issues). In pairs where one of these changes did *not* take place, we should not expect the other change either.

Table 3 shows the changes that took place from the first to the last round in each of the two undergraduate groups. (In the two high school groups, disobedience was so infrequent that practically no cases were available to study changes.) The expected association between the changes in a pair of players' behavior does indeed emerge. Again the number of cases is small, but the consistency is strong. We may, then, accept these data as support for a proposition that the players developed strategies which were effective, given their partners' strategy.

Inspection of the marginals in Table 3 shows moreover that not only did the players tend to adapt to the partner's behavior but also that when such mutual adjustment took place it was mainly in the direction indicated by the general structure of the game — towards a mutually satisfactory arrangement, with reciprocal concessions. That is, not only was change in obedience contingent upon change in agreements and orders (or vice versa); the change was most frequently in the direction of less conflict, as indicated by less disobedience.

The findings have interesting substantive implications when the game is considered as a research tool for generating theoretical propositions on the process simulated (the family situation, or similar instances of social control; see, e.g., Schild and Coleman, 1966). Here it suffices to emphasize the implications for learning in a game-situation: that the players learn to select those strategies which are rewarded with success in the game. In this context the game can be viewed as an organized set of reinforcement-contingencies which shape the strategies of the players.

GAMES AS EDUCATIONAL DEVICES

In the sense of the present analysis a simulation game does not teach more than could have been learned in the real-life situation or process simulated. The meaning of a "simulation" is exactly that the contingencies in the game reflect those in real life. But the simulation has, from a teaching viewpoint,

TABLE 3: Changes in Obedience and in Content of Agreements and Orders— Number of Pairs

Undergraduates I:

		Obedience		
		Increasing	No Change	Decreasing	Total
Favorability-to-Parent of Agreements and Orders	Decreasing	5	3	1	9
	No Change	–	2	–	2
	Increasing	1	–	2	3
	Total	6	5	3	14

$\gamma = .58$

Undergraduates II:

		Obedience		
		Increasing	No Change	Decreasing	Total
Favorability-to-Parent of Agreements and Orders	Decreasing	3	–	–	3
	No Change	1	4	–	5
	Increasing	–	–	1	1
	Total	4	4	1	9

$\gamma = 1.00$

advantages over the real-life situation, even beyond the fact that the real-life process may not allow for repeated trials (cf. the Life Career Game described in this volume). First the simulation is less complex than real life, facilitating adaptation to the crucial factors which are included in the game. Second, feedback is usually much more rapid in the game than in real life. (That the rapidity of feedback is also perceived by some of the players is indicated by responses to the following question, asked subsequent to playing the Parent-Child Game: "What are the major differences between the game and real life in the family?" One player responded with the concise statement: "In the game you see the results of your behavior much faster.") Both of these factors should greatly facilitate learning.

While games may teach *more* than winning strategies, the learning of strategies has in a sense priority over other possible learning. It is the most direct outcome of playing a game and thus, I would conjecture, the point where the game is likely to have the strongest impact. Indeed, Inbar indicates that the most learning which occurred in the Disaster Game was in connection with strategies and "problems" (i.e., the aspects of the game where the player faces contingencies for which he must develop strategies). Moreover, he reports that the learning of strategies was essentially *un*affected by the predispositions and other attributes of the players themselves.[5] Both of these findings support the view of games here defended.

Psychologically, this is a rather simple-minded approach to educational games. At the same time it has several implications. For one thing, it means that a game should be construed so that the skill, insight or facts to be learned are clearly needed by the players *in order to succeed in the game*. Whatever properties a game may possess as a device for increasing general interest on the part of the players, the crux of the matter is that it teaches how to play.

A serious problem here is whether the behaviors learned during the game are generalized to the real-life situation simulated. Will the adolescent who learned to win in the Parent-Child Game behave more effectively at home? Will the player who learned planning in order to succeed in the Life Career Game make his own occupational choice with more insight? Although in some cases the question is irrelevant (where the insight in the situation simulated is a goal in itself — as in the game of Legislature described in Boocock and Coleman *op. cit.*), in other cases — particularly those in which the game teaches some interpersonal skill — the problem is crucial to an evaluation of the game.

Unfortunately, no evidence is available; indeed, it would seem difficult and costly to gather such evidence. As a very modest beginning we have raised a preliminary question: not "Do strategies generalize from game to real life?" but "Do they generalize from one game to another?" The tests with the two undergraduate groups also provided some clues on this problem. Group II had played the game of Legislature a week prior to the Parent-Child Game; Group I had not. The game of Legislature teaches exchange — the principle of conceding on relatively unimportant issues in return for concessions on important ones. Table 1 shows that Group II was superior to Group I in respect to this aspect of the Parent-Child Game. Since this a far step away from real evidence, these data must be taken as suggestive only.

GAMES AS RESEARCH TOOLS

The fact that the players' strategies are shaped by the contingencies of the game is of crucial importance for the use of game-simulations as stepping stones towards theory. Unless the researcher dares to make the heroic assumption that his game is isomorphic to nature (in which case the findings from the game are "hard evidence"), two major uses of games in research seem relevant.

First, a game may be used as a test of the parsimony of existing theory. A game typically will include only some of the variables considered in theory. If nevertheless the development of play corresponds with known real life patterns the importance of the additional variables becomes questionable. The burden of proof is shifted to the proponent of received theory to show why those variables, not included in the game, are necessary to explain the phenomenon under analysis. Thus, the Parent-Child Game may show that "children" tend to obey their "parents," even when motivated purely by expediency. In that case the theorist who relies on mechanisms such as internalization of filial respect to explain this obedience must adduce new evidence in order to maintain the importance of this mechanism.

This assumes however that strategies are indeed shaped by the game. Otherwise it might have been argued, e.g., that the obedience demonstrated in the game was not a result of the game-contingencies, but simply the generalization of the players' filial sentiments to the game-situation. This argument is contradicted by the fact that the observed obedience was a result of *change* in behavior. While the postulated generalization should be effective from the first round (and, if anything, presumably *de*crease over rounds), the data show that obedience *in*creased over repeated trials. In other words, if the development of play is to be considered explained by the structure of the game, it is a prior assumption that this structure indeed shapes the behavior of the players.

A second use of the game is to generate new theoretical propositions. Consider for instance the parent-child interaction in respect to the potential for commitments and counter-commitments and mutual destruction. It is not *a priori* clear how this situation should be analyzed, even in the framework of a theory assuming that people pursue their interests in a reasonably intelligent way. The outcome of the simulation does suggest a possible framework for analysis: that the two parties engage in an *exchange* (of obedience in return for concessions on agreements and orders). And this framework then allows for the formulation of more specific propositions. (Such application of the present simulation is illustrated in Schild and Coleman, *op. cit.*)[6]

But again, this application rests on the assumption that the behavior of the players is adapted to the contingencies of the game. (True, it also implies a belief that these contingencies at least to some extent reflect those in nature. But it is only a belief which is sufficiently strong for the theorist to bet his strategy of theory-*construction* on; not necessarily a faith that he would base his strategy of theory-*testing* on.)

There are two assumptions, then, that are the basis for the use of game simulations in research: first, that the simulation can reflect the important contingencies of real life, and second, that these contingencies shape the strategies of the players.

The first assumption will usually rely on indirect evidence only; the present paper has attempted to present direct evidence bearing on the second assumption.

NOTES

1. See most of the chapters in the present volume.

2. Copyright, 1966, by E. O. Schild and Sarane S. Boocock.

3. A later version of the game has *two* behavior-alternatives for each issue, as well as other modifications (not affecting the basic structure). The present data, however, are all derived from the earlier version of the game.

4. The two sets of scores used were: (2,5,8,10) and (−2,4,10,13). Maximum punishment was 12 points.

5. See Inbar's paper in Part III of the present volume.

6. This analysis demonstrates the potential interaction between games and theory. Not only was the theory influenced by the findings of the game; the revision of the game was undertaken in the light of theoretical inquiry into the nature of social control.

REFERENCES

Boocock, Sarane S. and Coleman, James S. "Games with Simulated Environments in Learning." *Sociology of Education,* 39, No. 32 (Summer, 1966), 215-236.

Cherryholmes, Cleo H. "Some Current Research on Effectiveness of Educational Simulations." *American Behavioral Scientist,* 10, No. 2 (October, 1966), 4-7.

Kinley, Holly J. "Development of Strategy in a Simulation of Internal Revolutionary Conflict." *American Behavioral Scientist,* 10, No. 3 (November, 1966), 5-9.

Rapoport, Anatol and Chammah, Albert M. *Prisoner's Dilemma.* Ann Arbor, Michigan: University of Michigan Press, 1965.

————. "The Game of Chicken." *American Behavioral Scientist,* 10, No. 3 (November, 1966), 10-28.

Schelling, Thomas C. *The Strategy of Conflict.* Cambridge, Massachusetts: Harvard University Press, 1960.

Schild, E. O. and Coleman, James S. "Individual Behavior and Collective Decisions." Paper presented at *American Sociological Association Meetings,* 1966.

Skinner, B. F. *Science and Human Behavior.* New York: Macmillan Co., 1963.

Two Computer-Based Economics Games for Sixth Graders

RICHARD L. WING

■ Since 1962 the Center for Educational Services and Research of the Board of Cooperative Educational Services (BOCES) in Northern Westchester County, New York, has been experimenting with the use of computer-based games with simulated environments as an instructional methodology.[1] This chapter will report on some of our experience with two of these games, both essentially one-person games in which the student plays "against" a computer program.

Perhaps the greatest potential virtue of combining simulation as a method and computer-based technology as a medium is its ability to provide *individualized instruction*. Unlike the typical classroom situation in which groups of students are training at a fixed rate with no particular attention to differences in abilities and interests, the computer games developed at BOCES allow in particular for:

AUTHOR'S NOTE: The first games were undertaken jointly by BOCES and IBM during the summer of 1962 and continued into 1964 under the terms of Cooperative Research Project 1948. This project was followed by another, #2841, devoted entirely to the development of economics games.

1. *Variation in pace*. Students proceed at their own pace, so that they are neither held back nor forced to keep up with other students.

2. *Variation in scope*. The segments presented to the students were of differing length, depending on the student's previous success in the game.

The games to be described also allowed for easy variations of content (it was possible to switch from one game to another merely by signing off one game and signing on the other); of style (e.g., one game starts with an explanation in question-and-answer form and continues with a multiple-choice technique); and of mode of presentation (the games used both typewriter printout and slide-display, while relying primarily on the former).

Computer techniques also make it possible to vary the sequence and difficulty of the problems presented in accordance with the progress of the individual students. This possibility, however, was not utilized in the games here discussed.

DESCRIPTION OF GAMES

The first of the games developed at BOCES was the Sumerian Game, designed to teach sixth graders some basic principles of economics as applied to the time of the Neolithic revolution in Mesopotamia. During an introductory programmed tape and slide presentation the child playing the game sees himself as a ruler's son in the city-state of Lagash about 3500 B.C. At the conclusion of this orientation, the rules and the initial economic conditions are given to the child by means of typewriter terminals controlled by the computer. He then assumes the role of Luduga I, priest-ruler of Lagash, and is presented with his first problematic situation: "We have harvested 5,000 bushels of grain to take care of 500 people. How much of this grain shall be set aside for the next season's planting, and how much will be stored in the warehouse? The remainder will be given to the people to eat."

The child makes decisions and enters his answers at the computer terminal. The computer immediately returns a progress report, including the harvest reaped from the seed grain set aside for planting, a verbal description of the standard of living, and a report on his inventory. This kind of problem is repeated throughout the entire game, each harvest representing six months in the life of a ruler. As the game progresses, it becomes more complicated: the ruler must take into account a changing population, and is also faced with the problem of expansion, which entails the acquisition of new land and irrigation. At intervals the ruler is presented with technological innovations and disasters which alter the outcomes of his decisions.

The rule of the first Luduga is devoted to the solution of problems pertaining to an agricultural economy. In the second phase of the game the child, as Luduga II, is given the opportunity to apply his surplus grain to the development of crafts. In the third and final stage he is introduced to trade and the more complex problems which confront a changing economy. The rate and trend of development are dependent upon the wisdom of the child's decisions. (A sample printout from the Sumerian Game is contained in Appendix A.)

The purpose of the second game, the "Sierra Leone Development Project," is to simulate the economic problems of a newly-emerging nation, with a secondary emphasis on a study of the country's culture. The simulated economic and social situations used in this game are drawn from actual problems discussed in the ten-year Social and Economic Development Plan now in effect. An example is the land reclamation program in which former marshland is used to cultivate rice in order to diversify agriculture and to decrease expenditures for imported food, and thereby to obtain a more favorable balance of trade.

The mechanics of the situation are briefly as follows: (a) The student must pass a preliminary examination testing basic and general economic and geographic information on Africa; (b) Upon successful completion of this examination, the student is placed in the role of Second Assistant Affairs Officer for the Agency for International Development located at the American Embassy in Freetown, Sierra Leone; (c) The student progresses from problem to problem, at times carefully studying a specific geographic area in order to see the peculiar nature of that area's problems; (d) As the student satisfactorily completes and shows an understanding of the problems presented

157

to him he is promoted to Assistant Affairs Officer and finally to Chief Affairs Officer in AID. The game is thus divided into three main parts, each part presenting new and different economic problems.

The Sumerian and Sierra Leone Games were played on three IBM 1050 terminals, two equipped with modified carousel projectors and the third with an experimental random access film strip projector. During each game about seventy five pictures were projected at appropriate times. The terminals were connected by Dataphone to a special-purpose 7090 Computer which was under supervision of a Time Sharing Monitor system (TSM). The coding language used was Fortran Assembly Program (FAP) with a few additional control cards for file loading purposes. To give some idea of the scope of the programs, the Sumerian Game uses about 15,000 lines of instructions and approximately 37,000 memory places in the computer system.

PROBLEMS INVESTIGATED AND
EXPERIMENTAL PROCEDURE

The present experiment was intended to supply information concerning two groups of problems.

1. *Applicability of the games.* Whether sixth-graders indeed could play the games on the computer and develop the same interest usually generated by games and how much teacher-intervention would be required to enable them to play.

2. *Learning-effectiveness.* How this technique for learning basic economic principles compared with conventional classroom teaching in terms of amount of learning and time invested by the student.

From October 1965 to March 1966, twenty-five sixth-grade students from the Mohansic School in Yorktown Heights, New York, played the two games on three terminals at the Center for Educational Services and Research of BOCES. All students played both games, some starting with the Sumerian Game; others with the Sierra Leone Game. Meanwhile a control class of equal ability[2] studied the economics of life in Sumer and

158

Sierra Leone by conventional classroom methods, with a teacher considered to be especially talented and creative. Each student in the experimental group played the game for about 90 minutes and then signed off, returning the following school day to continue. The three terminals were separated from each other in the same room with portable wall section dividers, so that in effect the pupils were separated from each other while playing the games.

Before the games, all students in both control and experimental classes were pretested with the "Test of Economic Principles Based on Ancient Sumer" and the "Test of Economic Principles Based on Sierra Leone" prepared for the project. As each student in the experimental class finished one of the games, he took the posttest based on the game. The students in the control class were posttested as they finished each of the two instructional units taught by the control class teacher. The same test was used for pretesting and posttesting. (A sample page from the Sumer test is reproduced as Appendix B.) Finally, the test was re-administered as a "retention-test" several weeks after the posttest.

Time on the computer was recorded for each player. Moreover, the supervisor kept an anecdotal record of incidents at the terminal and composed a summary describing the ways in which each student reacted to the experience of working with the computer. She also interviewed each student when he had completed both games and posttests.

FINDINGS

Applicability of the Games

It was found that instruction was self-sufficient to the extent that most of the students required no assistance with the instructional aspect of the games. Each student worked independently of other pupils and received no help from a teacher except in these cases:

1. When he had misplayed the game to the extent that the message "please call the teacher" appeared. In this case the student was started over again and required to read aloud the instructions.

2. Whenever any program errors or system failures occurred.

3. Whenever he failed entirely to understand a question, assignment or paragraph within the games. These occasions were rare.

4. When, in one particular instance, the terminal supervisor read aloud the bulk of the printout to a student with very low reading ability.

As distinct from the act of manipulating the typewriter terminal the gaming part of the program presented no real problem to the students. The rules of procedure were simple and explicit enough so that they had no trouble playing the game. Whatever rules there are in these games are explained or made evident as the instruction progresses.

With the exception of two students who had very low reading ability, the sixth graders seemed to have no trouble in reading the printout or following instructions.

The fact that the games are apparently self-sufficient does not mean that they could not be used to greater profit in conjunction with a teacher for one of many possible combinations. It does mean, however, that it is possible to instruct pupils with some degree of success on a completely independent basis.

In regard to the *interest* which students had in the game we found that almost without exception the pupils said they enjoyed playing these economic games on the computer and that this high interest was maintained throughout the two games, which lasted an average of 15 hours in total. Working with a computer terminal is such a novel experience for young students that they undoubtedly experience a rather exaggerated Hawthorne effect. We do feel confident that their interest in working games at the terminal lasts at least 15 hours; we do not know whether it could last for 1,000 hours.

Learning-Effectiveness

Amount of Learning. Table 1 presents the mean pretest, posttest and retention-test scores for experimental and control groups in respect to both the Sumer and the Sierra Leone test. (It may be noted that experimental and control groups do not differ significantly on the pretest, thus supporting the assumption that they were evenly matched.)

The results are ambiguous. While the gain from pretest to

TABLE 1: PRETEST, POSTTEST AND RETENTION TEST SCORES FOR EXPERIMENTAL AND CONTROL GROUPS

| | SUMER | | SIERRA LEONE | |
	Experimental	Control	Experimental	Control
Pretest	17.0	15.8	14.1	14.4
Posttest	24.2	19.3	24.9	26.9
Retention Test	23.9	22.5	21.8	25.4
Learning: Post-score — Prescore	+7.2	+3.5	+10.8	+12.5
Retention: Retention Score — Postscore	—.3	+3.2	—3.1	—1.5

posttest was larger in the experimental group than in the control group (statistically significant at the .01 level) in respect to the Sumer test, the opposite result (although not statistically significant) was found for the Sierra Leone test. The retention was slightly superior in the control group.

Although the only statistically significant difference is the one pertaining to the larger gain of the experimental group in respect to the Sumer test, the total of the data seem to impose a cautious conclusion: that no difference in amount of learning was demonstrated. Insofar as these data go, no claim to superiority can be made either by the computer game technique or by the conventional classroom method of instruction.

Time Invested Per Pupil. The picture is different when we turn to the time invested per pupil. Table 2 presents mean, minimum and maximum game-time per pupil for both games, compared with the classroom, where the teacher spent approximately an hour a day for three weeks on the subject matter of *each* game — i.e. approximately 30 hours in all.

TABLE 2: LEARNING TIME (HOURS) FOR SUMER AND SIERRA LEONE TOPICS

| | SUMER | | | SIERRA LEONE | | |
	Minimum	Maximum	Mean	Minimum	Maximum	Mean
Experimental	6:40	14:05	10:15	3:55	8:00	5:05
(Control)	(15:00)	(15:00)	(15:00)	(15:00)	(15:00)	(15:00)

It is seen that the mean game-time for both games is considerably smaller than the classroom-time (differences significant at the .01 level). Indeed, on neither game did any pupil spend as much time with the computer as the standard classroom-time. For both games together, game-time is only slightly more than half of classroom-time.

In other words, on the average, the students in the experimental group attained approximately the *same amount of learning* with considerably *less investment of time.* In this sense of "learning effectiveness," amount of learning by pupil time, the games appear superior to conventional classroom teaching.

DISCUSSION

It does appear that the computer can be used as a technology for enabling sixth grade students to play educational games and that these games are teaching something. Considering that the Sumerian Game, for example, requires about 16,000 lines of instruction, we feel that we are to a certain extent making use of the power of the computer to deliver programs of considerable complexity.

In addition to being a device for providing instruction, the computer offers a wonderful opportunity to compare methods or teaching logics under stable conditions, that is, conditions which are not influenced by the variable personality and teaching techniques of the human teacher. The computer also provides us with complete records of the student's performance and can, of course, be programmed to make calculations of any sort we desire regarding such things as success and failure, number of repetitions, time elapsed, etc.

The game technique used in this experiment needs a great deal of further testing and revision. At the same time we feel that our findings so far offer encouragement for such further effort. That is, insofar as our experience goes, computer-based games *can* be used in practice even with sixth graders; they do teach as well as conventional classroom methods; and they seem considerably more effective than conventional methods, when the time investment of the student is taken into consideration.

APPENDIX A

SAMPLE PRINTOUT FOR SUMERIAN GAME

Hello! Before we begin, will you please type your name, first name first, then your last name, and then press the Return key.

Ed Smith

Now, Ed, you are ready to operate the Sumerian Economic Model.

Imagine that you have just been made Ruler of Lagash, a City-State of Sumer, in the year 3500 B.C. Twice yearly your Royal Steward, Urbaba, will report to you the economic condition of the kingdom. Guided by these reports, you will decide the use of your grain and other resources, trying to keep your population stable and well fed. Between reports, your court advisor will come to you with news of your kingdom.

The Steward will use the typewriter to report and ask for your decisions. When the "Proceed" light comes on, type your answer in figures and press "Return." (If you make a mistake, press "Cancel" instead and try again.) Good luck!

Initial Economic Report made to the New Ruler of Lagash by his Humble Steward:

Total population now	500
Total farm land under cultivation, acres	600
Total grain in inventory, bushels	900
one season old	900
two seasons old	0
three seasons old	0
Total grain just harvested, bushels	13000
Total resources, harvest + inventory	13900

You must now decide how to use your resources.
How many bushels of grain do you wish to FEED your people?

4000

How many bushels of grain do you want PLANTED for the next crop?

9000

This means that zero bushels must be removed from storage. Is this all right? Do you wish to 1 — let your decisions stand or 2 — revise them?

¹Resulting inventory   900

The steward will execute the royal commands and return in 6 months.

Sir, I am sorry to report that 225 bushels of grain have rotted or been eaten by rats this past season.

Economic Report of the Ruler's Steward for the SPRING Season in the year 1 of Luduga 1.

163

Population at previous report	500
Change in Population	—55
Total population now	445

The quantity of food the people received last season was far too little.

Harvest last season	13000
Harvest this season	14396
Previous inventory	900
Change in inventory	—225
Present inventory	675
Total resources, harvest + inventory	15071

You must now decide how to use your resources.
How many bushels of grain do you wish to FEED your people?

     5000

How many bushels of grain do you want PLANTED for the next crop?

     9000

This means that 396 bushels must be placed in storage. Is this all right? Do you wish to 1 — let your decisions stand or 2 — revise them?

APPENDIX B

SAMPLE PAGE FROM TEST ON ECONOMICS PRINCIPLES BASED ON ANCIENT SUMER

PART A: Multiple Choice

For each of the following questions or incomplete statements, choose the one best answer and place the corresponding letter in the parentheses at the right.

1. If the supply of a product increases at the same time the demand for it decreases, its market value will a. fall; b. rise; c. be undetermined; d. remain exactly the same. ( )

2. If the demand for a product increases, the increase in value which follows usually causes a. more of the product to be produced; b. less of the product to be produced; c. no change in production; d. the making of the product to be stopped. ( )

3. Specialization and trade between countries usually leads to a. the interdependence of both countries; b. the production of fewer goods; c. the economic instability of both countries; d. the fame of both countries. ( )

4. If the demand for a product declines a. the hiring of more workers follows; b. the rate of production slows temporarily; c. the value of the product increases; d. the product is worthless. ( )

5. Compared with the economy of the United States today, the economy of

Sumer at about 3000 B.C. a. was much more productive; b. had more government ownership and control; c. better satisfied the wants of the people; d. had more private businesses.   (   )

6. When a country overproduces a. trade for luxuries is made possible; b. the waging of offensive wars is encouraged; c. the worth of the craftsmen is increased; d. none of these.   (   )

7. When a large company that manufactures television sets finds its profit has become very high due to a great demand for its sets, it will probably a. fire many workers so as to reduce the cost of making television sets; b. distribute all of the profits to the workers as a bonus; c. spend money on research so as to build better sets or different products; d. sell some of the machines in the factory in order to reduce the cost of staying in business.   (   )

8. When technological inventions are encouraged a. production is increased; b. the study of science is no longer required; c. the standard of living is lowered; d. none of these.   (   )

NOTES

1. The games were prepared in consultation with experts in economics, ancient Middle East history, and modern Sierra Leone. Other persons who were instrumental in planning these games were Mabel Addis, a fourth grade teacher at the Katonah Elementary School; Walter Goodman, Chairman of the Social Studies Department at Briarcliff High School; and Jimmer Leonard, graduate student in the Department of Social Relations, The Johns Hopkins University. Programming has been done by William McKay of IBM.

2. As determined by scores on intelligence tests and the Reading Section of the Iowa Test of Basic Skills.

Part III

THE PARAMETERS

■ While it does seem clear that gaming can be an effective educational device, we still know little about the specific mechanisms which make them work or about the conditions (including the type of student) which facilitate or hamper their impact. The chapters in Part III investigate some of the parameters which may affect the impact of simulation games.

The individual characteristics of the players is one type of parameter. Zaltman investigates the importance of the age and social status of the players; he also shows how learning is effected by differential intensity of participation in the game. Farran postulates some special functions of simulations for the academic underachiever. Inbar also presents evidence on the effect of individual characteristics, in particular pre-dispositions; at the same time his major conclusion refers to the *social* nature of gaming and the development of a group atmosphere favorable or unfavorable to learning and enjoyment.

Other chapters consider parameters pertaining to the structure of the gaming session. Farran shows that different results may be obtained when competition is on an individual basis than when competition is between groups. The two chapters on the use of business management games with college students (McKenney & Dill and Starbuck & Kobrow) refer to the role of game administrators and advisors, and McKenney and Dill also consider the composition of player teams.

Clearly these papers represent only a sampling of the relevant variables. Indeed, there is no single game for which we can state precisely the most appropriate type of student-player and the optimum conditions for administration. It is probably in this area of games research that there is the greatest need for a large number of additional empirical studies.

Individual and Group Effects on Enjoyment and Learning in a Game Simulating a Community Disaster

MICHAEL INBAR

■ As we are often reminded, many things are still unclear on the topic of games with simulated environments. Thus, for instance, the question of how such games compare with alternative teaching methods, or how effective they are with different populations of players, are some of the problems which are still unsettled.

That such problems deserve further investigation is beyond

AUTHOR'S NOTE: The findings to be reported in this paper are a summary of part of a dissertation written under the main supervision of Professor J. S. Coleman. The reader familiar with his work in the field of simulations and of collective decisions will easily infer and is not likely to exaggerate how much this study owes to him.

In addition the author is grateful to Professors R. Breton, A. L. Stinchcombe and E. Schild for helpful comments and suggestions on earlier drafts of the study.

The investigation as well as the development of the simulation were part of a general research program supported since 1962 by grants from the Carnegie Corporation of New York. In addition to the grantor, the author wishes to express his indebtedness to Mr. Edgar Reeves, Jr., of the U.S. Department of Agriculture, for valuable suggestions made during the developmental stage of the game, and for providing opportunities to test it with large numbers of adolescents. Finally, the care with which the data of this study were collected, is to be credited to the efforts of G. K. Klein, L. Oester, W. Matson, and their staff of the Oregon State University 4-H Cooperative Extension Service.

discussion. At the same time, however, there is growing consensus on two things: First, that games have a striking impact on the participants; second, that this impact is differential,[1] i.e., different players react differently to the sessions, both in terms of learning and of enjoyment. In this paper we present the results of a study on the precise nature of one game's impact, and some of the reasons for this differential effectiveness on players.

On analytical grounds, the differential impact of a game can stem from any of the following main factors:

1. Variations in the players' background characteristics;
2. Differences in the predispositions;
3. Differences in their experience and behavior while the game is going on;
4. Differences in the characteristics of the groups of which they are members.

Our interest will be in determining how important each of these types of variables is for understanding variations in enjoyment and learning, over individuals and over groups.

Concretely, we shall first ask how much of the impact of the game can be explained by the characteristics of the individual players (background and predispositions) — and how much is explained by what happened in the game itself. This is the type of analysis usually found in the literature.

But then we shall take into account the fact that the game is played in *groups*, and show the importance of group membership on response to the game; this will highlight the insufficiency of the previous analysis by individuals only. Subsequently we shall inquire into the major determinants of the group effects, and finally return to an analysis of individuals, but this time controlling for membership in the relevant types of groups.

PROCEDURE

The Research Design

The sample on which our findings are based consisted of 220 4-H club members organized into twenty-three groups of eight to eleven players. These young people played the first phase of the Disaster Game in two and one-half hour sessions in Oregon during the last week of February, 1966, and the first week of

March, 1966.[2] "Before" and "after" questionnaires were given to all players, the first to assess players' predispositions and their original level of knowledge on the learning variables, the second to measure the impact of the game. Also, measures of the players' understanding of the rules and of their interest and active participation in the game were obtained while it was going on. The questions (with a few exceptions, which will be mentioned when appropriate) took the form of a seven-point scale.[3]

As the study is concerned with *differential* learning — i.e., differences *within* the sample, not whether the game teaches more than an alternative stimulus — all players in a sense are "controls" for each other.

The Dependent Variables

The before-after questionnaires each contained twenty-four items pertaining to some aspect of learning which could be affected by the game. For each item, a measure of learning was constructed which was the ratio of actual change (between the before and after responses) to maximum possible change (in the direction intended by the game designer).[4] The after questionnaire also included ten items pertaining to the player's enjoyment of the game.

Factor-analysis of all of these items generated six factors, and the high-loading items on each factor were used to construct an index. Thus, the study concerns six dependent variables defined as follows:

Learning the Problem of Community Organization (Items: "Lack of organization is a problem;" "Lack of cooperation is a problem;" "Lack of discipline is a problem").

Learning a Feeling of Potency (Items: "Feels 'experienced' in the topic;" "Would know what to do in a disaster;" "Perceived level of knowledge").

Learning Strategies (Single Item).

Learning the Problem of Communication (Items: "Lack of communication is a problem;" "Lack of availability of telephone lines is a problem").

Learning Motivation (Items: "Interest in the subject;" "Willingness to learn more").

171

Enjoyment (Items: "Enjoyment of the game in general;" "Enjoyment of the newness of the experience;" "Enjoyment of the situation challenge;" "Personally, the game was interesting").[5]

The Independent Variables

These were measured in the before-questionnaire (Background-characteristics, Predispositions) or based on measures after the introduction to the game (but before first play) and during the play itself (Experience in Game). They included the following items:

Background: age, sex, grades in school.

Predispositions: liking of games in general, liking of competitions, degree to which participation in game was voluntary, preferences for studying alone vs. with friends, interest in the subject of the simulation.[6]

Game Experience: understanding of rules, interest in the game, active participation in the game — as reported by the subject. In respect to the first two variables we distinguished between the *original* level of understanding and interest (prior to the actual play) — and the *change* in these (during play).

FINDINGS

In the factor-analysis "Enjoyment" emerged as the first and major factor. We shall therefore initially consider the impact of the game in respect to this variable, and subsequently consider the other dependent variables. (These are all, except for "Learning Strategies," significantly associated with Enjoyment.) Our purpose is to see to which extent the independent variables can explain the differential enjoyment found. We shall at this stage group the independent variables in their major categories (Background, Predispositions, Original Level of Game Variables, Changes in Game Variables) and only later refine the presentation.

All of the independent variables were introduced in a forced stepwise multiple regression. It was found that these variables together could account for 40 per cent of the total variance of enjoyment[7] (R = .63). With this *explained variance* as basis, Figure 1 shows how much was explained by each category of variables; that is, *relatively* how much of differential enjoyment is explained by each category.

The first remark that one should make is that the amount of variance explained by all the variables is only moderate. This points to the fact that important variables affecting the process studied were not measured. Within these limitations, however, it is striking to see that once they are controlled for the preceeding variables, changes in the understanding of the rules, in interest in the game, and in active participation in it, account for only 16 per cent of the explained variance. At this point it looks as if the differential impact of the game was largely pre-determined before the beginning of the session, for not only do background, pre-depositions and the original level of the game variables account for almost all the explained variance, but in addition they explain over one third of the total variance (.337).

We shall see shortly how misleading such a conclusion can be. But for this purpose we must turn to the usually unreported question of the group effects on the impact of the game.

The regression analysis has shown how different categories of variables are related to the differential enjoyment of the game. A simple one way analysis of variance, however, shows that enjoyment is also very significantly conditioned by group membership.[8] We partitioned the sample into those groups which highly enjoyed the game, and those which did not (respectively 12 and 11 groups). Table 1 shows the averages *over individuals* on the various variables for those who belonged to groups with high and those who belonged to groups with low averages of enjoyment.[9]

The most important result apparent in this table is that the differences in enjoyment between the groups are not due to their being composed of players predisposed to a differential enjoyment of the game. Thus none of the predispositions which at the previous level of analysis explained the bulk of the variance of the dependent variable come close to being significantly different in the two categories of groups, even at the .05 level [10] and with one-tailed tests. It is only with regard to age that the groups are different, but we have seen in the regression analysis that in terms of its explanatory value this variable can safely be disregarded in this sample.[11]

We are therefore in a situation where for all practical purposes the background and predispositions of the players, although related in their own right to the impact of the game, are of no value in explaining the different average of enjoyment of the players who were in high and low enjoyment groups (6.51 versus 5.47, respectively, $P < .01$). On the other hand there is unambiguous evidence that the groups differ with regard to the way the games developed, for *changes* in active participation, in interest in the game and in understanding of the rules, as well as learning, are clearly different in the two categories of groups.[12] Moreover, it is interesting that the original levels of the game variables already come close to being significantly different in the two categories of groups.

It should here be recalled that the "original level" of the game variables was measured *after* the players read the rules and were given explanations by their game administrator — (but before the actual play). In other words, although the original level of the game variables is logically prior to the impact of the game, it nevertheless already bears the mark of the table manager, whose performance may be crucial for the development of the whole game.[13] We may then summarize Table 1 by stating that the closer we get to actual play, the more the groups differ.

If so, we may reinterpret Figure 1 by grouping the "original level" of the game variables together with the changes in these variables, all pertaining to the game *session*. These variables then account for 35 per cent of the explained impact. Note that with this interpretation of the "original level" of the game variable, the first few minutes of the session, preceding actual play, assume great importance: they determine some 20 per cent of the explained impact of the game.

In any case, Table 2 shows the importance of group membership for the learning and enjoyment in the game. We may ask whether the effect of the group is itself dependent on the predispositions of the players: Does the group uniformly increase (or decrease) learning and enjoyment for all players — or does it affect players with positive predispositions differentially from the effect on players with negative predispositions? Table 2 indicates that the effect is differential.[14]

Thus in the groups with a high enjoyment mean the predisposition is of almost no value in predicting the final score of the individuals; roughly speaking, 90 per cent will enjoy the session

TABLE 1: Comparative Averages of Players in High and Low Enjoyment Groups

VARIABLES	AVERAGES		P.
	High enjoyment groups (N=110)	Low enjoyment groups (N=110)	
Age	14.78	14.08	<.01
Grades	2.23	2.33	N.S.
how much more would like to learn on the topic	5.99	5.81	N.S.
would be willing to participate in meetings on the topic	5.73	5.53	N.S.
would know what to do in case of a disaster	4.08	3.93	N.S.
how much feels that he knows of the subject	3.88	4.08	N.S.
games and learning should be merged activities	5.54	5.21	N.S.
likes games in general	5.68	5.51	N.S.
participated freely in the game	6.02	5.81	N.S.
feels experienced in community disaster problems	3.53	3.46	N.S.
how much is interested in the subject	5.41	5.52	N.S.
original level of understanding of the rules	2.52	2.08	(<.05)
original level of interest	5.11	4.63	(<.05)
change in the understanding of the rules	7.86	6.34	<.01
change in interest in the game	8.08	6.02	<.01
change in active participation	7.74	6.23	<.01
learning the problem of organization	3.78	1.98	<.01
learning the problem of communication	6.48	4.87	<.01
learning potency	2.64	1.31	<.01
learning motivation	4.03	1.61	<.01
learning strategies	2.99	2.80	N.S.

TABLE 2: Differential Enjoyment, in Groups with High and Low Enjoyment, of the Players who Started at Different Levels of a Predisposition

A. Predisposition "How much would like to learn of the topic."

		Low enjoyment groups	
		individuals with	
		High pred.	Low pred.
Individuals with	High enj.	32	25
	Low enj.	16	36
		$Q = .48$	

		High enjoyment groups	
		individuals with	
		High pred.	Low pred.
Individuals with	High enj.	48	52
	Low enj.	4	6
		$Q = .16$	

B. Predisposition "Likes games in general."

		Low enjoyment groups	
		individuals with	
		High pred.	Low pred.
Individuals with	High enj.	40	17
	Low enj.	22	30
		$Q = .52$	

		High enjoyment groups	
		individuals with	
		High pred.	Low pred.
Individuals with	High enj.	63	37
	Low enj.	5	5
		$Q = .26$	

regardless of whether or not they were predisposed to do so. On the other hand, in the low-enjoyment groups the predispositions affect the final score of the individuals quite strongly (roughly speaking, two-thirds of those who were predisposed either to like or to dislike the game in fact do so).

This difference of pattern between the two categories of groups, which is general although we have illustrated it with only two predispositions, raises a crucial question.

FIGURE 1: Percentage of **explained variance** accounted for by each category of variables.

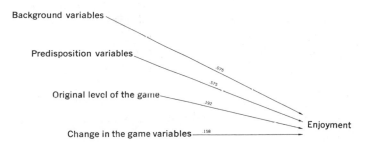

Background variables

Predisposition variables

.075

.575

Original level of the game

.192

Change in the game variables —.158

Enjoyment

Total: **1.00** of explained variance (.40)

FIGURE 2: Percentage of **explained variance** accounted for by each category of variables

A) **High Enjoyment Groups**

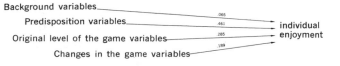

Background variables

Predisposition variables

Original level of the game variables

Changes in the game variables

.065

.461

.285

.189

individual enjoyment

Total: **1.00** of explained variance (.334)

B) **Low Enjoyment Groups**

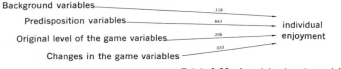

Background variables

Predisposition variables

Original level of the game variables

Changes in the game variables

.118

.643

.206

.033

individual enjoyment

Total: **1.00** of explained variance (.431)

Our findings on the group effects indicate that we are faced with two different phenomena: In the high-enjoyment groups, a general "landslide" seems to have occurred, so that the scores have very little relation to the predispositions; in the low-enjoyment groups, however, the impact of the game is to a considerable extent predetermined by the predispositions. If so, the amount of "explained variance" reported in Figure 1 is misleading. We must now expect that the explanatory power of the various variables will be quite different when we analyze high-enjoyment and low-enjoyment groups separately.

Figure 2 shows that this is indeed the case. It will be noted that for the high-enjoyment groups only .33 of the differential impact of the game over individuals is now explained by the independent variables, while the figure rises to .43 for the players who belonged to the other category of groups. In other words, when the game develops unsuccessfully,[15] when "nothing happens," individual differences in the response of players is increasingly predictable; moreover it is so increasingly on the basis of their background and predispositions, which alone account for over 75 per cent of the explained variance. On the other hand, when the game develops normally we have seen that a unipolarization of responses tends to occur.

It would then be only natural, that in the high-enjoyment groups, where there is relatively little difference among players, i.e., variance is small, the predictive power of *all* the independent variables should be lowered. *But this is not the case.* As a matter of fact, the game variables (original level and change) in this case explain .158 of the *total* variance, as against .093 for the low-enjoyment groups. In other words, when the game is played under favorable conditions, the events of the game become *increasingly* important — not only relatively, but also absolutely — in determining differential enjoyment (see Figure 3).

We believe that in the foregoing analysis we have shown that group membership is a crucial dimension for understanding the differential impact of the game. But we still have to specify the *extent* to which group membership affects enjoyment and learning.

Table 3 shows how much of the total variance of enjoyment and of learning is accounted for by the group average of each player on these dimensions (i.e., by group membership).[16]

It will be noted that in all cases group membership is the

FIGURE 3: Comparative percentages of the **total variance**
accounted for by each category of variables

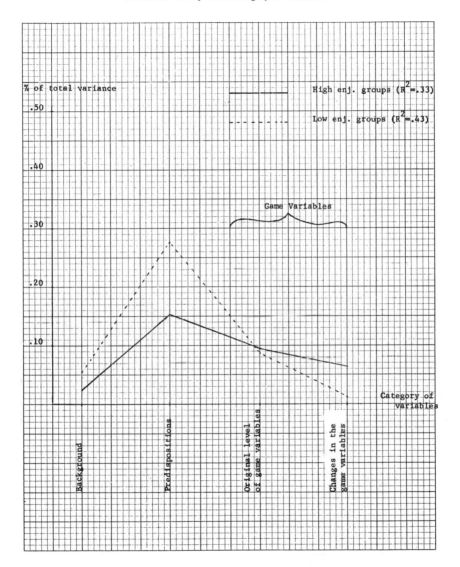

TABLE 3: The Group Effect on Players

INDEPENDENT VARIABLE	Individual Enjoyment	DEPENDENT VARIABLE				
		Individual Learning of "Organization"	Individual Learning of "Communication"	Individual Learning of "Potency"	Individual Learning of "Motivation"	Individual Learning of "Strategies"
Group Average	.262	.176	.117	.129	.116	.096
Background	.007	.002	.032	.009	.008	.002
Predispositions	.178	.014	.052	.052	.045	.041
Original Level of the Game Variables	.053	.019	.022	.009	.021	.005
Changes in the Game Variables	.020	.002	.012	.020	.003	.009
Individual Enjoyment	—	.004	.001	.007	.057	.000
Percentage of Total Variance	.520	.217	.236	.226	.250	.153

TABLE 4: Between Groups Variance Explained by Size

INDEPENDENT VARIABLE	Group Averages of Enjoyment	DEPENDENT VARIABLE				
		Group Averages of Learning "Organization"	Group Averages of Learning "Communication"	Group Averages of Learning "Potency"	Group Averages of Learning "Motivation"	Group Averages of Learning "Strategies"
Group Sizes	.444	.015	.193	.171	.018	.019
Background	.005	.050	.003	.006	.012	.020
Predispositions	.013	.026	.026	.037	.025	.029
Original Level of the Game Variables	.008	.018	.014	.005	.012	.001
Changes in the Game Variables	.018	.014	.027	.000	.057	.047
Individual Enjoyment	—	.061	.005	.015	.043	.002
Explained Between Variance	.488	.184	.268	.234	.167	.118

leading explanatory variable, even for learning strategies for which, as already noted, we are unable to explain much variance in the first place. Although the players' predispositions retain the status of a relevant dimension for the problem at hand, their importance never comes close to that of group membership. This fact has clear implications for the interpretation of the findings about game non-enjoyers which are commonly reported in the literature in disregard of group membership. We shall elaborate on this point in the next section.

It is important to note that (except for "learning motivation"), once the group level of learning is taken into account, the *individual* enjoyment of the player is of no importance for learning. This contradicts a simple hypothesis that the individual player learns as a function of his own enjoyment of the game. Rather, it would seem that enjoyment and learning covary for the individuals, because they both are dependent on the group effect. In other words, we are not dealing with a straight psychological process in the individual, where his "fun" makes him learn; the process of learning is mediated by *the general atmosphere in the group:* favorable group atmosphere induces general high enjoyment — as well as high individual learning.

We may then, finally, consider the differences between the groups in respect to enjoyment and learning as dependent variables. Why are some groups more successful than others? Table 4 presents the proportion of between group variance explained by group size and by group means on the independent variables.

Turning now to the between group variance it appears that, as in the previous case, we are able to explain the most variance for enjoyment and the least for learning strategies. In any case, group size assumes the explanatory value expected; thus, in three cases, (i.e., for enjoyment, learning communication and learning potency), group size accounts for a minimum of 72 per cent and up to 91 per cent of the explained variance. With regard to the other dependent variables, it will be noted first that they are those for which we explain the least variance, and second that the bulk of whatever amount of variance we do explain, is accounted for by game variables rather than by the players' characteristics. Thus the overall conclusion to which one is led is that the groups were indeed homogeneous as far as the players were concerned, and that to the extent that we were able to explain the between group variance at all, the major effect was due overwhelmingly to group size.[17]

DISCUSSION

Our major finding is undoubtedly that both for learning and enjoyment the group effect is the major determinant of the impact of the session upon the players. It is interesting to note, however, that after the powerful group effect has been extracted, the players' predispositions remain an important explanatory dimension, accounting for one third of the explained total variance of enjoyment and approximately one fourth of the learning variance. It is therefore of interest to inquire more closely into the nature of these predispositions.

On the basis of a stepwise multiple regression it turns out that the following three predispositions make the greatest contribution to our understanding of the process under study:

1. Wants to learn more on the topic? (.20);
2. Engaged voluntarily in the game. (.20);
3. Willing to participate in meetings on the topic. (.19).

The figures in parentheses show the partial correlation of each item with enjoyment, controlling only for the background and for the other predispositions.[18] The first thing to be noticed is that the first and third of these predispositions reflect a general interest in the topic to be simulated. Second, liking competitions, studying preferences (in groups or alone) and liking games in general or as a teaching device, as well as more generally all the predispositions which reflect in all probability basic attitudes, are conspicuously absent from the set of the leading predispositions. The trend which emerges seems therefore to be that the most influential predispositions are those which enhance the players' specific interest in the session, rather than those which reflect more rooted values. In other words, there is evidence that willingness to take part in the simulation because of aroused interest in the topic, rather than, for instance, studying preferences or even liking of games in general, is the best warrant of a positive reaction to the session.

We believe that this fact has important policy implications for the administration of games. Indeed, of all the predispositions, interest in the simulation and willingness to participate voluntarily in the session are probably the variables which are the most readily influenced by the person in charge of presenting the game. That they are also the most important predispositions is therefore of extreme relevance. In particular one is led to the conclusion that the differential impact of the game is much less predetermined than it seems at first sight, or more accurately, that to the secondary extent to which it is so, the players' characteristics which are involved are not beyond reach. Thus a careful handling of the players before the session starts might be all that is needed to induce those predispositions which seem to produce desired results in the playing session. In this respect, and recalling our previous finding on the unexpected importance of the first few minutes which preceed the beginning of the play, one cannot avoid reaching the general conclusion that the person in charge of the session is of tremendous importance, at least for games which are not really self-taught and/or self-administered.

Turning now to the differential impact of the game over groups, we have seen that the size of the playing groups stands out as the major explanatory variable. In overcrowded groups the players learn the rules of the games less efficiently, interact less, are less interested in the session and participate less actively in it; as a consequence they tend to play a lesser number of moves and the impact of the game is weaker. In this particular game these processes tend to be effective as soon as the size of the groups exceed nine players. This breaking point undoubtedly varies from game to game. However, such a point probably exists for most games. Thus, it would seem fruitful to pay special attention to the conditions in which games are played. In the long run the success of games as a teaching device might depend on such an allocation of our efforts. Indeed, to the extent that the wide adoption of games as a teaching medium rests on the reaction of its first users, it would seem wise to insure that we do not generate *unnecessarily* an important subpopulation of game non-enjoyers, especially since the evidence seems to indicate that in normal conditions of play we may expect a strong and almost unanimously favorable response to the session.

As for the nature of the impact of the game, we have seen that the extent of learning was different for different topics. Most learning was found in respect to the "problems" of the situation simulated, followed by learning of strategies, motivation and potency, in this order.

In all cases, however, much variance was left unexplained — more for learning than for enjoyment. Obviously, then, important variables for the problem at hand have not been measured in this study. In particular one is surprised to see that the players' experience in the game seems to be of such little explanatory value. It is why we believe that we have been far less successful in either defining or measuring the really influential game variables than we have been in the case of those which measure the players' predispositions. Indeed, it does not seem reasonable to accept without further investigation the proposition that the players' experience in the game bears the secondary and erratic relationship to the impact of the game that they seem to do on the basis of this study. Rather, we are inclined to think that additional and carefully measured variables, such as the players' perception of their winning chances and their sociometric position while the session develops, should substantially increase the amount of explained variance that we were able to account for in the present investigation.

But this is not the only point on which additional research is needed. Because of the very exploratory nature of the present investigation replications are clearly essential to tell the extent to which our findings were idiosyncratically affected by, among other things, the fact that we used a small, highly selective sample which played a single game only once. We would suggest that two problems which arise from our findings be given special attention by the researchers.

The first concerns the players' predispositions and their reactions to the first few minutes which precede the game properly speaking. We have seen that these two dimensions are important for the differential impact of the game. On the basis of the nature of these variables we have concluded that they could be influenced by the person in charge of the session. The present data do not, however, establish whether this is indeed the case, and if it is, to what extent. Clearly the final choice between a policy of selective diffusion of games with the relative slowness that it implies, and a widespread but necessarily more careless one, depends on the cost incurred in the latter case, and only further research can provide us with the evidence needed to solve the dilemma — if indeed it turns out that such a dilemma really exists.

184

The second problem stems from the amount of variance that was left unexplained in our study. Its origin is certainly intriguing. We are inclined to believe that much of it can be accounted for by additional or better-measured game variables at both the individual and group levels. But as things stand no real answer can be given to those who would argue that the unexplained variance will be accounted for predominantly by socioeconomic or personality variables that we have not measured (e.g., socioeconomic status, ambiguity tolerance, frustration tolerance, etc.). We believe this potential issue is of great importance, and deserves further study.

SUMMARY

We have seen that, within the limits of the variance that we were able to explain, the group effect is the major determinant of the differential impact of the game over players, as group size is the major determinant of variations among groups. In other words, the impact of a game seems very much to be a *group phenomenon,* rather than a purely individual learning process.

It follows, moreover, that inferences from studies which do not take group effects into account should be accepted with caution. Thus, estimates from such studies (and they are typical of the literature) of a magnitude of non-enjoyers usually encountered in games, cannot be accepted at face value. Indeed, it was shown that the major difference between the groups where only 50 per cent of the participants responded favorably to the game, versus those where over 90 per cent did so, was group size.

It was then pointed out that given the nature of the players' most influential predispositions for the problem at hand, and given the importance of the first few minutes which precede the beginning of the play proper, the impact of games with simulated environments[19] depends more on the capability of the person in charge of the session than one would have suspected. It was therefore suggested that more attention than is now usual should be paid to holding sessions in favorable conditions. Indeed, while the overall reaction of the participants is generally very positive, it is quite likely that even the minority of players who react negatively to a game can be substantially reduced by relying less on the "magic" effect of games and more on the proper presentation and handling of the sessions.

185

APPENDIX

Overview of the Simulation

In its present version the game requires optimally seven to nine players. At the beginning of the game they sit together around a table on which a board is unfolded. It reproduces schematically the map of what could be a medium-sized town or an area of a large town. For instance, the map gives the location of two residential areas, a police station, a fire department, a shopping center, two hospitals, an industrial area, a city park, etc. These points are spread over the board and are connected by a network of roads which are subdivided in little squares. It takes a unit of "energy" to move from one to the other.

Each player is given a role in the simulated community. This role includes the player's location at the beginning of the game, the relatives and friends he has in the community, his job and eventually such special obligations or interests as appointments to keep or property owned.

When the game starts the players are informed that a catastrophe has occurred in an unspecified part of the town. People may have been wounded and property might have been destroyed. Each player is therefore anxious to an extent specified on the role card about the fate of the persons and things he cares for. To alleviate this anxiety, the players may try to find out what happened by listening to radio broadcasts, by telephoning to relatives, to friends or to official agencies, by asking people with whom they meet or by getting to the disaster area. In the course of these actions, the experience of the players will be that road and switchboard jams, if they occur, are a *direct* function of their behavior. Similarly, they will face the fact that the public agencies whose services they might require perform their functions only if the persons (players) who are in charge perform theirs. Thus the community will be without a communication network if the phone company or the police cars are not operated (i.e., the players are not allowed to communicate with each other and they must remove their pawn from the board — there is a state of complete blackout, except for the players who happen to meet in the streets or in a building and who are informed of the occurrence by the director of the game who centralizes all the moves on a special board). Likewise, the radio will be silent if the speaker does not broadcast, the ambulance will be pinned down if there is no gas supply, etc.

When the players gather reliable information on the location of the disaster area and on the extent of the damages, community organization becomes imperative. Indeed, some players are faced with the fact that they have relatives trapped in the disaster area. To evacuate them they must enter the impact area, and this requires the intervention of the department of public works to clear the roads, of the fire department to master the blaze, of the police station to fight road jams, etc.

If the community cannot organize itself quickly enough or efficiently enough its failure leads to the taking over by outsiders of the rescue activities, or even worse to the spread of the disaster area, which might cause damages beyond repair.

At the end of the game the players elect among themselves the three who did most for the community. Among these three, the winner is the player who was the most efficient, i.e., who accumulated the least amount of anxiety points and spent the least amount of energy points.

Once the players have played this version of the game and have gained some familiarity with the basic problems involved in a disaster they are in a position to play phase two of the game. In this phase they are allowed to engage in emergency preparations before the disaster strikes. They can duplicate some agencies and material resources as well as get trained in special tasks to increase their potential efficiency. The preparedness policy is then tested when the disaster strikes, i.e., when the basic version of the game is played once more.

NOTES

1. In the case of the Disaster Game, we know from extensive testing with several thousand youngsters that on the average 20 per cent of the players enjoy the session little or not at all. For a similar observation over games and populations see J. A. Robinson, "Simulation and Games," (mimeographed,) Northwestern University (Department of Political Science), 1965, p. 19.

2. See appendix for a description of the game. In this particular test no winner was elected.

3. The underlying assumption is that the players' responses form an equal interval scale, which of course is only an approximation.

4. i.e., $L = St_{+1} - St$, where St is the score on an item before the
$$\overline{\lambda - St}$$
game, and λ is the maximum possible score, i.e., 7. See R. Bush and F. Mosteller: *Stochastic Models for Learning*, New York: Wiley, 1955, especially Chapters 2 and 3.

5. The detailed report on the factor analysis, as well as item-correlations for each index, are reported in the author's dissertation.

6. The choice of these predispositions was based on a review of the literature. See for instance J. Huizinga, *Homo Ludens*. Boston: The Beacon Press, 1962; O. K. Moore and A. R. Anderson, "Some Puzzling Aspects of Social Interaction" in *Mathematical Methods in Small Group Processes,* J. H. Criswell, H. Solomon and P. Suppes (eds.), Stanford University Press, 1962; R. Caillois, *Man, Play and Games.* New York: The Free Press of Glencoe Inc., 1961; H. C. Lehman and P. A. Witty, *The Psychology of Play Activities.* New York: Barnes and Company, 1927; T. Leary, "How to Change Behavior" in *Interpersonal Dynamics.* Schein, Berlew and Steele (eds.), The Dorsey Press, 1964; J. S. Coleman, *The Adolescent Society.* New York: The Free Press of Glencoe, 1961, Chapter 11; and E. Berne, *Games People Play.* New York: Grove Press Inc., 1964.
The same rationale led us to estimate the players' experience and behavior in the game by measures of the following three "game variables": understanding of the rules, interest in the game, and active participation in it. (The critical evaluation of these as well as of the other independent variables is postponed until the last section.) Finally, the characteristics of the group include such measures as group size, level of interaction among the players, number of moves played, etc.

7. The variables were forced into the multiple regression in the following order: background variables, predispositions, original level of the game variables and finally changes in the game variables. By including in an additional step the dimensions of learning to extract whatever the feedback between learning and enjoyment can explain of the variance of the latter, the explained variance raises to .46.

8. $F = 7.85, P < 01$.

9. Only a subset of the players' predispositions is presented. Those who did not contribute at all to the explanation of the variance of the dependent variable are omitted.

10. In this study we adopted the .01 level as our level of significance.

11. From previous pre-tests we have evidence that when the range of ages is greater than is the case in this sample, age becomes a much more relevant variable.

12. As the reader will undoubtedly have noticed, this does not hold true for strategies whose differential learning by the players we have been unable to explain in this study. It may be pointed out that under the hypothesis that games excel in teaching strategies, we would expect the variance of this variable to be high and the sample to achieve a high score on it. That this is, indeed, what happened might therefore serve as a basis for such an interpretation (i.e., the variance of "strategies" is the highest by far among the dependent variables, and the example achieved its second highest score of learning on it).

13. This interpretation is corroborated by the fact that the two categories of groups differ significantly with regard to the number of complaints the players voiced against their table manager. It may be pointed out that by means of a controlling procedure, which is beyond the scope of this paper, we were able to obtain evidence that enjoyment did not contaminate the players' perception of the managers' performance.

14. This table presents *number of individuals* with high vs. low enjoyment, rather than *means* of enjoyment. This measure is preferable because a given group average of enjoyment can be the product of various combinations of individual enjoyments. In particular, it could well be the case that the same proportion of players with a high predisposition to enjoy the game will end up enjoying it highly, independently of the group in which they play. In such a case the differences in group averages would simply be due to a montonically different level of enjoyment of the players, depending on the group to which they belong.

15. In an analysis not reported here it was found that group enjoyment is very strongly related to group size and number of moves played ($Q = .90$ and $.86$ respectively). In addition, and as was suspected on the basis of previous pre-tests, group size turns out to be causally related to the number of moves played ($Q = 1.0$). The picture that emerges is therefore that an inappropriate number of players (over 9 players in the case of this game), makes it difficult to play the game, which consequently tends to develop unsuccessfully; apparently from the very start the rules cannot be explained sufficiently on an individual basis, they are therefore less understood, the interest is lower (see Table 1), fewer moves are played and the over-loaded manager is perceived as performing inadequately, which is objectively true. An additional cue of this general breakdown in the groups which tend to be oversized can be found in the comparison of the perceived level of interaction among the players (5.81 and 5.10 in the high and low enjoyment groups, respectively; $P < .01$).

16. As mentioned in the previous footnote, group size emerges as the major explanatory variable of the between-groups differences when the analysis is carried out by means of cross-tabulations.

189

17. With regard to the relative magnitude of the between to the within variances, we have already mentioned that the F ratio for enjoyment is 7.85. For learning, the F ratios range from 1.95 to 4.71 and are all significant at the .01 level or better, except for learning strategies (F = 1.95), which is significant only at the .05 level.

18. Two other predispositions — "would know what to do in case of a disaster" and "like games in general" — have a partial correlation of some magnitude with the dependent variable (.15 and .10, respectively); the contribution of the other predispositions is negligible.

19. At least of those which are not self-taught and/or self-administered.

Competition and Learning for Underachievers

DALE C. FARRAN

■ This paper describes research on the effects of three simulation games on eighth grade boys at the North Carolina Advancement School. Two parameters affecting the game situation will be studied. One involves the structure of the situation in which the games are introduced — more specifically, the way in which game competition is structured. The first section of this chapter is an account of an experiment conducted to test the effects of different types of competition on the amount of learning in these games.

The second section considers the type of student involved in the games. The Advancement School is a residential school, set up to provide intensive remedial instruction and educational enrichment to eighth grade boys designated as having average or above intellectual ability but low academic achievement relative to their ability. Boys are referred to the school by their own school principals, and most stay at the school for sessions of approximately three months. The policy of the school is oriented toward innovation and experimentation in dealing with these boys' learning problems. This section will postulate some of the special functions of the simulation technique for the underachiever, supporting these arguments with observations from classroom experience with games during the past year. Unlike the first section, this discussion is not based upon data from an experiment, but is a more descriptive discussion of the effects of simulation gaming upon a special type of student.

The three games which were used in these tests are the Con-

191

sumer Game, the Life Career Game, and the Legislative Game, all developed at the Johns Hopkins University. (The Consumer Game is described in the appendix to the chapter by Zaltman, in this part of the book. The other two games are both described in the chapter by Boocock, in Part II.) No other simulation games have yet been introduced at the Advancement School.

GROUP COMPETITION AND INDIVIDUAL COMPETITION AS LEARNING CONDITIONS FOR UNDERACHIEVERS

Whatever the specific aspects of simulation games which facilitate (or hamper) learning, the fact that they involve *competition* is presumably of considerable importance. Indeed, much of the impetus to present research on games is derived from Coleman's observations on the functions of competition for the social climate of high schools in which he proposed that interscholastic athletic competition produces an emphasis on sports in the value system of the "adolescent society."[1] A student's achievement in athletics contributes to the prestige of his group (his school) and is hence rewarded with status. There is usually no such intergroup competition in academic studies; students are not interdependent in respect to intellectual pursuits and hence these do not play a central role in the value and status system of the student collectivity.

This analysis gives rise to the hypothesis that intergroup competition in intellectual achievements should raise the importance of these in the social climate of the schools. Moreover, as actual effort and achievement has been found to be contingent on this social climate, the students should also learn more in such a competitive situation. The hypothesis thus predicts increased learning as the result of intergroup competition, mediated by more favorable attitudes to study. *Individual,* i.e., intragroup competition, on the other hand, should have no such effect.

Note that such a hypothesis cannot easily be studied in the laboratory. The hypothesized effect of group competition on the value and status system (a) pertains to collectivities which develop some sense of group identity, and (b) is presumably a time consuming process.

The present experiment is, therefore, a field experiment with all the problems this implies, in particular lack of control over many events which might have occurred differently for the different experimental groups.

Method

One hundred twenty-three students, accepted for the summer session, were divided, randomly, into two groups. Each group was then assigned, randomly, into four house groups. (A "house group" is the living unit at the Advancement School. Students live together, and attend activities and classes as house units.) Four houses played games in a group competitive situation, and four played games competing individually.

All students played two days a week for two hours at a time. The first three sessions were spent on the Consumer Game. In the group-competitive houses, each house totaled the scores made by its house members at the end of a game and compared that total score with those of the other three houses. In the individually-competitive houses, a winner was named in each house and the houses did not compare total scores. Much the same procedure was followed for the Life Career Game to which five sessions were devoted.

The number of sessions allocated for each game allowed for one orientation session and two complete plays of the game.

In respect to study outside game sessions, houses were randomly assigned to classes, teachers, etc.

The learning effect investigated was the content to be learned for the games themselves. Two tests were developed to measure this. Each test had two sections: Game Knowledge, and Applicability. The Game Knowledge section covered the content as it was specifically presented in the game; the Applicability section covered the content as it might apply outside the game. Each question on the Game Knowledge section had a matching question on the Applicability section. Since no questionnaires of this sort existed for either of the games, the research staff at the school devised the questionnaires used.

The tests were administered upon completion of the sessions devoted to the corresponding game, i.e., the Consumer test (31 items) at the fourth session and the Career test (62 items) at the final (tenth) session.

Attitudes to learning were measured by the California Study Methods Survey. This survey was administered during the first week at school and again after completion of all game sessions.

Findings

Table 1 presents mean learning scores on the Consumer and Career tests, for those students who played under group competition and for those who competed individually.

TABLE 1

Mean Scores on Consumer and Career Tests, for Each of the Two Experimental Conditions

	Inter-group Competition	Individual Competition
Consumer, Total*	14.73	16.98
(Knowledge)	7.30	8.68
(Application)	7.43	8.30
Career, Total*	20.03	22.97
(Knowledge)	12.16	13.62
(Application)	7.87	9.35

*difference significant at .01 level, two-tailed test

The data in Table 1 unequivocally contradict the initial hypothesis; the students who competed individually learned *more* than those who were in intergroup competition.

Table 2 presents mean pre- and post-test scores on the CSMS for the two experimental conditions.

The initial hypothesis again fails to receive support. The students who competed individually increased their score more than the students in group competition.

TABLE 2

Pre- and Post-Test Scores on CSMS, for Each of the Two Experimental Conditions

	Inter-group Competition	Individual Competition
Pre*	70.83	71.90
Post*	72.02	78.84

*difference between pre-post differences significant at .01 level, two-tailed test

194

The data of Tables 1 and 2 together raise the question of whether the better learning in the individual competition condition can be explained by the greater attitude change in this group. Therefore the means of the game learning scores for the two experimental conditions were adjusted (for each game test) so as to control for the influence of the CSMS.[2] This, however, did not affect the findings of Table 1. (In no case did the adjusted mean differ from the raw mean by as much as .10.)[3]

Conclusions

The initial hypothesis was clearly contradicted. Several interpretations may be offered.

One trivial possibility is that, unknown to the researchers, uncontrolled events took place during the five weeks of the experiment which induced greater learning in the houses with individual competition, and that these events had so strong effects that they balanced and overpowered the positive effects of intergroup competition. This does not seem a satisfactory explanation. The original data on which Coleman's analysis is based were also taken from the field, rather than from a controlled laboratory condition, and the hypothesized effect is supposed to be strong enough to overcome the impact of confounding variables. (Nor do we have any positive reason to believe that such strong uncontrolled events in fact did occur differentially.)

A second possibility is that the hypothesis does not apply to the type of learning studied — i.e., learning in *games*. The low correlation between learning in games and learning in a conventional context has often been noted. The motivating forces in games may be so different from those in the ordinary classroom situation that the rationale of the hypothesis becomes irrelevant. (This difference may also be implied by the absence of relationship between the attitudes measured by the CSMS and game learning.)

The hypothesized superiority of intergroup competition implied a process whereby academic achievement became a criterion for status among peers, mediated by the contribution of this achievement to the success of the peer group in competition with other groups. But in the condition with individual competition, success in the game gave such status directly and immediately (given the high motivation of the students to succeed in the game); and as success in the game is — at least in part — contingent on learning,

195

the status rewards did induce learning insofar as game knowledge and understanding is concerned. This process might then be stronger, because it is more direct, than the comparable process in the condition with group competition.

If this interpretation is valid, we may have reached the "wrong results" for the "right reasons." That is, the Coleman-mechanism of status rewards from peers *is* an important factor for learning; but insofar as *game* learning is concerned, its effect is more direct and more powerful in individual competition than in group competition.

Whether this specific interpretation is true or not, it seems highly important to distinguish clearly between learning in games and learning in conventional contexts. In particular this is true for the kind of students with whom this experiment was concerned: underachievers. The observation of the players during and after the game sessions gave rise to a number of impressions concerning the special functions of games for these students. While it must be kept in mind that the present sample does not include any comparison group — i.e., boys who are *not* underachievers, or even boys who have not been exposed to the special environment of the Advancement School — it still seems worthwhile to speculate upon the special educational needs of the boys who attend the school and on the extent to which simulation games can meet these needs.

THE EFFECTS OF SIMULATION GAMES
ON THE UNDERACHIEVER

Description of the Problem

Before one can attempt to deal educationally with under-achievers, one must be able to identify their problems. Identification of the problem is not easy. While one should begin with a fairly homogeneous group one can label "underachievers," Advancement School boys are not such a population. They come from vastly different areas of the state of North Carolina; they come from widely varying socioeconomic levels; and they have differing ability, attitude, and achievement levels. In short, they seem to have little that would unite them as a group.

The thing each entering student does have in common with all other Advancement School students is that he has not performed well in the school situation. For some reason, or many reasons, he is an educational "misfit," recognized by his parents, teachers,

196

guidance counselors, or principal as "different" from the rest of the students. What makes him seen as different often depends upon the individual school system. He may be defined as a behavior problem, a motivational problem, a remedial problem, or all three.

These boys bring with them to the Advancement School a history of failures: failures to make the right decisions, failures to make any decision at all, failures to find the strategy for moving effectively through the educational system. All such failures make the underachiever skeptical of his own ability. He responds to his failures in various ways: by being afraid to attack a problem at all; by treating every situation, especially an educational situation, as a joke; or by doing any problems as quickly as possible, hoping that by intuition he will have come up with the answer that pleases a teacher.

Research statistics from testing done after the boys arrive at the school, indicate that the mean reading and arithmetic levels of the students are usually sixth grade; their mean verbal and non-verbal I.Q. scores are near 100; and the mean scholastic attitude percentile is at the 25 percentile level. However, a complete picture of these boys includes something that test statistics do not reveal. This something, a common feeling of being completely disinterested in the educational process, is the core of the under-achievement problem with which the Advancement School must deal.

In order for any educational technique, course, or system to be effective with underachieving boys, it must combat the core problem shared by all these students. It is not possible to rely on traditional remedial materials to get these students back into the educational mainstream. Instead, materials must be found or developed which have the following characteristics: they must be interesting, exciting, and "fun." *For Advancement School students, these three words are contradictory to the very meaning of education as they have experienced it.* In addition, the new material must carry with it an educational value that will be meaningful once the students return to their own school systems.

As part of its total drive to accomplish these goals, the Advancement School turned to the simulations developed at Johns Hopkins University, since these games seem designed to counter some of the important problems of underachievement. The following sections will point to several of these problems and describe how simulation games seemed to affect them.

The Effects of Three Games

1. *Content learning.* Games are an arresting way of helping the underachiever learn content, because the game situation allows him to experience the content directly. Although these students have difficulty verbalizing what they have learned, one boy may have come close when he said:

> There's three things you can take in high school: you can take business education, general education, or college prep. If you hadn't had this game [Life Career], they would tell you about it ... but you wouldn't quite know which to take. It might make the difference whether somebody dropped out of school or not.

From this boy's point of view, the difference between being told about something and experiencing it himself is a crucial one.

Another content effect of games which is important for underachievers is that they serve as a frame of reference to unite various separate ideas students have learned prior to encountering the games. Like other young people, they have picked up many separate ideas, but what they lack is a frame of reference for these ideas so that they "make sense" together. Games, often inadvertently, furnish that frame of reference.

In fact, players often attribute more learning to a game than it could possibly have taught them. During the spring term of 1966, two games administrators had a discussion with a group of students who had played the Consumer Game one day a week throughout the term. Several students argued that games were valuable as teachers of facts alone, citing examples of knowledge they had gained to support their claims. The administrators were rather astonished at how much these boys were crediting the game with teaching them, until they realized what the game had in fact done for these students. That is, it had served to bring into focus much information that heretofore had not been related for these students in any meaningful manner.

2. *Other Effects of Games.* Game play has a value which goes beyond the content imparted to the player. The content in a game could be taught in a number of different ways, but there is a combination of elements inherent in games, regardless of their con-

tent, which cannot be imparted by any other means: strategic decision-making, relational thinking, and planning.

a. Strategic Decision-Making.

Games engage these students in a rather unique way. The game presents a problem to the student, but the problem is contained within the defined boundaries of the game, and the student usually feels that he can understand these boundaries. The student also knows that should he make a mistake, it is not a *real* mistake. He can always replay the game; he can always change his strategy in the middle of the game to try something new. The games are not capricious the way teachers, parents, or friends often seem. They represent to the student an orderly, constant system with which he can cope.

For example, a team of four sixteen-year-old eighth-graders in competition with other teams in the same room played the Life Career Game. They were playing with a profile of a low ability student, and their first reaction to the whole situation was to treat the game as a joke. By the end of the sixth round, midway through the game, they had planned their profile into deep troubles — he had quit school, had a low paying job, had married early, and was continually being "blessed" with unplanned children. In fact, they had done with their profile much the same things that had happened or were likely to happen to themselves. But, at the beginning of the seventh round, they began to be interested in the problem they had created. The game was not punishing them for what they had done, nor was anyone else. They simply were falling behind the other teams in the room. One boy in particular suddenly became quite determined that he and his team were going to solve the problem. The team sent the profile back to night school, had him take a second job, part-time, and gave him almost no leisure for two years. They managed to "pull him out of it" and the excitement and elation that followed is seldom displayed by an underachiever in a learning situation.

Underachievers do become quite excited by being successful in the game situation. Once a student has uncovered a strategy for winning a particular game, he resents any interference with his strategy. In the Consumer Game, "unexpected event" cards (usually bills) are drawn at the end of every round. These cards can be devastating to a well-designed strategy, and for the underachiever, they are intolerable. He has just experienced success;

he has just realized that by careful planning he has a chance to win — and then, by *chance,* he draws a card which he thinks ruins his strategy. His reaction is immediate: he withdraws from the situation and refuses to play. The problem became so acute at the Advancement School when students played the game individually that it seemed desirable to have them play in teams of two, on the theory that two could handle chance better than one.

Games help develop problem-solving abilities by engaging the student in an interesting and understandable problem which demands solution. They allow him to experience success in forming strategies and making decisions. For students who have never successfully coped with a problem in education, games provide the opportunity to see that planning leads to proportionate amount of control over a situation.

b. Relational Thinking.

Students, for perhaps the first time, are involved in observing the result an action produces and in directing the cause and effect. One student, a poor reader, had attacked in a blind fashion the problem of allotting study time for his Life Career profile in high school. He kept getting extremely low grades, although he was playing with a high ability profile. Questioned about the way he continued to adopt the same schedule when as far as grades were concerned, he was far from successful, he answered, "It doesn't matter; it's all luck." Shown the score card by which his grades had been computed, he discovered on what basis he had been receiving his low grades up to that point. He was astounded to find out that the study time he had been scheduling for the profile actually had affected the academic results he got in each round. He was so delighted with his knowledge that he professionally explained the relationship between study time and grades to several other students in the room.

The ability to see the relationship between past and present, and present and future is another new experience for most of these students. One class which had just completed its first session with the Life Career Game was clamoring to replay the game because, as they put it, "now we know what to do." They explained they now understood the effect the decisions they had made for their profile in high school had on the results they were getting at the end of the game. They wanted to go back and replay the high school years to see if they could make better decisions during that period in order to yield better results later. One student voted against doing this, however, for, as he put it, "you can't live your life over again." For him the consequences of the game had been very real ones all along.

Students, having played the Life Career Game, can look back and point out the relationships between the various decisions they have made, and they can begin to project the consequences of the decisions they are currently making.

A second aspect or definition of relational thinking is the ability to unite disparate pieces into a complete strategy, and this is perhaps the most important aspect of this type of thinking. This definition treats relational thinking as an active rather than a passive process; it is the act of relating. The student's mind must be reaching out; it must be actively engaged for relational thinking to occur. This active relational thinking is rare for underachievers, even with the games, but when it occurs there is a major breakthrough. The student has become a strategic thinker.

The clearest example of this type of thinking took place during a "play off" tournament in the Life Career Game when the winning team worked out an incredibly complex schedule that would allow the profile with which they were working (a girl in this case) to work, be married, do the necessary housework, *and* have sufficient time for leisure, a feat no team had been able to accomplish before and the rules for which were not spelled out in the rule book. So aware were they that they had indeed accomplished something unique and quite creative they jealously guarded the plan from the other teams.

As one school administrator put it in viewing a video tape film of this tournament, "And these are the 'sitters' in a classroom. These are the students who 'don't' respond."

c. Planning.

Learning to make a strategic decision, to see relationships between events in time, to understand cause and effect, and to piece ideas together all lead to the ability to formulate and carry through a plan or strategy. The student begins to develop a sense of control over his environment; he begins to be aware of his relationship to his environment. He is no longer so convinced that things "just happen"; he is aware that he can achieve certain goals for himself. The student in the following quotation is aware of the

201

effect the game is having in enabling him to plan and the consequences this newly developed ability could have: "You learn how to study more and plan your life, and I think we should start playing now because when we start planning our life now, which college we want to go to, we'll get better grades."

Students begin to experience and understand the importance of planning, not just in its effect on what happens immediately, but in its consequences for the future. In another student's words: "Life Career, that sort of shows us how our life will be in the future, if we don't watch out. It shows us how we can plan our future, how to get a job and everything like that."

It is important that the games enable students to see the value of planning, but it is more important that the games allow the student the opportunity to formulate a plan and to follow it through. Experience in strategic planning is one of the most fundamental experiences the games provide for the underachiever.

DISCUSSION

The games have produced some remarkable effects — and seem a step in the direction of solving the core problem of underachievement — but there are still difficulties associated with their use. While these difficulties have not been major enough to destroy the enthusiasm the staff feels for the values of games, they are great enough to require serious consideration before game playing can be totally espoused as an effective educational experience for the underachiever.

The games are not manageable with a group of more than twelve to fifteen underachievers at a time. Playing games in the classroom is essentially an individual rather than a group situation requiring initially much individual attention from the administrators.

With a small group, this individual attention can be accomplished easily: eventually the games will carry themselves and the administrator will have less function in the classroom. With larger groups the games have never reached this point. A greal deal of guidance is required from administrators in large groups regardless of how much experience the students have had with games. The School has found that three administrators are essential in a game session involving over twenty students.

A second major problem thus far in our use of the games is that they still need much refinement mechanically. This is particularly true of the Life Career Game. Underachievers must be involved in an educational experience which flows smoothly. If the underachiever is to reap the full benefit of the game, he must be immediately involved in it. He must be engaged in the problem-solving experience from the very beginning or he is not likely to become involved at all. If mechanical problems, i.e., the way the game is played, interfere with his involvement, then the benefit of the game is greatly diminished.

The underachiever becomes severely frustrated if he cannot get involved in the game. It is almost as though he can sense the experience he should and could be having if the game were going well, but the material itself is prohibiting him from reaching that point.

The game technique is a powerful one; the possibilities inherent in it are extremely exciting. However, for underachieving eighth grade boys those possibilities have not yet been realized. The technique is worthwhile, but much work needs to be done to make it as powerful as it might be.

NOTES

1. J. S. Coleman, *The Adolescent Society*, New York: Free Press, 1961.

2. The formula used was:
$$y_{ij} = y_{ij} - b_{ix}(x_j - x.)$$
where y_{ij} = the adjusted mean of condition j on test i;
y_{ij} = the corresponding raw mean;
b_{ix} = the regression coefficient of test i on the CSMS;
x_j = the mean of condition j on the CSMS;
$x.$ = the grand mean on the CSMS.

3. Similar adjustments were carried out for initial differences between the students in the two experimental conditions in respect to non-verbal intelligence, reading ability, and arithmetic ability. In no case did these adjustments eliminate the superiority of the students who competed individually.

Degree of Participation and Learning in a Consumer Economics Game

GERALD ZALTMAN

■ Among the rationales supporting games as useful teaching devices is the idea that simulated environments provide participants with experience and that experience is a highly effective teacher.[1] The more involved and active a player is in a game the more experience he gains with various facets of the game. Accordingly, if games are effective teaching tools we would expect, first of all, some learning to take place and, secondly, that there would be differences in amounts of learning associated with differences in the extent to which players undertake or experience certain key activities.

Experience may induce learning in two ways. The first results simply from a player's exposure to certain facts not necessarily related to the outcome of the game. At some point, after sufficient exposure (i.e., after going "through the motions" often enough), a player learns about some feature of the game. The second way experience may induce learning is by demonstrating that certain consequences (winning or losing) are contingent upon certain behavior (the play of the participant). This encourages players to

AUTHOR'S NOTE: There are two persons to whom I am very heavily indebted: Mrs. Audrey Suhr and Mrs. Lynn Trowbridge. Their assistance in the designing and testing of *Consumer* has been invaluable, and their extra-ordinary efforts in gathering the data for this paper are also very much appreciated!

discriminate between different behaviors or strategies in order to find the strategy providing the most favorable consequences.[2]

It can be stated as a general hypothesis that experience-induced learning (of either type) is associated with the degree of participation in basic game processes. This chapter will explore this hypothesis but with regard to the more specific notion that experiencing the consequences of certain behavior is related to the amount of learning. We shall look at a particular facet of a simulation which has an important bearing on the outcome of the game and which requires discrimination by players between alternate courses of action. The basic question being posed is whether the learning of strategies occurs and is associated with the degree of participation in the basic game processes? The game considered here is Consumer.[3] An overview of this simulation is provided below.

OVERVIEW OF THE SIMULATION

The purpose of the Consumer Game is to teach adolescents about the economics and problems of installment buying. This is accomplished by placing students in an artificial or simulated environment which presents a number of situations requiring many of the same decisions players will eventually make in real life. In the game, as in real life, a wise decision or strategy is more rewarding than an unwise one and increases the chances of winning. The competitive nature of the simulation encourages students to develop a good credit-use strategy on the basis of their experience in the game. The basic game calls for eight to sixteen players and takes about one and a half hours. Players are assigned to one of the following three types of roles:

1. *Consumers:* Consumers receive a monthly income with which they may buy certain products. Satisfaction (utility) points are received for each item purchased. The price of these goods is generally constant, varying only when there is a sale or when another player finds it necessary to auction off something he has purchased or when a repossessed good is resold. However, for a number of items, the utility points vary according to a prearranged schedule so that the decision as to when to buy a particular product and whether or not it is worth going into debt for it becomes important. The buying period in which an item is of greatest value

may not coincide with a time when the consumer has the necessary amount of money. The occurrence of unplanned or random events in the game makes this especially likely. Thus, players are often confronted with a situation in which it may be necessary to borrow money in order to purchase a product, pay an accident bill or even pay off other installment debts during an unanticipated period of unemployment. Consumers compete by trying to maximize their utility points while at the same time minimizing credit or interest charges for which they are penalized.

2. *Credit and Loan Managers:* If a consumer finds it necessary or feasible to borrow money he may go to the bank, the finance company, or to the department store for credit. Players representing these institutions compete against one another receiving points for each transaction and losing points under certain other conditions. Each credit and loan officer has his own rate schedule, contracts, may require (and repossess) collateral, etc.

3. *Salesman:* At present there is one salesman in the game. His chief functions are to disburse items purchased, act as auctioneer and as judge in the event of a legal dispute between a consumer and credit manager.

The game is structured in such a way as to encourage consumers to:

1. Weigh the added cost of financing a purchase against the the additional value to them of having the item now;
2. Consider the opportunity costs of their purchases, i.e., to ask themselves whether there is another use of their money which will yield greater utility; and
3. Guard against unanticipated events not generally covered by insurance.

As a result of interactions in the game between consumers and credit loan managers players should learn:

1. To compare the interest rates charged by different financial institutions;
2. That their credit rating can affect their ability to borrow;
3. To understand fully the implications of contracts before signing; and
4. To appreciate the mechanics of that sector of the economic system concerned with consumer credit.

STUDY DESIGN

A total of 166 persons played the role of consumer. These included teenagers from various high schools in the Baltimore, Maryland area and adults from various neighborhood action groups and from university and federal government adult education programs. None of the adults or teenagers had been involved in consumer education programs prior to the game. Players were classified according to their age and the occupation of the major wage earner in their family. Table 1 shows the number of people in each of the four possible categories. All players completed a questionnaire after the game. Some players also completed a pre-game questionnaire.

TABLE 1: Classification of Game Participants[4]

Occupation of Major Wage Earner in Family	Age		Total
	Adult	Teenager	
Professional	41	29	70
Non-Professional	42	54	96
Total	83	83	166

LEARNING AND DEGREE OF GAME PARTICIPATION

As stated earlier the purpose of the game is to teach players *how* to borrow, i.e., what a good strategy is once the decision to borrow money or buy on credit has been reached. One of the most important strategies the game was designed to highlight was the value of comparison shopping for credit.[5] It is not the intent of the game to teach players that one particular financial institution has higher or lower rates than another, since there is too much variation in actual rates charged by different lending institutions to make this type of "factual" instruction possible. For example, rates charged by different finance companies vary from one-half per cent to three per cent per month on the unpaid balance.[6]

A player's standing at the end of the game is affected by the total number of credit or interest charges he incurs. Each dollar in credit charges means a loss of one utility point in the final score.

It therefore behooves players to shop around and compare rates when borrowing money to settle "unplanned" expenses which occur randomly throughout the game. Such behavior is important for still other reasons relating to buying strategies. Given the situation in which borrowing is necessary if a player is to obtain a particular product at some point in the game, and given that the utility received for some items varies throughout the game, a player will want to compare rates for two related reasons. If, for example, deferment of a purchase until the next buying period means a loss of 10 utility points (to reflect the "cost" of going without a desired item) a player should borrow only from the institution which will charge him less than $10 in interest. Consequently, whether he is able to purchase "now" is affected by his finding a source of credit whose charges will not offset any gain in utility he receives by buying now. Moreover, the extent to which he is better off is determined by his getting the lowest available rates. The lower the credit charges the greater the person's net gain in satisfaction (utility). It is, thus, very important for players to discriminate — to look for differences — among alternative sources of credit.

Players were informed prior to the game that the three agents did charge interest and that the total interest charges would be deducted from their total utility points to determine their final score. They were not told that the three agents charged different rates. The "true" rates of interest in the game were between 11 per cent and 36 per cent and remained fixed for each agent.

Given the hypothesis that activity in the game produces learning, we would expect those players who do borrow more frequently to learn more about the differences in rates charged in the game by the various lending institutions. The more experience they get in borrowing the more likely they are to find out that different rates are charged and who it is that has the highest (lowest) charges.

To test this hypothesis and the effectiveness of the game in teaching discrimination among different agents, players were asked the following question: "Whose interest or credit charges in this game were the highest?" The three agents and a "don't know" category were listed after this question.

Table 2 shows the proportion of each of four groups who, after one play of the game, were able to identify the agent in the game charging the highest rate of interest.

The major differences in Table 2 are between teenagers and

TABLE 2: Proportion of Each Group Selecting Correct Agent

TEENAGERS		ADULTS	
Professional Background	Non-Professional Background	Professional Background	Non-Professional Background
(n=29)	(n=54)	(n=41)	(n=42)
.55	.54	.27	.29

adults. Interestingly enough, there are essentially no differences with regard to occupational background of the family. According to our hypothesis that degree of game participation affects learning, we would expect teenagers as a whole to have borrowed more frequently than adults. Table 3 presents information concerning the average number of borrowing transactions for each group. Teenagers did indeed tend to borrow more frequently on the average than adults. As in Table 2 there are no differences with regard to occupational background.

TABLE 3: Average Number of Borrowing Transactions

TEENAGERS		ADULTS	
Professional Background	Non-Professional Background	Professional Background	Non-Professional Background
(n=29)	(n=54)	(n=41)	(n=42)
1.72	2.11	1.52	1.39

However, the crucial test of the hypothesis that learning in a game is associated with degree of participation is to consider these two variables simultaneously. Rather than look at the average number of transactions for a group we shall go a step farther and classify each group according to high, medium, and low borrowers. Table 4 shows the proportion of each of the four groups further classified by the frequency with which they borrowed who gave the correct answer.

The effect of each independent variable and its statistical significance is summarized in Table 5.[7]

TABLE 4: Proportion of Four Groups Borrowing to Different Degrees
Who Gave Correct Answer

TEENAGERS			ADULTS		
Professional Background			Professional Background		
Hi	Med	Lo	Hi	Med	Lo
(n=9)	(n=13)	(n=7)	(n=8)	(n=26)	(n=7)
.79	.54	.14	.63	.15	.29
Non-Professional Background			Non-Professional Background		
Hi	Med	Lo	Hi	Med	Lo
(n=21)	(n=27)	(n=6)	(n=9)	(n=25)	(n=8)
.71	.56	.00	.44	.28	.13

TABLE 5: Values of Coleman's "a" for Multi-Variate Analysis
and Level of Significance, Controlling for Frequency
of Borrowing, Occupation, Background and Age[s]

Variable	Effect Parameter: a	P
Frequency of Borrowing*	.332	P<.01
Occupational Background of Major Wage Earner in Family	.051	Not Significant
Age	.204	P<.01

*standardized to dichotomy

There is a very strong and statistically significant (at the .01 level) effect of one's participation in the game as measured by the frequency with which he borrows on his learning which of the three agents charge the highest interest. In all cases high borrowers were more likely to know the correct answers than those who borrowed less frequently.[9] For example, 76 per cent of all teenagers from non-professional backgrounds who borrowed very frequently correctly identified the agent charging the highest rates whereas none of their peers who were low borrowers were able to do so.

It should be noted that there are no significant differences in learning associated with family occupational background. This is an especially interesting finding in connection with the teenagers, since more research evidence indicates that youngsters from lower status backgrounds come to school with lower pre-dispositions to learn and do in fact perform at a lower academic level than their higher status peers.[10] The data here indicate that these students were not at a disadvantage in the game situation. An age-associated difference remains even when controlling for participation in the game; teenagers generally did better than adults.

The following conclusions can be drawn from Tables 4 and 5. First, the general hypothesis that extent of game participation affects learning is confirmed. Furthermore, teenagers do better than adults. This latter situation is both because teenagers participate more (which is consistent with the general hypothesis) and because they learn more for any given level of participation. This raises the possibility that the same degree of quantitative participation, i.e., same number of transactions, may actually reflect different qualitative involvement (with the teenagers being more involved than the adults).

GAME IMPACT ON BASIC ATTITUDES

The impact of a simulation game is mediated, in part, by engaging in various behaviors resulting in certain consequences. The question that arises at this point is whether, in adopting the set of behaviors characteristic of a given role as defined in a simulation, players also adopt the attitudes associated with such behavior and by implication come to "approve" such *behavior*.

If this generalization from behavior to attitude does in fact take place, we might expect some over-all change, in a more permissive direction, in attitudes toward borrowing. Such change is to be more expected, if at all, among high borrowers in general and among teenagers in particular.

In order to determine whether there was any change in attitude toward borrowing the following question was asked on both the pre-game and post-game questionnaire. "In general, do you think borrowing: (Check one) ...... Should be Avoided Altogether ...... Should be Used Only for Necessities ...... Should be Used for Anything You Really Want." Since pre-game and post-game questionnaire data are somewhat more complete here for the same respondents this before-after data is tentatively presented.

TABLE 6: Change in Attitude Toward Borrowing by Age and Borrowing Frequency

| | TEENAGERS | | |
	More Favorable	No Change	Less Favorable
Frequency of Borrowing			
Low	—	8	1
Medium	1	23	2
High	3	22	2
Total	4	53	5

| | ADULTS | | |
	More Favorable	No Change	Less Favorable
Frequency of Borrowing			
Low	1	5	6
Medium	6	26	2
High	—	8	2
Total	7	39	10

Table 6 shows change in attitude toward borrowing among the two age groups according to the frequency with which they borrowed. The great majority of players showed no change at all. What change did occur tended to be toward a more conservative position. Holding age constant, it is evident that high borrowers followed this same pattern. When we look at age, holding constant differences in borrowing we see the same tendency. What Table 6 seems to indicate is that gaining insight does not require or result in a change in attitudes, that is, there is no evidence in Table 6 to support the often expressed fear that games, by placing a person in a role or position which requires or encourages certain behaviors, induces approval of those behaviors.

CONCLUSION

The evidence presented here supports the hypothesis that experience-induced learning is associated with the degree of participation in basic game processes. The kind of experience-induced learning with which this hypothesis is concerned is that in which the consequences of certain behaviors are demonstrated to players. It was shown that the more players undertook a particular activity having important consequences on their standing at the end of the game, the better able they were to discriminate accurately between alternative strategies in carrying out this activity. Although the game involves activities which, at least if undertaken frequently, may be inconsistent with players' own attitudes, there were no discernable changes in those attitudes.

NOTES

1. Sarane S. Boocock and James S. Coleman, "Games with Simulated Environments in Learning," *Sociology of Education,* Vol. 39, No. 3, (Summer, 1966).

2. For a more expanded discussion of this see, E. O. Schild, "The Shaping of Strategies," *American Behavioral Scientist,* Vol. 10, No. 3, (November, 1966).

3. Copyright, 1966 by Gerald Zaltman.

4. Examples of occupations classified as professional in this study are physician, teacher, and banker; occupations such as janitor and truck driver were classified as non-professional.

5. There is a great wealth of information showing that most consumers do not compare interest or credit charges levied by various financial institutions despite the very wide range in rates charged nor do users of credit generally know what the "true" rate of interest is that they do pay. See, for example, Arch W. Troelstrup, *Consumer Problems and Personal Finance,* 3rd ed., New York: McGraw-Hill, 1965, p. 95; and Wallace P. Mors, *Consumer Credit and Finance Charges,* New York: National Bureau of Economic Research, 1965, pp. 80-91.

6. Troelstrup, *op. cit.,* p. 106.

7. Table 5 shows weighted measures of the parameter effects. With unweighted measures the effect of age is not significant.

8. James S. Coleman, *Introduction to Mathematical Sociology,* New York: The Free Press, 1964, Chapter 6.

9. The possibility exists that with only one play of the game, pre-game opinions could affect post-game responses and that the results in Table 2 simply reflect pre-game opinions. The ideal way to test this would be to examine turnover of response to the same question. This, of course, was not possible since post-game question referred to what was best *game* strategy and this could not have been asked before players had had

game experience. The next best way to approach this problem is to see if responses to a pre-game question is related to game participation. A pre-game question was asked concerning the source of credit a hypothetical family would likely find charging the highest interest. If pre-game opinions did not influence post-game responses the proportion of high borrowers naming a finance company prior to the game should not be very different than the proportion of low borrowers naming a finance company. It was this situation that characterized pre-game responses (although the data are very sketchy in this case and there was no way of knowing which of several different kinds of "real life" financial institutions — e.g., sales finance company, consumer finance company, credit union, etc. — respondents had in mind when considering a finance company on the pre-game questionnaire).

10. See, for example, Sarane S. Boocock, "Toward a Sociology of Learning: A Selective Review of Existing Research," *Sociology of Education* (Winter, 1966), 32-37.

Variation in Administrative Techniques in Two Business Games

1. The Effects of Team Assignment and Faculty Boards on Student Attitudes and Learning

JAMES L. McKENNEY and
WILLIAM R. DILL

■ *Books is th' roon iv people . . . There's more life on a Saturdah night in th' Ar-rchy Road thin in all th' books fr'm Shakespeare to th' rayport iv th' drainage thrustees.*
— MR. DOOLEY IN PEACE AND IN WAR

■ In the spirit of Mr. Dooley, management simulation games were welcomed in business education as a more exciting and realistic introduction than text or casebooks could provide to the job that a manager must do.[1] Most of the simulations were simple in concept, designed more to stimulate the players to recognize a few issues like the interactions between production and marketing decisions than to provide a rich environment for sustained exploration and learning. Since the games were

217

self-contained and fun to participate in for their own sake, players often got little more faculty supervision than they would expect "on a Saturdah night in th' Ar-rchy Road." On this basis simulation games proved easy to add to business school curricula or to industrial training programs but, as the novelty wore off, hard to justify keeping. The attrition among casual users has been high.

Where strong commitments to simulation exercises have developed we find both more complex models and supplemental efforts beyond the models to make the exercises effective educational experiences. Detail and realism in the models let members of a simulated firm go beyond the "Aha!" experience of learning that managers have problems to the act of developing and testing strategies for solving the problems. Complexity in the model helps force hierarchial organization and role specialization within student firms and puts a premium on the firm's ability to lay out goals, competitive strategies, record systems and controls. Complexity also permits the use of tools of analysis like regression, or decision aids like inventory models, to improve decisions. The more elaborate simulation models pose substantial intellectual and emotional challenges even to experienced business executives.[2]

The simulated environment that a game model provides, however, is only one resource for building a meaningful educational experience. In the view of most players learning comes predominantly from the organizational experiences of working with their teammates to make decisions rather than from the specific nature of the decisions they are asked to make.[3] It comes from reflecting on their actions and experiences and from trying to justify their decisions and the resulting economic consequences to faculty members who serve as boards of directors to the firms. Learning is also enriched by assignments relating to the game in other courses before, during or after the students play. Where simulation games are embedded into a curriculum, faculty behavior is at least as important as characteristics of the simulation model in stimulating learning.

There are still many unanswered questions about how to involve faculty effectively and about how to organize the players as firms in a complex simulation exercise. Many choices exist, and many have been tried, but with relatively little investment to measure the effects of different approaches on what the player learns. In the study summarized here we collected measurements in an exercise involving 650 graduate students of business administration with the goal of testing a few ideas for helping players learn.

The first of these concerned the "attitude" which students adopted at the beginning of the game. If some players were asked to write about what they intended to learn from the experience before they began to play, would this affect performance, satisfaction or post-game testimony about what had been learned? We hoped that even a brief assignment for some of the players to describe their personal learning agenda would lead them to be more experimental and more reflective as they played the game.

The second idea was intended to reinforce the first. It has been demonstrated in a variety of settings that one of the most productive ways to have faculty members involved in a management simulation exercise is to have them serve as boards of directors to the player firms.[4] Many methods for establishing boards have been used, including the teaming of faculty members with top-level executives from the local business community. Relatively little has been done, though, to control the posture that boards adopt in dealing with the teams. Our study was designed to measure the effects of three different faculty orientations as board members: one group of directors to stress profits, another to stress experimentation in group organization for decision-making and the third to stress activities that would maximize the learning which teams could take from the game into other courses. As the results of the study show, however, we became involved with a different but equally significant question — one concerning the ability of faculty members to assume and of students to recognize and accept different board orientations.

Our third concern was with the assignment of men to firms. Earlier studies suggest that firm performance is independent of firm averages on aptitude and certain personality tests and that satisfaction is higher among students when they have a voice in selecting and organizing the firms on which they play.[5] But many other facets have not been explored.

One possibility — based on recent arguments that the best

way to train managers to work as a team is to train them as a team — led us to compare experienced vs. newly formed groups. During the term preceding play, all the students had participated in an experimental, group-based human relations course. In setting up firms for the game it was possible to keep some of the groups intact as firms and to contrast them with firms that were formed without reference to prior group assignments. The experienced groups should get off to a faster start and should work together more effectively in the game.

With the firms that were not organized on the basis of prior group assignments a second proposition could be explored. Firms could be assembled so that their members were homogeneous in ability or in past scholastic performance. It has been argued by some that equality of ability among members of a firm would stimulate learning by providing greater equality of opportunity to share in the jobs that the firm must do. Hence, homogeneous groups should show greater satisfaction, better performance, and more learning.

DESCRIPTION AND PURPOSE OF THE SIMULATION GAME

The students we observed participated in a game exercise during their first year in the MBA curriculum of Harvard Business School. The game had been developed and used over a six-year period to serve as a laboratory experience in decision-making with these goals:

1. To integrate concepts and experiences from the first-year courses.
2. To let students try analytical approaches that they have studied in the context of static case problems in a dynamic, uncertain environment with feed-back.
3. To involve students in a small, task-oriented group.
4. To provide experience in planning over an extended period of "time."

The game was required late in the first year program. Students were organized into 21 independent industries, and each industry included six or seven five-man firms. The firms competed against each other for three simulated years in an industry modeled by computer to represent a stylized version of

220

the consumer appliance business. Each decision set or move represented one quarter of simulated time and specified the financial, marketing and production activities of the firm for the entire quarter. Up to 76 decisions were to be made each quarter to define product quality, to budget marketing effort and production volume, to set prices and to determine the source and amount of outside financing.

EXPERIMENTAL DESIGN

The organization of the first-year MBA program had some convenient experimental design features. At the beginning of the year the 650 students were divided into seven equally sized classes, each of which was to represent the geographic origins, academic backgrounds and social makeup of the total group. Each of the 90-man classes met together throughout the first year with a single set of faculty. These arrangements gave us a base against which to introduce variations in team organization and in the roles of faculty members as directors for the student firms.

For students in three of the seven classes the assignment to firms perpetuated groups that had been set up randomly the term before in the human relations course. These groups faced a change in mission but not in membership. For students in the other four classes the assignment to firms was made with the objective of contrasting homogeneous teams with different levels of capability. The specific measures varied from class to class; but essentially men were matched within teams on prior undergraduate performance, graduate entrance examination scores and first-term grades at Harvard.

Each of the seven classes was split into three independent industries of six or seven firms, and each industry had its own faculty board of directors to introduce the simulation exercise and to guide the students as they tried to master it. Each board was to encourage rational play and reflection on experience, but each of the three boards within a given class had a different emphasis to impart. One was to stress profits. A second was to encourage experimentation in team organization and decision-making. The third was to emphasize the use of the game to exploit learning opportunities which had implications for future courses or the students' job goals.

We sampled students' attitudes and understanding of the simulation by questionnaires before, during and after play. An attitude questionnaire, to poll reactions to team assignments, and to measure students' anxiety was given at the beginning of the game. After the fourth move four classes were given an ungraded examination to test their understanding of the simulated environment and of the rules for play. At the same time the other three classes were asked to describe their learning agenda; improvements in knowledge, skill, perspective and attitudes that they would like to accomplish in the game.

At the conclusion of play all classes filled out the attitude questionnaire again and took a new test on understanding of the simulation and the rules of play. They also completed a questionnaire rating what they thought they had learned. Each faculty board documented the progress and behavior of their firms in accordance with a standard set of instructions. These responses, along with the economic results attained by the student firms, comprise the data base for our study.

LEARNING AGENDA AND THEIR EFFECTS

The effort to get students to think out their agenda for learning from the game was disappointing. Although information about the game was available from second-year students and although the game was looked on positively by most students as they began to play, students' lists of things to be learned were not particularly rich or specific. They did not read as if they reflected much prior thought or personal commitment. No relations were found between either the length or content of the pre-game learning agenda and players' satisfactions, performance and post-game testimony about learning.

Experience on a smaller scale with business executives, subsequent to this experiment, suggests that pre-game discussion and analysis of what players hope to learn can be valuable, but that the effort must go beyond simply writing agenda. Ways must be found to review the agenda against the opportunities that the game will provide and to refer back to the agenda as play progresses.

THE INFLUENCE OF FACULTY BOARDS

Our hope in asking the faculty directors to emphasize different things was to measure the effects of these differences on how students approached and reacted to the game. The boards which stressed profits were to make it clear that they would grade the teams on their success as money-makers. Students were to be measured not by style and strategies but by economic results. The boards which stressed experimentation in team organization and operation took a more direct counseling role. They were to grade students by how well they functioned as teams, with little or no emphasis on actual economic results. The boards which stressed using the game as a vehicle for long-term learning were supposed to encourage radical variations in students' play, using the game less as a competitive economic exercise than as a setting in which each man could practice things that would improve his future capabilities as a manager.

The differences in role were subtle, and after the game students were checked by questionnaire about the role that they *perceived* their board to play. We learned that the communication of intended roles had not gone according to plan. Table 1 provides a concise statement of differences between intention and result.

The profit message was most consistently received. The experimental, counseling role seems to have been communicated effectively by only one of the seven boards who were asked to take that emphasis. The emphasis on future learning was communicated with reasonable consistency. It was not clear from our data how much of the failure to communicate rested on the faculty's inability to assume a role and how much on the unreceptiveness of the students. Because the model itself tends to reinforce a competitive interest in profits, both factors were probably involved.

The HBS faculty seems to accommodate best to a profit-oriented role, and the students seem to anticipate that this is the role they should take. Counseling by faculty on how to make decisions was misunderstood and resented by students as interference with their freedom as "managers" in the game. The students expected the faculty to question their plans and actions critically after the fact, but they did not want to be limited in their freedom to frame plans and try different courses of action.

The moderate success of the future-oriented emphasis by

faculty boards suggests, though, that directors can do more than evaluate the short-term profitability of student actions. By relating profit-seeking activity within the game to broader business questions from outside the game faculty directors can help students generalize the game experience in ways that will be helpful after play is over. If this sort of reflective activity can be fostered during the game we believe students will take more from the game. Finding ways to promote transfer of game experience into subsequent course and job experiences is important to showing that investments in simulation exercises are justified.

EXPERIENCED VS. NEWLY FORMED TEAMS

Our expectation that experienced teams would have an advantage over newly-formed teams was not confirmed. In three of the 90-man classes teams perpetuated groups that had worked together during the previous term in an experimental human relations course. In the other four classes teams were assembled on other criteria, in ways that broke up groupings from the human relations course.

Thus while all players had received the same human relations training, only those from three of the classes could apply what they had learned to the same groups that they had been trained with. We expected that firms with a previous history of working together might start with a better attitude toward each other and, over the course of the exercise, maintain higher levels of satisfaction with the group and produce better results. On the other hand, since team assignments in both the human relations course and the game were involuntary, many individuals might feel frustrated in their inability to change group membership when starting the game. Such frustration might have negative effects on satisfaction, performance and learning. Our hypothesis was that the advantages of continued association would outweigh the disadvantages.

The results suggest that instead advantages and disadvantages may cancel each other. Experienced firms were neither higher nor more variable in pre-game satisfaction than newly-established firms. Through the game changes in level of satisfaction on a variety of measures were comparable in direction

TABLE 1: COMMUNICATION OF INTENDED FACULTY ROLES

	MESSAGE RECEIVED BY INDIVIDUAL				
MESSAGE INTENDED	PROFIT	EXPERIMENT	FUTURE LEARNING	NONE	TOTAL
Profit	112	7	19	25	164
Experiment	48	27	45	33	153
Future Learning	62	27	74	15	178
Total	222	61	138	73	495

χ^2 of equal opportunity = 76.5
Overall R (message intended/message received) = .24
Overall R (message received/message intended) = .06

TABLE 2: NORMALIZED PROFIT AND SALES PERFORMANCE AGAINST ABILITY MEASURES

		ABILITY CLASSIFICATION OF TEAMS			
		ABOVE AVERAGE	AVERAGE	BELOW AVERAGE	RANDOMIZED ABILITY (CONTROL)
Normalized Profits	Upper Third	13*	11	3	19
	Middle Third	6	13	9	18
	Lower Third	0	15	9	22
Normalized Sales	Upper Third	11	9	3	23
	Middle Third	5	14	9	18
	Lower Third	3	16	9	18

*Entries indicate number of teams.

and magnitude for both kinds of firms. While firms with prior history together showed slightly less of a decline in satisfaction with the way they worked together as a team than did newly established firms, the difference was not large enough to be significant. Experienced groups also failed to show any superiority in profit and sales performance or in the amounts they reported having learned from participation in the game.

Generalizations from the results — or lack of results — are difficult. Perhaps differences were washed out by the sharp change in task assignments from the human relations course to the game. Both established and newly-formed groups faced new levels of challenge and uncertainty as they entered the simulation exercise. In the face of these, specific things learned during the human relations course may not have seemed to apply. The results cast doubt on arguments for training managers as teams unless the team training makes direct and specific reference to the environment and challenges that the team will face when it returns to its regular job.

ORGANIZING FIRMS BY ABILITY

Our alternative method of grouping was based on intellectual ability as measured by undergraduate grades, scores on the E.T.S. Admission Test for Graduate Study in Business, and first-term grades at Harvard Business School. A different combination was used in each of four classes to separate the class into firms of above average, average and below average ability:

1. First-term Harvard grades alone.
2. Predicted first-year Harvard grades. (Predictions were made using an estimating equation that was derived on the basis of regression analysis for recent classes. It relates A.T.G.S.B. scores and undergraduate grades to first-year Business School grades and has predicted accurately about 72 per cent of all recent student grades.[6])
3. A comparison of first-term grades with predicted grades. (All students whose grades were appreciably higher than the predicator were considered over-achievers — above average. Those whose grades were appreciably lower were considered under-achievers, or below average, and the remainder achievers or average.)

226

TABLE 3: AVERAGE MEASURES OF INDIVIDUAL ATTITUDES AND PERCEPTIONS AGAINST ABILITY LEVEL OF GROUP

ABILITY LEVEL OF GROUP	ATTITUDES						PRE-GAME LEARNING AGENDA (MEDIAN LENGTH)	POST-GAME CLAIMS OF LEARNING		
	SATISFACTION WITH GAME		SATISFACTION WITH RESULTS		SATISFACTION WITH GROUP			ABOUT FUNCTIONS OF FIRM	ABOUT ANALYSIS OF DATA	ABOUT LEARNING FROM EXPERIENCE
	Before	After	Before	After	Before	After				
Above Average	7.4*	6.9*	6.4*	5.9*	8.0*	7.2*	63	6.1	5.6*	5.8*
Average	7.0	6.2	5.7	5.3	7.2*	6.3	56	6.4	5.0	5.7*
Below Average	7.0	6.1	5.3	5.7	7.1*	6.3	58	6.3	5.3	4.9
Randomized (Control)	7.0	6.0	5.8	5.3	7.6	6.5	62	6.4	5.0	5.1
	.18**	.01	.004	.06	.001	.001		.41	.17	.09

*/"t" test value significant at .10 level or better for difference between group measures and control group measures.

**/Probability all grouping the same by F-test noted below each column.

4. A combination of first-term grades and achievement level. (This gave firms that represented both high grade performance and over-achievement, average grade performance and over-achievement, low grade performance and over-achievement, high grade performance and average achievement, etc. This method of classification was intended to test the discriminating power of two measures versus one.)

To compare team performance we used several measures: operating profit, sales volume and faculty appraisals. Because teams played against three slightly different computer models of the environment all sales and profit results were normalized for each of the models. Table 2 shows profit and sales positions for the above average, average, and below average groups (with the established groups, holding over from the human relations course, as controls). Profits were significantly better for the above average groups and significantly poorer for the below average groups. Average groups did about as well as the randomly assigned ex-human-relations teams. The picture for sales is less clear than for profits, perhaps because of controllable factors in the simulation. It was much easier for teams in general to generate sales than profits.

Table 3 shows results on the pre-game and post-game attitude questionnaires. These suggest that grouping individuals on the basis of ability or talent affects what they learn from the game. Players were fairly equally satisfied with the game as part of their curriculum as play started, but over the course of the game satisfaction held up much better for the above average groups than for the average, below average or control groups. This may reflect superior performance, but it may also mean that only the above average groups had the spark of leadership and individual initiative which generates and sustains morale.

The difference did not lie in understanding of the basic rules of play or in the size and complexity of learning agenda. Learning objectives for the groups were similar, and all seemed to understand the rules equally well. The above average groups, though, used their knowledge to better effect.

What do the results mean? In the initial stages any simulation game poses mainly an intellectual task, to learn the rules and to discriminate among masses of information, and an organizational task, to accommodate to others on the teams and to develop a decision-making style. The above average students were able to learn faster than their classmates and this capacity made them more confident, more satisfied and less anxious from the start of the game. The below-average groups seemed to be overwhelmed by the task. Few had leadership capability within the group to show the way through early problem situations. Early dissatisfaction with poor results led in turn to reduced effort, either in trying to learn the simulation or to cope with the problems that the competitive situation posed. The end result was both poor performance and low satisfaction.

The differences in ability, while not affecting pre-game aspirations to learn, did affect post-game statements about what was learned. All groups were about the same in claims for having learned about the interrelationship of functional activities in the business firm. On methods of analyzing data and on evidence of learning from their experience, the above average groups claimed they had more to show than the below average or control groups. The measures of post-game learning were crude, but the differences do suggest that high satisfaction and high sense of learning from the simulation experience do go together.

Some of the differences between the high and low ability groups may have stemmed from the transparency of the assignments. Because high performers and over-achievers tended to be people recognized within the class as discussion leaders in other courses, the class knew that the team assignments were not random. There was some resentment toward the game administrators for what was perceived as an obvious bias in the groupings.

The anticipated differences between different classes, based on the measure of ability that we used to set up teams, proved too subtle to pull from the data. We can only note that the class which was sorted both on measures of over and under-achievement and on academic record produced, as we expected, the most and the least profitable firms in the game.

CONCLUSION

What we have been learning in general — and what this study was particularly designed to confirm — is that simulation experiences in themselves are not enough. In fact, some of the very things that make such experiences engrossing and exciting may diminish their educational effectiveness. The competitive aspects of a management game, for example, do arouse motivation and help sustain effort. But they may also detract from long-term learning by leading students to play conservative strategies instead of experimenting with new approaches, to emphasize short-term profits within the game context at the expense of building and trying to achieve long-term strategic plans, and to let anxieties about relative performance and grades interfere with efforts to learn.

We have tried to highlight through this study two of the important factors in making simulation experiences more productive as opportunities for learning. First, we have stressed attention to the way in which teams are organized. Keeping groups together simply because they have worked together before does not seem to enhance what they get from the game. Grouping them so that they are homogeneous in ability or prior performance has serious drawbacks. It is especially detrimental to both satisfaction and performance to make teams that reflect obvious differences in potential compete against each other in the same industry.

We would recommend against any method of grouping that puts the weaker members of the class together on teams, and would suggest that each team should have at least a couple of men with above average ability or leadership potential. To the extent possible, student resentment against having team structure imposed can be removed by letting the students decide themselves how team assignments should be made and how teams should be organized.

Our other concern was experimentation with the role of faculty boards of directors. Our results emphasize that the role which is chosen should be one that the faculty members can play with comfort and conviction and one that the students will see as legitimate, both relative to the game and to the general environment of the school. In an MBA program such as the one we have worked with we conclude that the faculty member serves best as a critic and questioner of the role that the students are trying to assume — not as an active counselor or consultant on how to manage. The role can be augmented usefully by encouraging students to look at their activities in the game against the perspective of their future aspirations as business executives.

The restrained role of questioner and critic is most appropriate when, as was the case at Harvard, the amount of time a faculty director can spend with his team is limited. If the director can work closely enough with the team to understand the simulated environment, their organization and their strategic plans as well as they do, he may be able to win their respect and trust as a counselor. Otherwise his advice too often seems like irrelevant interference.

With the improvement of simulation techniques and languages and with expansions both in the capacity of computers and in the flexibility of arrangements by which students can interact with the machine, we can look ahead to simulation games that will be many stages more complex and realistic than the ones we have today. At the same time the future of simulation in education probably rests less on these kinds of developments than it does on efforts to tie the use of models more closely into the total curriculum and the total environment of student-faculty relationships.

NOTES

1. For early overviews of the potential of management games, see Greenlaw, Paul S. *et al. Business Simulation.* Englewood Cliffs, N. J.: Prentice-Hall, 1962; Cohen, K. J. and Rhenman, Eric. "The Role of Management Games in Education and Research," *Management Science,* 7 (1961), 131-166; Dill, W. R. *et al.* (eds.). *Proceedings of the Conference on Business Games as Teaching Devices.* New Orleans: Tulane University, 1961.

2. Cohen, K. J. *et al. The Carnegie Tech Management Game: An Experiment in Business Education.* Homewood, Ill.: Richard D. Irwin, 1964; Thorelli, H. B. and Graves, R. L. *International Operations Simulation.* New York: The Free Press, 1964.

3. Dill, W. R. and Doppelt, Neil. "The Acquisition of Experience in a Complex Management Game," *Management Science,* 10 (1963), 30-46.

4. Cangelosi, V. E. and Dill, W. R. "Organizational Learning: Observations toward a Theory," *Administrative Science Quarterly,* 10 (1965), 175-203; Cohen *et al., op. cit.,* chs. 3, 6 and 9.

5. Cohen *et al., op. cit.,* ch. 8.

6. Rosenbloom, R. S. "A Progress Report on a Study of First-Year Grades for the Experimental Section." (Unpublished report, Harvard Business School, March 4, 1961.)

2. The Effects of Advisors on Team Performance

WILLIAM H. STARBUCK and
ERNEST KOBROW

■ During the summer of 1963 a group at Purdue University conducted a fairly elaborate study of business game play. The study was motivated primarily by a desire to learn more about small group decision-making, but their was a secondary interest in pedagogical technique. The latter led us to assign "advisors" — advanced doctoral students who had shown exceptional promise in their academic work and who had strong interests in pragmatic business decision-making — to some of the student teams. This paper discusses the consequences of adding advisors to the teams.

PROCEDURES

Eighty-eight graduate students were randomly assigned to eighteen teams, two teams having four members and the rest five. The students were candidates for Master's degrees in industrial administration, and had nearly completed their course of study at the time the game was played.

The eighteen teams were divided into three industries of six teams each. Teams within an industry competed directly with one another, but there was no competition between industries. Three teams from each industry were assigned an advisor, and three were permitted to make decisions as they pleased.

AUTHORS' NOTE: This study was supported in part by National Science Foundation grants G24199 and GS-370. Faculty and graduate students who have contributed to this study include John Dutton, Clarke Johnson, Donald Rice, Vernon Smith, John Walter, Norman Weldon, John Wertz, and especially Ronald James and Donald King.

Each of the three advisors was assigned one team from each of the three industries. The advisors were told that their primary function was to encourage and facilitate the use of rational, quantitative decision models by the players, but that they could serve as generalized resources to the extent that their teams solicited such help.

The teams played the UCLA Executive Decision Game (Version 3), making two decisions a week for six weeks. It was announced initially that the teams would make fifteen decisions; but the game was terminated after twelve decisions to thwart end-game strategies. Two hours of the regular class schedules were allotted for each decision, but teams could spend more or less time as they saw fit. Although participation was required as part of a concurrent course in business policy, no specifications were laid down for what constituted adequate participation; game activities had no effect on the students' course grades.

Aside from the sheer fun of the game, the primary reward for participation was monetary. Before the teams began to play a formula was announced by which the fictitious profits in the game could be translated into dollars. The formula was based on the profits achieved by undergraduate teams in a previous play of the same game, and was intended to pay an average team about $55. In fact, the graduate students achieved nearly three times the profits we had forecast, with earnings ranging from $85 to $179.

RESULTS

The advisors were surprised and disappointed that their teams made almost the same profits as the unadvised teams. The advised teams earned $1,315 and the unadvised teams earned $1,221, and the variances among teams were so large that the difference is not statistically significant.

Of course, one question is whether the length of the experiment affected the apparent difference between advised and unadvised teams' profits. The answer is "possibly." We ran the regression

$$\text{Profit} = (C_0 + C_1\gamma) + (C_2 + C_3\gamma)\,(\text{Time})$$

where γ equals one for advised teams and equals zero for unadvised teams. The estimates for C_1 and C_3 are given in Table 1. They indicate that — if there was a difference between advised and unadvised teams' profits — the advised teams made less profit early in the game but increased their profits more rapidly and were making more profit late in the game. Thus the difference between advised and unadvised teams' profits might well have been statistically significant had the experiment continued for a longer period.

TABLE 1: Profit Coefficients

Effect	Coefficient Estimate	Standard Deviation	t Ratio
C_1	−51.9	177.9	−.292
C_3	32.1	37.4	.860

If the advisors were surprised that their teams did not earn significantly more profit than the unadvised teams, they were astounded by the content which they found themselves teaching. Before the game began the advisors saw themselves as technical experts whose task was to facilitate the use of mathematical decision models. They shortly discovered that they had to teach some more elementary subjects. The following observations by one advisor are typical:

> At the start of the game, a surprising number of team members did not understand what the numbers in financial statements meant. There was much confusion over cash-flow versus the profit-and-loss statement.

> Practically none of the team members had any affinity for marginal analysis. They were prone to rely on average figures, and I found myself, several times, delivering brief lectures on the advantages and correctness of using marginal analysis. In truth, many of the students did not seem to know what marginal analysis was.

> In the early part of the game, most players were wont to look no further ahead than the next decision.

The advised teams also had some opportunity to work with quantitative decision-making techniques. The models were quite simple, chiefly composed of elasticity calculations and change-in-profit calculations. A small amount of work was done with subjective probability assignments, and some use was made of break-

TABLE 2: Evaluative Items from the End-of-Game Questionnaire

Questions	Responses		Differences Between Advised and Unadvised Teams
	Members of Advised Teams	Members of Unadvised Teams	
1. Do you feel that the play of this game was worthwhile?	75% Yes	69% Yes	Not Significant
2. If you had an opportunity to play the game again with the **same** group of people, do you feel that your team would perform significantly better?	57% Yes	67% Yes	Not Significant
3. If you had an opportunity to play the game again with a **different, randomly-selected** group of people, do you feel that your team would perform significantly better than this one did?	39% Yes	29% Yes	Not Significant
4. If you had an opportunity to play the game again, would you prefer to play on a team (with/without) an advisor?	53% With	10% With	Members of unadvised teams are less likely to select an advised team next time ($X^2 = 19$ and d.f. = 1.)

TABLE 3: Team Structure and Decision-Making Items from the End-of-Game Questionnaire*

Items	Differences Between Advised and Unadvised Teams**
1. Allocations of teams' earnings among individual team members.	No interpretable differences except, of course, the allocations to advisors by the advised teams.
2. Rank orderings within a team on Bales characteristics: activity, task-ability and likeability.	No significant differences.
3. Time spent on the game by each student during the final week of play.	Insignificant difference in means. Significantly less variance among **members** of unadvised teams.
4. Characterizations of the relationships among team members on four, nine-point scales:	
a) Friendly — Unfriendly.	Unadvised teams rated significantly more friendly. Significantly less variance among unadvised **teams**.
b) Formal — Informal.	Insignificant difference in means. Significantly less variance among advised **teams**.
c) Cooperative — Uncooperative.	Insignificant difference in means. Significantly less variance among advised teams.
d) Specialized — Unspecialized.	No significant differences.
5. Characterizations of the teams' decision-making on five, nine-point scales:	
a) Few changes in organization over time — Numerous changes in organization over time.	Insignificant difference in means. Significantly less variance among advised **teams**.
b) Few changes in policy over time — Numerous changes in policy over time.	No significant differences.
c) Emphasis on next period's results — Emphasis on results several plays hence.	Unadvised teams rated significantly higher in emphasis on next quarter results. Insignificant difference in variance among **teams**.
d) Most decisions made by group discussion during regular meetings — Most decisions made by individuals or groups outside regular meetings.	Unadvised teams rated significantly more inclined to have decisions made by individuals or groups outside regular meetings. Insignificant difference in variance among **teams**.
e) Desire to conserve assets — Desire to take risks.	No significant differences.

* Questionnaire responses were scaled for each student to give a zero mean and unit variance.

** 95% confidence, 5% type I error.

even calculations. We tried to use marginal analysis as best we could.

In other words, the advisors found themselves teaching material which they felt the students should already know. One advisor described the game play as "a singular indictment of a management program which prides itself on its widespread use of quantitative methods." It is not hard to imagine how the first meetings of the advised teams went, or to hypothesize a reason for the lower initial profits of the advised teams.

The students were ambivalent about the advisors. At the end of the game, the teams allocated their cash earnings among the individual players. The three advisors were allocated $100, or 7.6% of the $1,315 earned by the advised teams. Had the advisors been allocated equal shares with the students, they would have received about $219. It is interesting, however, that $100 is approximately the difference in the total earnings of advised and unadvised teams: $1,315 − $1,221, = $94. Thus the advisors were paid their marginal value!

The players completed an end-of-game questionnaire in which they evaluated their experience and described their teams' structures. The four evaluative items are shown in Table 2. The only significant difference between the responses by advised and unadvised students was on the fourth item, advised students being more likely to prefer an advised team on a subsequent play.

The team structure and decision-making items are shown in Table 3. Possibly as a result of the fact that each advisor participated with three teams there was generally less variance among advised teams than among unadvised teams. The advised teams varied significantly less in their degrees of formality and cooperation and in their perceived number of organizational changes.

There were only two exceptions to the general pattern of greater conformity among advised teams. Unadvised teams were significantly more friendly, and — probably because the rating scales were bounded — there was less variance in friendliness among unadvised teams. There was also significantly less variance among unadvised students in the amount of time they spent on the game.

Besides the greater friendliness within unadvised teams, there were two significant differences in the mean ratings. First, the unadvised teams were more inclined to make decisions on the basis of next period's results. This is consistent with the advisors' attention to long-range planning, but could also be a perceptual consequence of the more rapid increase in the advised teams' profits over time.

Second, the unadvised teams were more inclined to have decisions made by individuals or groups meeting outside the regular team meetings. This is probably a difference in *when* decisions got made, not in *who* made them. The greater variance in time spent by advised students suggests that the advisors actually decreased the uniformity or participation. And, while the average time spent by advised students was slightly greater than the average time spent by unadvised students, the difference was not statistically significant.

CONCLUSIONS

The difference in profit earned by the advised and unadvised teams was not large enough to be significant with the sample sizes used and with the number of decisions played. Nevertheless, the authors believe that the difference was real and that the advised students learned more from their experience. But we base these conclusions on the subjective reports of the advisors as much as on the profits earned. The experimenter who undertakes discrimination in terms of a generalized criterion like profit has a tough problem indeed. In the present case, every student had had at least seventeen years of schooling, the last year of which was devoted exclusively to business management. The average student was very bright, and every team played the game extremely well. Even the worst team made more profit than the best undergraduate team we had seen. If one wanted to establish statistical significance he should have undergraduates play the game before they begin to study business management.

The advisors had little success in making the game a laboratory for sophisticated decision models, but they found the game an excellent medium for driving home fundamental concepts and for uncovering and correcting gaps in basic understanding. Of course, the latter are more important objectives than the former, and they are objectives difficult to achieve in a classroom.

Consider marginal analysis. These students had heard teachers expound on marginal analysis for a year. They had had at least eighty exposures to the basic idea. Yet a large proportion of the students still did not buy what the faculty was trying to sell — possibly because they did not understand, but probably because they did not accept the pragmatic applicability of the idea. The students need a situation in which opportunities to use marginal analysis would arise naturally, and a tutor who could help them recognize these opportunities and who could reduce the frustration of first efforts with a new tool. Those are the functions which we think the business game and the advisors performed.

The imposition of advisors did reduce the degree of perceived friendliness in the teams' interpersonal relations, but friendliness *per se* is not an important criterion in teaching. The most serious negative consequence of adding advisors was the higher variance in time spent by advised students. Since advised students spent little more time on the game, the higher variance means that some advised students spent a great deal of time and some spent practically no time at all. However, the proportion of students who found the game "worthwhile" was essentially the same in both advised and unadvised teams, so it is plausible that the lower variance in participation by unadvised students was produced by friendship, not by interest in the game itself.

Part IV

PERSPECTIVES FOR THE

FUTURE

■ The chapters in this final section speculate on the directions the field may take in the future. Burgess and Robinson make some predictions about the nature of our society — particularly our political and business organizations — in the years ahead, and suggest how simulation games can be used to prepare young people to cope with such a society. Their theme of problem-solving and decision-making is echoed in Varenhorst's chapter, which suggests a way to integrate game sessions and supplementary materials in a career guidance program organized around such a concept. This seems the most promising use of games in the future.

In the concluding chapter we have drawn from our own and our colleagues' experiences with games whatever facts, ideas, or hunches might enable us to forecast the future. In particular we have dwelt upon what seems to us the most valuable contribution games could make to educational institutions — i.e., to help the "unsuccessful" student catch up to his classmates, while challenging the bright student to full use of his abilities — and upon the difficulties we foresee which could prevent widespread adoption of learning games by educators.

The need for further research is so obvious that it has hardly been mentioned in these final chapters. Indeed, the function of this section is to whet the appetite of educators and behavioral scientists to add new contributions to the field.

Political Science Games
and the
Problem-Solver State

PHILIP M. BURGESS and
JAMES A. ROBINSON

■ Two fundamental questions must be asked when attempting to forecast the future use of games in educational settings: *What do we want our games to do?* And on the basis of both our accumulated research and folk wisdom about gaming: *What can we expect games to do for the student and to his classroom environment?*

With regard to the first question — our goals when introducing the gaming supplement — we may be underestimating our potential impact by emphasizing variables such as recall and fact mastery. However difficult to measure, we might raise our sights and broaden our goals. We should expect well designed and rigorously administered games to enrich the variety of social and political experience of our students. The political and social experiences in the social science classroom game can be as real as student government or athletics.[1] Games are accessible to more students and the possible classes of experience are more varied.

Given the low status of student government, it is more reasonable to expect students to acquire self-confidence from sharpening their decision-making, problem-solving, and information-processing skills as a result of the integrated decision sequences and trial-error-feedback characteristics of games. We can use games as well as campus organizations to introduce students to unusual social and political situations and to make salient the significant "non-event" choices (e.g., career "decisions") that people make.

We are not suggesting that these classroom gaming goals are exhaustive or that they are intrinsically more significant goals than retention or fact mastery. Rather, they are of a different class of pedagogical aims, a class perhaps more susceptible to gaming stimuli than traditional methods of instruction. In other words, by altering and modifying our goals for classroom gaming, we may open an area in which gaming techniques do indeed "make a difference."

Thus, we are faced with the second question posed above: What can we expect gaming techniques to do — how will they "make a difference"?

If our aim is to increase basic social and political skills, we might use either simple games or the complex, highly abstracted simulation depending on our specific concerns and our estimates of future developments.

Our stress on abstract and multi-issue decision-making simulations derives from our expectations concerning the importance of certain emerging and future organizational roles that many students will occupy and/or be affected by.

THE PROBLEM-SOLVER STATE

Various forecasts, or hypothetical developmental constructs, have been offered about the elite characteristics that are likely to dominate the organizations of the present and the future. Burnham (1941) summarized prospective developments in corporate business and finance as "the managerial revolution"; the legal and economic evidence previously amassed by Berle and Means (1932) was congenial to such a formulation. This "developmental construct" emphasized that the skills at managing the new organizations are different from the skills at making large fortunes in the post-Industrial Revolutionary period. Lasswell (1941, 1962) projected the rise of the "garrison state," in which "specialists in violence" exercise influence at critical posts in organizations other than military or quasi-military (e.g., police, intelligence, scientific organizations applying knowledge to defense). He forecast a spill-over effect in which these specialists influence organizations concerned with communication, education, research, and business.

Additional competitive, constructs deserve to be formulated. Their formulation serves a normative purpose: they alert scientists and others to an alternative future that may be as possible as any other, providing policies are invented to contribute to its realization rather than to that of another possible future. Descriptive, or scientific, purposes are also served: such constructs may be investigated with a view to some prediction of which is more probable, given certain concurrent trends.

We hypothesize the coming of the "problem-solver state," in which organizations, public and private, will be managed less by lawyers and financiers and more by an emerging profession of decision-makers and problem-solvers who can handle large amounts of information about quite different issues (or subjects), each quite complicated and each with its own experts and expertise. This "profession" will, not unexpectedly, emerge from among fields now identified with operations research, computer technology, information theory, and related interests. It will also be skilled in designing organizations and, perhaps more importantly, in reshaping and reorganizing them to meet current and changing demands in an organization's history.

People skilled at problem-solving — that is working on social, political, and business problems of great variety — will be in increasing demand in the next quarter- or half-century. Politicians will need them; the private sector will use them even more than at present. Political parties, executive branches, bureaucracies, international organizations, and legislatures will call for their skills. These problem-solving skills are not specialized by conventional issues — pollution, labor relations, housing, voting, welfare, defense, etc. Rather they are specialized to using, for purposes of making decisions, the immense volume of specialized knowledge on such subjects as we have enumerated. Problem-solvers will move from issue to issue, and in and out from the public to the private sector.

In short, we expect that in the last half of the twentieth century, political power — in parties, bureaucracies, executive offices, and eventually even in legislatures — will be exercised by persons skilled in handling large amounts of information on a variety of political issues. The "information processing specialists," possessing ancillary skills in operations research and data processing, will be able to move from one substantive problem to another, as lawyers and financiers have heretofore notably done. Not by virtue of their authority as economists, or agronomists, or physicists, but by virtue of their skills as effective processors of the information provided by substantive specialists, they will be able to weld together and evaluate the contributions of the specialists and link the demands of political groups to the available resources of the authoritative decision-makers.

If such a "development construct" of political and social trends is postulated, then complex simulations, in which time is compressed, roles are differentiated, and a large volume and variety of information is generated, seem particularly appropriate as a medium for inculcating, developing, and testing these future skill requirements.

GAMES AND POLITICAL SOCIALIZATION

If, on the other hand, we have less specialized aims, such as inducing self-confidence or a sense of efficacy, the complex simulations may be appropriate for other reasons. These kinds of aims, however, suggest a form of learning in which the implications of gaming are most far-reaching and least considered: the processes of political socialization.

The processes of political socialization, considered for their effects on individuals, essentially constitute a learning experience (Dawson, 1966; Hyman, 1959). The agents, or instruments, of socialization include, among others, the family, the formal education process, social groups — primary and secondary, and instruments that inhere in the political systems, such as the mass media. While some controversy exists as to just when political beliefs, attitudes, and orientation become ingrained — during pre-adolescence, adolescence, or post-adolescence — virtual agreement exists that the family plays a crucial, if not the most important, role. However, the influence of the family is mediated (sometimes reinforced, sometimes challenged) by other agents of socialization in the political system. Therefore, even if it is assumed that the individual remains malleable through the post-adolescent period of his chronological development, the potential role of the school and the classroom is underscored (Parsons, 1959).

In this regard, then, it may be that gaming and simulation in the classroom have two potentially far-reaching effects on the political socialization of the individual. First, the gaming process itself may operate to increase the saliency and impact of primary and secondary groups on the socialization of the individual. And second, the content and play of games over many years may operate to modify certain dimensions of the personality of the individual — his self-esteem, his self-confidence and feelings of efficacy, which are known to be important variables in the political behavior of the adult (Milbrath, 1965).

The influence of the groups, and especially the peer group, on the attitudes, values, and opinions of the individual at all stages of his development is well-documented in the social sciences (Verba, 1961; Milbrath, 1965; Coleman, 1961; Lane and Sears, 1964). But because individuals tend to choose friends "like themselves," it might be argued that peers simply reinforce the political and social norms that the individual already possesses (Hyman, 1959). In the school, however, and especially in the classroom, the individual's choice of friends — his peers — is limited, and it might be expected, especially in the elementary and secondary school, that the student would be more likely to find himself in heterogeneous peer groups, thereby increasing the chances of resocialization rather than reinforcement (Langton, 1966). It is beyond the scope of our purpose here to discuss the direction that this resocialization process might take. The point is to underscore the largely unnoticed potentiality of classroom games and simulations for reinforcing and stimulating the mediating role of the peer group in the socialization process, especially if gaming were introduced at the elementary level and continued through the secondary school, or if gaming were given the status and priority of intramural athletics (Ziblatt, 1965; Coleman, 1961). Gaming alters classroom interaction patterns, and some evidence (Boocock, 1963) supports what many of us have observed: that student-student and student-instructor interactions are affected by gaming techniques. Furthermore, in the gaming process, the student is learning from and being "judged" by rules of the game and by the other participants in the game. The instructor is relieved — at least during the period of the game — of his potentially disruptive role in the learning process, that of judge. Rather, the students' peers become more salient in the learning process because cues about performance emerge from peer interaction in the context of the gaming environment.

247

Gaming may also have a potentially significant impact on the development of the student's personality traits that relate to subsequent political behavior. For example, if over a period of years, the student is exposed to a series of games that is closely related to various referent systems and that contains information that is easily translatable to the "real world," then it would be reasonable to expect that he would possess a more realistic understanding of real world processes. Sigel (1966) has pointed out that many contemporary Americans eschew political involvement and participation because they feel that the political world, and especially that part of it dealing with foreign policy, is "too complicated" for them to cope with. One would expect that as the individual gains a more realistic understanding of the "way the world works," as he gains an ability to empathize, that he would gain increased self-confidence in his ability to control and manipulate his environment. If these expectations are sound, then we might have reason to expect dramatic changes in subsequent political behavior of students subjected to the cumulative impact of gaming experience from primary school through the university.

NOTE

1. It should be noted here that an exciting innovation in the form of intramural gaming has been initiated at the Nova High School in Fort Lauderdale, Florida, under the direction of Robert W. Allen.

REFERENCES

Berle, Adolph, and Means, Gardiner. *The Modern Corporation and Private Property.* New York: Macmillan, 1932.

Boocock, Sarane S. *Effects of Election Campaign Game in Four High School Classes.* Baltimore, Maryland: The Johns Hopkins University, Department of Social Relations, 1963. (Mimeographed report.)

Burnham, James. *The Managerial Revolution.* Originally published in 1941; now available from Bloomington: Indiana University Press.

Coleman, James S. *The Adolescent Society.* New York: Free Press, 1961.

Dawson, Richard E. "Political Socialization." In Robinson, James A. (ed.), *Political Science Annual,* Vol. I. Indianapolis: Bobbs-Merrill, 1966.

Hyman, Herbert. *Political Socialization*. Glencoe, Ill.: Free Press, 1959.

Lane, Robert and Sears, David. *Public Opinion*. Englewood Cliffs, New Jersey: Prentice-Hall, 1964.

Langton, Kenneth P. "Informed Publics and Political Socialization: Some Foreign Policy Implications." Paper delivered at *Midwest Political Science Association Meeting,* Chicago, Illinois, 1966.

Lasswell, Harold D. "The Garrison State," *American Journal of Sociology,* 46 (1941), 455-468.

————. "The Garrison-State Hypothesis Today." In Huntington, Samuel P. (ed.), *Changing Patterns of Military Politics.* New York: Free Press, 1962, 51-70.

Milbrath, Lester. *Political Participation*. Chicago: Rand McNally, 1965.

Parsons, Talcott. "The School Class as a Social System: Some of Its Functions in American Society." *Harvard Educational Review,* 29 (1959), 297-318.

Sigel, Roberta S. "Image of the American Presidency — Part II of an Exploration into Popular Views of Presidential Power." *Midwest Journal of Political Science,* 10 (February, 1966), 123-137.

Verba, Sidney. *Small Groups and Political Behavior*. Princeton, New Jersey: Princeton University Press, 1961.

Ziblatt, David "High School Extra Curricular Activities and Political Socialization," *The Annals,* 361 (September, 1965), 21-31.

The Life Career Game

Practice in Decision-Making

BARBARA B. VARENHORST

■ Vocational and educational guidance has always been a difficult task for guidance counselors because there are so many variables that must be taken into consideration in planning for the future — job opportunities, labor market demands and trends, educational requirements, social trends, and so on. In addition to the amount and complexity of the factual information that must be assimilated, variables associated with the relationship between the counselor and the student must be considered. As a consequence, efforts in this area have been somewhat haphazard; including testing, individual counseling interviews, career pamphlets and "courses," and career "days" or "fairs."

At the most general level, guidance is essentially training in *decision-making;* as such its purpose is to provide information, to make alternative choices meaningful, and to provide practice in making decisions. The guidance program at the Palo Alto Unified School District is based upon such a framework. Working on the assumption that we do know at least some of the kinds of information needed for intelligent career decision-making, we have been trying to answer the questions: how is such information to be collected, and how is it to be dealt with in a guidance program? Supported by a NDEA research grant, we have been compiling a pool of data — both on the career opportunities in the surrounding area and on the actual job and education experiences of students who graduated from the Palo Alto high schools. We have also been experimenting with a series of group guidance sessions for all stu-

251

dents at the ninth and eleventh grade levels, in which this information is given to the students, along with visual materials and test scores.

While the evaluatory data gathered indicate that, for some students, the sessions did result in more considered decision-making with respect to educational choices (e.g., selecting a different course, changing choice of college, or studying harder for certain classes), they also indicated that the sessions did not fully involve many students nor produce the level of learning and understanding which seemed desirable. We felt that if the kinds of information about their future lives we wished to communicate to students could be presented in such a way that students actually *interacted with* the components of that future environment, they would not only be exposed to some of the realities of the future, but would also gain some practical experience in how to deal with them. The technique of simulation gaming seemed to offer a possible solution to these needs. Consequently, in the spring of 1966, we began investigating the potential of the Life Career Game.[1]

We are now in the process of evaluating the game, on a variety of criteria, with respect to the goals of the total guidance program. Attempts are being made to estimate not only immediate short-term effects, but also effects after a period of years (which will necessitate a follow-up study of students who have had experience with the game). We shall here describe only a few of the results of this exploratory phase which seem to have important implications for the future both of educational simulations in general and of this game in particular.

First, the game worked with students covering a wide range of achievement and ability levels. In particular, we had successful experiences with three types of students who represented guidance or classroom "problems," at this particular school (which has a national reputation for academic achievement and college attendance, and which is characterized by a high level of social sophistication as well as fierce academic competition):

1. high ability students performing well below their ability, often out of rebellion against their parents, the school, or life in general;

2. a group of Negro students, who represent a small minority group in the school, who differ from the rest of the student

252

body in family income, previous academic performance, and social skills, and who have thus had difficulty adapting to the social system of the school; and

3. a group of students who are average to slightly below average in achievement (sometimes with rather higher ability), who tend to be ignored in a school where they do not fit the school "image," but also do not make enough trouble to draw attention to themselves.

Another interesting sidelight is that in these first tests players worked in teams combining a boy and girl. Not only was an interest factor introduced, since boy-girl relations are extremely important to high school students, but it also simulated some of the potential conflicts that must be resolved in family units when decisions are made.

Second, because the Life Career Game is structured in an open-ended way, it can be expanded, revised, or varied in a number of ways, to suit the particular group. For example, in our tests actual catalogs from the local colleges and universities most frequently attended by Palo Alto students were used in the game. If teams wished their person to attend one of these schools, they had to meet the admission requirements and select courses from the offerings of that particular school. Likewise, the job table contained information on actual job opportunities in the surrounding country, as well as details about the district's work experience program. Job applications were based upon typical forms used at the employment office. In addition, teams were given bonus points for finding a job through newspaper advertisements or by consulting a local employment office. The game was further expanded by allowing group discussion, at the end of rounds of play, during which players could compare scores and strategies, challenge each other's decisions, and even question the values expressed by certain decisions. A further variation of the game is suggested by the fact that each group eventually asked to play the game again using themselves as "profiles."

Third, the game can be incorporated into a larger guidance unit or course. Our feeling is that for the game to be utilized fully, it must be anchored in some type of related, ongoing program. Curricular materials are now being written that will incorporate the game at certain key points. For example, we have designed a workbook, "Invitation to Decisions," which includes "experience tables" (reporting the experience of previous Palo Alto students with regard to post-high school education or training and job experience), as well as a record of the individual student's test scores, grade point averages, and so on.

Other plans for the future include:

1. Using the game in large groups, such as social studies classes. This would involve more students, would eliminate the problems connected with calling students out of different classes for game sessions, and would still allow for group discussion.

2. Adapting the game for use at the junior high, and perhaps at the elementary school level. Thus, a student who graduated from high school would have had considerable practice in decision-making and would hopefully have gained some skills and confidence regarding his own future planning.

3. In-service training for counselors and teachers.

4. A symposium for parents, at which time they will play the game and be given an opportunity to discuss its implications for their children.

NOTE

1. Copyright, 1966, Sarane S. Boocock. For a description see the chapter by Boocock in Part II.

Conclusion

The Future of Simulation Games

■ We have called this volume a "progress report." The word "progress" implies some future desirable state toward which we are moving. We shall now speculate a little on the nature of this future. Given the experience with simulation games so far — what would we like and/or expect to occur in the next decade or so. We shall be conjecturing; whatever the phrasing — we do not mean to assert or conclude, but merely hypothesize.

GAMES FOR WHOM?

One of the dominant concerns of education in recent years has been the problem of the "learning gap" between the "unsuccessful" student and his more successful peers. We believe that games can be a powerful means to reduce this gap.

In the category of "unsuccessful," we include the "underachiever," the "non-motivated," the "culturally deprived," the "inner city," and various other types of "problem" students. This does not mean that we consider these various subcategories as synonymous (although there tends to be considerable overlap); nor do we accept all of the terms as accurate or fruitful descriptions of the learning problem designated. Whatever the specific nature and causes of the problem, most other innovations in teaching have been unable to close the gap; on the contrary, they typically provide the able student with additional tools with which he can move even further ahead of his peers.

Simulation games seem to have a quite different effect. The lore of games research is full of exciting instances of "learning breakthroughs": a previously withdrawn, unresponsive, non-achieving, troublemaking, etc. student comes to life in a game session and proves himself surprisingly active and effective in planning strategy, participating in (or even leading) team activities, etc. (Boocock, 1963; Blaxall, 1965). But there are also "hard data" available. Consistent empirical evidence shows that the relationship between learning in a game situation and performance in the conventional school setting (Boocock, 1966; Inbar, 1965; Cohen, 1964) is very weak. Note that it is not a *negative* relationship which is indicated; games are not a purely compensatory device suitable for those students unable to learn by conventional methods and equally unsuitable for the successful students. They are rather a *different* way of learning. The zero-magnitude correlation with conventional classroom work implies, of course, that the use of games together with conventional methods will decrease the variance of achievement, (without decreasing the mean).[1]

This finding on learning in games is one more in the series of discoveries that have contradicted the notion of given and rigid learning-ability (and inability) which forever freezes the hierarchy of students by intellectual achievement. It has been a repeated observation by sociologists and psychologists entering the field of education that educators frequently display a strange skepticism in respect to children's ability to learn. Bruner has argued the point forcefully with regard to developmental "readiness": that you can teach something of any subject matter — in an honest way — to a child at any age. The impact of simulation games is another case in point: the unsuccessful student *can* learn — if you provide him with the appropriate tools. This learning, as measured in studies so far, is not a result of psychological treatment of the individual; the studies have not used games for therapeutic purposes to remove personality blocks and motivational obstacles in order to release a suppressed learning ability. They have simply placed the student, as he is, with whatever motivational, psychological, cultural problems he may have, in a different learning situation — and he learns.

At the same time the use of games with unsuccessful students does encounter some special problems. It is frequently difficult, for one thing, to demonstrate their learning relative to other students, because they test poorly on standard tests of achievement (or aptitude). In addition to whatever bias may be inherent in the test itself, it has been shown that unsuccessful students may accept the role of "failure" and develop a psychological set which makes them do poorly (cf. the discussion of Negro scores on intelligence tests, in Pettigrew, 1964). It may well be that this self-image of being an academic failure is one cause of the relative impact of games: the perceived difference between the game and the conventional learning methods relieves them of the "obligation" to fail. But in any case, the negative set toward testing imposes considerable problems on the measure of actual learning.

A second difficulty is more substantive than methodological. A particular problem is often observed when unsuccessful students play games. One sees them making very shrewd moves — and making them repeatedly so as to show that they are not simply random or lucky moves. Such students are, however, seldom able to explain in words what they did. This phenomenon has been discussed by Bruner, who found that students are often able to perform intellectual tasks requiring the use of quite abstract rules or theories well before they can say what these rules or theories are. For example:

> It can be demonstrated that fifth-grade children can play mathematical games with rules modeled on highly advanced mathematics; indeed they can arrive at these rules inductively and learn how to work with them. They will flounder, however, if one attempts to force upon them a formal mathematical description of what they have been doing, though they are perfectly capable of guiding their behavior by these rules (Bruner, 1960, p. 38).

Of course, the highest order of understanding means not only being able to act effectively but also being able to say what you are doing. What we wish to make clear here, though, is that these are two distinguishable kinds of performance, and for young people with academic backgrounds of deprivation and failure, the former alone may represent a real intellectual victory. The more general implication is that it will not be possible to test our belief in the great importance of simulation gaming for the poor school performer without designing some ways to measure different kinds of learning.

It may also be — and this should not be overlooked — that games *per se* are intrinsically limited in their effect: that, in Bruner's terms, they may induce "enactive" and "iconic" learning but do not lead the player to *symbolic* representation. If so, the games should be linked to other devices — e.g., "post mortems" in group discussion — which may produce the symbolic learning desired.

But games may also have a more far-reaching impact on the unsuccessful student, beyond teaching him whatever knowledge and skill is contained in a specific game. A growing body of theory and evidence supports the view that behavior in general and learning in particular is strongly affected by the individual's sense of "control of his own destiny" (Rotter, 1966; Seeman, 1966). Most recently, impressive evidence was presented by Coleman and Campbell in their large-scale survey of education in the United States (Coleman, Campbell, *et al.* 1966). This survey was intended *inter alia* to discover, on a large national sample, the factors which make for high versus low achievement in school. Among the major findings were those pertaining to a variable defined as "belief in control of environment":

— that the extent of this belief was a major differentiating factor between white and Negro school children (at grades one, three, six, nine, and twelve);

— that this belief is the best predictor of school achievement for Negro children and the second best predictor for white children; this finding holds when other relevant variables, such as family background and characteristics of the school and faculty, are held constant;

— that the zero-order correlation of this belief with achievement, is as high as the correlation of achievement with ability measures.

The antecedents of the presence or absence of this belief are still not known. One possibility is that the absence of sense of control is derived from insufficient experience with situations where the actor clearly *has* control — that is, from a past where outcomes in fact have not been highly contingent on the actor's behavior or the contingencies have been too complex for easy perception. Extended experience in simulated environments may remedy this deficiency. (For an elaboration of this view, see Schild's chapter in Part I.) Most of the research to date, however, has concentrated upon one game and mainly over relatively short periods of time, and it seems clear that any real effect upon such a deep-seated feeling as one's sense of control would require a much longer exposure to the simulation technique, preferably with a number of different games. Hopefully, what might be built up from long-term experience with a number of games is a kind of "game attitude," and outlook on life which can be described as:

> ... first of all an attitude in which the child learns that the outcomes of various activities are not as extreme as he either hoped or feared ... In time, the attitude of play is converted into what may best be called a game attitude, in which the child gets a sense not only that consequences are limited but that the limitation comes by virtue of a set of rules that govern a procedure, whether it be checkers or arithmetic or baseball (Bruner, 1966, pp. 134-135).

And we would add: that these consequences are to some extent under the actor's own control. Ideally, this would mean teaching students games varying not only in content but also in such structural features as number of players, the nature of the interaction, the structure of the competition, and so on. It means that the goal is not only the essentials of play but also the understanding of the underlying models of the games, so that students could see that even very complex situations and events have an underlying order and that seemingly different situations and institutions may have similar structural characteristics and arrangements. It could mean including as a part of the simulation experience the correction or revision of games or parts of games, and perhaps even having students try their hand at designing games. Whatever the players may learn from a simulation game, it is clear that its designer has learned a great deal about the social process simulated. It is almost axiomatic that in order to design a good simulation of some social institution or process you need a pretty good understanding of the basic principles of its operation.

An example of such an experiment is being developed by Cherryholmes. In this exercise:

> Students will be *presented* with a completed simulation of the United States Congress in the 1960's. Students will simulate a contemporary Congress at the beginning of a year course in American history. Later in the school year they will be presented with historical materials describing Congress at the turn of the century, from which they will *re-design* the simulation to repre-

sent that period, then *operate* and *evaluate* their model of Congress on the basis of historical materials. This procedure will be repeated still later in the school year for Congress as it existed in the early nineteenth century (Cherryholmes, 1966, p. 7).

The passage quoted above raises several other points about the future use of simulation gaming. First, while we in this chapter so far have argued the special value of this technique for the weak student, one can formulate an equally strong argument for the appropriateness of gaming for the *gifted* student. We shall not dwell on this side of the coin, because the Burgess-Robinson paper in the preceding chapter has presented a cogent argument of the potential value of simulations in preparing future "decision-makers." The Varenhorst paper in this section also suggests that games can capture the involvement of the very bright, (including those bright students who have become alienated from the school system). In fact, Sprague and Shirts, who have been experimenting with relatively long and complicated simulations, feel that these may work significantly better with very able students (Sprague and Shirts, 1966).

The Cherryholmes exercise suggests a special appeal of gaming for the bright, imaginative student. Used in the way he describes, games can free this kind of student from the rigidity of the typical class assignment, rewarding him for independence, creativity, and special effort, and encouraging him both to develop ideas and theories of his own and to test them against "reality" (actual historical or other factual materials). At the same time the task does not generate into the empty non-work of some "creative assignments": hard learning and concrete knowledge is needed in order to do the job.

Thus, it would seem that the single teaching technique of simulation gaming can appeal to both the very able and to the non-achieving student. This points to a generalization of considerable importance for the future use of this technique: that simulation games seem to be an effective learning tool for a great variety of participants. An overview of the players in the studies reported in Parts II and III suggests some of this variety. Moreover, in several cases the *same* game has been tested successfully with players varying greatly in age, ability, and motivation. For example, the Life Career Game, discussed in both the Boocock and Varenhorst chapters, has been used with students ranging from sixth through college level, and also with adult education groups; it has been played by students in the highest academic "tracks" in very competitive suburban high schools and by students in the "basics" classes in inner city schools; it has been used in outside-school youth organizations ranging from 4-H clubs to federal job corps camps. Moreover, it has been found that youngsters of quite different interests and abilities, and even ages) can participate in the same game sessions. A similar broad applicability of a single game is reported in the Abt chapter in Part I. As Abt sees it, not only can "... both slow and rapid learners ... share social interactions in the game while learning from it at quite different levels," but that "the slower students also learn from the faster ones, sometimes better than from teachers." Any teaching tool which not only narrows the gap between the high and the low achiever, but also enables slow and fast learners to work together and to help and learn from each other, certainly deserves serious attention from educators.

DISSEMINATION OF GAMES

The problem is to which extent such "serious attention" is indeed forthcoming and whether it will be translated into actual large-scale adoption of the gaming technique. It would be naive to assume that because a handful of researchers have had some gratifying successes with the technique and can produce some evidence of its educational worth, that it will automatically be adopted by school systems and correctly used by classroom teachers. Educational history is full of good ideas that never got beyond the superintendent's office.

It should be further recognized that the more innovative a new technique is, the greater the difficulties of dissemination — and games certainly fall toward the "more" end of the innovation continuum. Their physical format alone demands significant departures from standard classroom arrangements. Chairs and tables get moved around, students move about the room freely or gather in small groups to argue over points of strategy. The very fact that gaming so closely fits Dewey's ideal of the "active learner" means that the classroom is often noisy and apparently less well organized than in the conventional lecture-recitation situation. (And

261

such a change in the physical setting has obvious implications for the social definition of the situation.)

A second, and perhaps more radical, change is in the teacher-student relationship. If the teacher is to use a simulation game in the manner intended, he must not only familiarize himself with the equipment and the rules, but also change his perception of the students in some rather basic respects. An important assumption underlying the technique is that students *can* be autonomous, self-motivating, and self-regulating with regard to their own learning to a much greater extent than is normally assumed — and allowed. Because the rules are in the game itself, rather than being imposed by the teacher's authority, and because the outcome of the game, not the teacher, decides the winner, control of the class shifts from the teacher to the learning materials themselves — and in a sense ultimately to the students. While this shift in control could lead to a more productive exchange between students and teachers, it could also be very threatening to those (both teachers and students) accustomed to more authoritarian methods of teaching.

Third, the type of intellectual problem posed by a simulation game differs from the type of problem usually presented in the classroom. Teachers and students alike are familiar with the textbook problem which covers one or a few specific points and has one unambiguous "right answer." They will probably also have tried "discussions" about complex attitudinal issues, where no one opinion is superior to another (and the discussion frequently degenerates into empty generalizations devoid of substantive content or intellectual challenges). A simulation presents a rather complex problem (albeit simplified relative to real life) and there is, in contrast to the textbook problem, usually more than one winning strategy. At the same time, unlike the "discussion," some strategies are clearly much superior to others. This kind of problem is encountered much more frequently in life than in the classroom.

This structuring of the "problem" does, however, introduce ambiguity in evaluating students, because standard verbal tests are not entirely appropriate to measure many of the skills learned in the game. And what teacher would allow success in a *game* of all things to determine his evaluation of a student?

Finally, resistance to the simulation technique may be expected simply because the games present the world as it *is* rather than as it "ought to be."[2] While this touches upon the question of the

262

values which are or are not taught by games, an issue far too complex to be handled satisfactorily here, several observations relating to the possible future use of games can be noted. It is, as Coleman's paper in Part I has indicated, possible "to devise games that represent innovations in social organizations" — i.e., to experiment with idealized versions of social institutions and processes. Even with the current games, however, it is possible to give students some meaningful way of confronting the real vs. the ideal world, using the game as a model of the former and then encouraging students to discuss whether or not they "like" this model.

An implication of these innovative aspects is that if simulations are incorporated into the school system, they are likely to work to *change* the system. Giving students greater freedom, and at the same time making them more responsible for their own learning, can have a marked effect upon the value climate of a school, as well as changing its structure of interpersonal relations.

Given that games are built upon a number of assumptions that run counter to traditional notions of teaching, can we really expect them to be widely accepted? One proponent of the technique, in a moment of pessimism, suggested that we simply contend ourselves with reaching those teachers or schools which are most receptive to innovation — perhaps 10 per cent of the total.[3] Our own view tends to be more optimistic, although it seems clear that the imagination needed to introduce games and the gaming technique into school systems is as great as that required to design the games themselves. It also seems clear that until we know much more about the appropriate design of simulation "kits," including instructions to teachers on how to fit a particular game into the regular school curriculum and, in some cases, additional materials to supplement the game, we cannot leave the dissemination function to publishing or other commercial companies that may produce educational games. Like the "new math," games will be most effective where teachers are adequately trained in their use, and, at least in the near future, this will have to be done by those directly involved in their design and development.

The most intensive work in this area is currently being done by Project Simile, at the Western Behavorial Sciences Institute. Just before the opening of the school years 1965 and 1966, two-week workshops for teachers were held. The workshop members took part in four simulations, discussed the theory underlying each as well as its merits and shortcomings, and developed a plan for trying the simulation exercises in classrooms during the succeeding year. In the 1966 workshop, participants also tried their hand at designing new games.

For the actual school trials, the project staff printed and distributed game materials and were present in the classroom as observers and to help students and teachers with any problems. As Sprague, the director of Project Simile, describes the first year's experience:

> We tried to work ourselves out of the consulting job as soon as we could by preparing additional written or visual materials. In some cases, our help was not required at all; most often we answered questions about details of the simulations and coached student teams in tasks associated with management of the simulations (Sprague and Shirts, 1966, p. 5).

The report as a whole gives an idea of the imagination and improvisation required in the introductory stages of a new educational technique. The researchers made no attempt to reach a representative sample of teachers at this point: participants in the workshop were chosen by their principals and were paid for attendance.

The problems of dissemination raise a related but different question: In what *form* can simulation games be most effectively disseminated? The actual use of games by classroom teachers will depend partly upon the ease with which they can be combined with other class work. While many games have been added to social studies courses and guidance programs without much conscious concern for the exact nature of integration, the widespread adoption of games will clearly require more systematic attention to this problem.

Sprague has suggested the following as possible strategies:

(a) We should design and try packaged units of study built around simulations with suggested readings, guides for incorporating the units into existing standard social studies courses, and suggestions for ways in which the simulations can be varied in form and content to meet demands of different settings.

(b) Whole courses should be constructed around one or more simulations and tried in a variety of situations.

(c) Taking an even broader look, we might envision a whole series of, for example, international relations simulations, the simplest of which could be tried by first graders, slightly more complex varieties by more advanced students, and so on. By the time a student reached his senior year in high school, he might be taking part in a simulation far more elaborate and demanding than the present Inter-Nation Simulation, having had ten years of simulation experience. (This last idea is based partly on a hunch: one of the things participants seem to learn in a simulation is how to take part in a simulation; we have some intuitive evidence that they can jump into a later exercise with more speed and skill.) (Sprague, 1966, pp. 27-28.)

Sprague also emphasizes that while it is important for new materials to fit fairly comfortably within the existing curriculum and classroom procedure, it is also important that a game not be so structured and self-contained that resourceful teachers (and students) cannot make modifications to suit the particular kind of learning desired. Indeed, one of the most interesting features of simulations is their relative open-endedness and adaptability, and the purpose of designating supplementary materials to go with a particular game is to enhance, not to bury, this quality.

The addition of supplementary materials also would allow testing of another hunch. It seems plausible — and we have a small amount of supporting empirical clues — that students can not only acquire knowledge from the game itself, but that the interest and involvement aroused in the game may have a "carry-over" effect, such that they also learn related materials more efficiently. For example, in an experiment with a simulation of a national Presidential election, it was found that players scored significantly higher than a control group of non-players on test items referring to a municipal election then going on in Baltimore, *although this information was not contained in the game itself* (Boocock, 1963). The finding suggests that the game experience sensitized players to the general problems of elections, so that they either read more newspaper or magazine reports or listened to more television or radio news pertaining to the coming election, or that they simply "saw" or "heard" more of the mass media reports that they already read or listened to.

The general pedagogical implication is that games, via their carry-over potential, may make subsequent conventional instruction more effective. A further implication is that using a simulation game alone is to make only partial use of its learning potential. By supplementing the game with readings and other correlated activities, the additional potential can be utilized. The strength of carry-over certainly seems worthy of further investigation.

FURTHER RESEARCH ON GAMING

Most research reports conclude with a few paragraphs on gaps in the existing knowledge in the field and suggestions for further research. We shall not follow this line in any detail because it is so obvious that the set of papers comprising this book is not comprehensive in any sense. Indeed the newness and complexities of the field are such that virtually any well-thought-out evaluative research will make a genuine contribution to our knowledge (and, of course, replications of much of the work reported here would be of great use).

Let us just point out how much we still have to learn about the very core of this field: how to design a good simulation game. Beyond the obvious requirement that the designer have substantive knowledge about the topic of simulation, little can as yet be said. Games design is not only not a science, it is hardly a craft, but rather an "art" in the sense that we have no explicit rules to transmit.

We need two types of knowledge: a better sociological theory (which tells us what to include in the game and what not) and a better theory of gaming (which would tell us which aspects of the game have what effects). The search for this knowledge is — to us — intrinsically rewarding. If we are right it is also a way to satisfy a desire latent in many social scientists: to do something which can have a major impact on a social institution, in this case education.

NOTES

1. Actually the absence of relationship found may in part be due to the fact that no study included the full range from the very gifted to the very unsuccessful student. But even if the true correlation is positive but low, there is to our knowledge no other technology which can claim this.

2. Our experience has been that this kind of "moral" objection is more widespread among educators than might be assumed. For

example, at a recent meeting on new educational techniques, a member of the panel took violent exception to Abt's Game of Empire (a simulation of trade patterns and practices in the eighteenth century British Empire) on the grounds that winning players often "re-invented" smuggling, piracy, and slavery. In point of fact, such practices did exist, and an institution like slavery was supported over a long period of time by many respectable citizens, probably largely because it represented a "rational" solution to certain economic problems. This critic apparently felt that a more favorable image of our national heritage should be presented to school children.

3. R. Garry Shirts, at the conference "Educational Realities," sponsored by the American Management Association, August, 1966. Mr. Shirts also predicted that it was the members of his audience — school administrators, teachers and counselors, and business executives from companies involved in the production and marketing of educational materials — who would keep games out of the schools, while if the decisions about purchasing of materials were left up to the actual users (i.e., the students) educational games would be readily adopted. This claim is supported by an incident which occurred recently in an Allegheny County, Pennsylvania, high school. Following trials of games in several social studies and math classes, the faculty group evaluating the project hesitated so long over whether or not to adopt games for general school use that the student body, via a formal student council action, petitioned the school administration to continue the use of games in class, offering to do additional homework assignments if necessary.

REFERENCES

Blaxall, John. "Game Learning and Disadvantaged Groups." Cambridge, Massachusetts; Abt Associates, 1965. (Unpublished paper.)

Boocock, Sarane S. *Effects of Election Campaign in Four High School Classes.* Baltimore: The Johns Hopkins University, 1963. (Mimeographed report.)

————. *The Effects of Games with Simulated Environments upon Student Learning.* Baltimore: The Johns Hopkins University, Department of Social Relations, 1966. (Unpublished Ph.D. dissertation.)

Bruner, Jerome. *The Process of Education.* Cambridge, Massachusetts: Harvard University Press, 1960.

————. *Toward a Theory of Instruction.* Cambridge, Massachusetts: Harvard University Press, 1966.

Cherryholmes, Cleo. "Some Current Research on Effectiveness of Educational Simulations: Implications for Alternative Strategies." *American Behavioral Scientist,* 10 (October, 1966), 4-7.

Cohen, K. J., Dill, W. R., Kuehn, A. A. and Winters, P. R. *The Carnegie Management Game: An Experiment in Business Education.* Homewood, Illinois: Irwin, Inc., 1964.

Coleman, James S., Campbell, Ernest Q. *et al. Equality of Educational Opportunity.* Washington, D.C.: U.S. Government Printing Office, 1966.

Inbar, Michael. "Simulations of Social Processes: The Disaster Game." Baltimore: The Johns Hopkins University, Department of Social Relations, 1965. (Unpublished paper.)

Pettigrew, Thomas F. *A Profile of the Negro American.* Princeton, New Jersey: Van Nostrand, 1964.

Rotter, J. B. "Generalized Expectancies for Internal vs. External Control of Reinforcements." *Psychological Monographs,* 80 (1966).

Seeman, Melvin. "Antidote to Alienation — Learning to Belong." *Trans-action,* 3 (May-June, 1966), 35-39.

Sprague, Hall. "Using Simulations to Teach International Relations." La Jolla, California: Western Behavioral Sciences Institute, 1966. (Mimeographed paper.)

Sprague, Hall and Shirts, R. Garry. "Exploring Classroom Uses of Simulations." La Jolla, California: Western Behavioral Sciences Institute, 1966. (Mimeographed paper.)

Appendix A

SELECTIVE BIBLIOGRAPHY ON
SIMULATION GAMES
AS LEARNING DEVICES

The following list contains only works relating to simulation games designed or used primarily for educational purposes. It does not contain references to simulations developed for theoretical or predictive purposes[1], or which do not have a game structure. Nor does it include references to the literature on "game theory," as developed by von Neumann and Morgenstern and their followers. There is also a body of literature on games in the anthopological literature, which is not included here.

In the case of games or research programs on which a number of papers and monographs have been published (e.g., the Carnegie Tech Management Game), we have tried to select those which are most recent and/or comprehensive.

GENERAL PERSPECTIVES ON GAMES

Berne, Eric. **Games People Play.** New York: Grove Press, 1964.

Caillois, Roger. **Man, Play, and Games.** New York: Free Press, 1961.

Huizinga, Johan. **Homo Ludens.** Boston: Beacon Press, 1955.

Long, Norton. "The Local Community as an Ecology of Games." **American Journal of Sociology,** 64 (1958), 251-256. Also available in Bobbs-Merrill Reprint Series.

Mead, George H. **Mind, Self and Society.** Chicago: University of Chicago Press, 1934, Chapter 20: "Play, The Game, and the Generalized Other."

Piaget, Jean. **The Moral Judgment of the Child.** Glencoe, Illinois: Free Press, 1948, Chapter 1.

————. **Play, Dreams and Imitation in Childhood.** New York: W. W. Norton and Company, 1962, Part 2.

Rapoport, Anatol. **Fights, Games and Debates.** Ann Arbor: The University of Michigan Press, 1960.

Schelling, Thomas C. **The Strategy of Conflict.** Cambridge, Massachusetts: Harvard University Press, 1960.

Simmel, Georg. "Sociability: An Example of Pure, or Formal Sociology." In Kurt Wolff (ed.), **The Sociology of Georg Simmel.** Glencoe, Illinois: Free Press, 1950, 40-57.

FUNCTIONS OF GAMES FOR LEARNING

Abt, Clark C. **Heuristic Games for Secondary Schools.** Cambridge, Massachusetts: Abt Associates, 1965, mimeographed report.

————. "The Rediscovery of Exploratory Play, Problem-Solving and Heuristic Gaming as a More Serious Form of Education." Paper presented at the Lake Arrowhead Conference on Innovation in Education, December, 1965.

————. **Games for Learning.** Cambridge, Massachusetts: Educational Services, Inc., 1966.

Bruner, Jerome S. **Toward a Theory of Instruction.** Cambridge, Massachusetts: Harvard University Press, 1966, especially 83-86, 92-96, 99, 117, 125-127, 134-135.

Coleman, James S. **The Adolescent Society.** New York: Free Press, 1961, Chapter XI.

————. **Adolescents and the Schools.** New York: Basic Books, 1965, especially Chapters 3, 5, and 6.

Editors of **Education USA, The Shape of Education for 1966-67.** Washington, D.C.: National School Public Relations Association, 1966, 48-51.

Gibson, John S. **New Frontiers in the Social Studies.** Medford, Massachusetts: Lincoln Filene Center for Citizenship and Public Affairs, 1965, 26-28.

Guetzkow, Harold S. (ed.) **Simulation in Social Science: Readings.** Englewood Cliffs, New Jersey: Prentice-Hall, 1962.

Moore, O. K., and Anderson, A. R. "Some Puzzling Aspects of Social Interaction." In J. Criswell, H. Solomon and P. Suppes (eds.) **Mathematical Methods in Small Group Processes.** Stanford, California: Stanford University Press, 1962.

Schild, E. O. "Learning in Simulated Environments." In **Proceedings of the Rider College School of Education Conference: New Approaches to Social Studies.** Trenton, New Jersey: Rider College, 1966.

FIELD TESTING OF SIMULATION GAMES AND EVALUATIONS OF THEIR LEARNING EFFECTS[2]

Many of the discussions of particular games in the following sections of this list also describe tests of the game.

Blaxall, John. "Game Learning and Disadvantaged Groups." Cambridge, Massachusetts: Abt Associates, 1965, unpublished paper.

Boocock, Sarane S., and Coleman, James S. "Games with Simulated Environments in Learning." **Sociology of Education,** 39 (Summer, 1960), 215-236.

Boocock, Sarane S. **"The Effects of Games with Simulated Environments upon Student Learning.** Baltimore: The Johns Hopkins University, Department of Social Relations, 1966, unpublished doctoral dissertation.

Garvey, Dale M., and Seiler, William H. "A Study of Effectiveness of Different Methods of Teaching International Relations to High School Students." Emporia, Kansas: Kansas State Teachers' College, 1965, mimeographed paper.

Inbar, Michael. **"The Differential Impact of a Game Simulating a Community Disaster and Its Implications for Games with Simulated Environments."** Baltimore: The Johns Hopkins University, Department of Social Relations, 1966, unpublished doctoral dissertation.

McKenny, J. C. "An Evaluation of a Business Game in a MBA Curriculum." **Journal of Business,** 35 (July, 1962), 278-286.

DESCRIPTIONS OF PARTICULAR SIMULATION GAMES

A. Political Games

Alperin, Robert J. "A Simulation in the Beginning Course in American Government and Politics." University of Maryland, 1962, mimeographed paper.

Anderson, L. F., Hermann, M. G., Robinson, J. A., and Snyder, R. C. **A Comparison of Simulation, Case Studies, and Problem Papers in Teaching Decision-Making.** Evanston, Illinois: Northwestern University, 1964, mimeographed report.

Barringer, Richard E., and Whaley, Barton. "The MIT Political-Military Gaming Experience." **Orbits,** 9 (Summer, 1965), 437-458.

Bloomfield, Lincoln P. "Political Gaming." **U. S. Naval Institute Proceedings,** 86 (September, 1960), 57-64.

Bloomfield, L. P., and Padelford, N. J. "Three Experiments in Political Gaming." **The American Political Science Review,** LIII (1959), 1105-1115.

Cherryholmes, Cleo. "Developments in Simulation of International Relations in High School Teaching." **Phi Delta Kappan** (January, 1965), 227-231.

Cohen, Bernard C. "Political Gaming in the Classroom," **Journal of Politics,** 24 (1962), 367-381.

Garvey, Dale M. "A Simulation of American Government." Emporia, Kansas: Kansas State Teachers' College, 1965, mimeographed paper.

Giffin, Sidney F. **The Crisis Game: Simulating International Conflict.** New York: Doubleday, 1965.

Goldhamer, H., and Speier, H. "Some Observations on Political Gaming." **World Politics,** XII (October, 1959), 71-83.

Guetzkow, Harold, et al. **Simulation in International Relations: Developments for Research and Teaching.** Englewood Cliffs, New Jersey: Prentice-Hall, 1963.

Robinson, James A. "Simulation and Games." Columbus, Ohio: Ohio State University, Department of Political Science, 1965, unpublished paper.

Robinson, James A., **et al.** "Teaching with Inter-Nation Simulation and Case Studies." **The Political Science Review,** 60 (March, 1966), 53-65.

B. Business Games

Cohen, K. J., and Rheuman, E. "The Role of Management Games in Education and Research." **Management Science.** 7 (1961), 131-166.

Cohen, K. J., Dill, W. R., Kuehn, A. A., and Winters, P. R. **The Carnegie Management Game: An Experiment in Business Education.** Homewood, Illinois: Irwin, Inc., 1964.

Dill, William R., Jackson, James R., and Sweeney, James M. **Proceedings of the Conference on Business Games.** New Orleans: Tulane University School of Business Administration, 1961.

Greenlaw, P. S., Herron, L. W., and Rawdon, R. H. **Business Simulation.** Englewood Cliffs, New Jersey: Prentice-Hall, 1962.

Kibbee, J. M., Craft, C. J., and Nanus, B. **Management Games: A New Technique for Executive Development.** New York: Reinhold, 1961.

Martin, Elizabeth (ed.). **Top Management Decision Simulation.** New York: American Management Association, 1957.

Rawdon, Richard H. **Learning Management Skills from Simulation Gaming.** Ann Arbor: University of Michigan, Bureau of Industrial Relations, 1960.

Thorelli, H. B., and Graves, R. L. **International Operations Simulation.** New York: Free Press, 1964.

C. Other Games

Blaxall, John. "Manchester." Cambridge, Massachusetts: Abt Associates, 1965, mimeographed report.

Davidson, W. P. "A Public Opinion Game." **Public Opinion Quarterly,** 25 (1961), 210-220.

Duke, Richard. "Gaming Urban Systems." Reprint Series of the Institute for Community Development, Michigan State University, No. 30, 1965-1966.

Feldt, Allan G. **The Cornell Land Use Game.** Miscellaneous Paper No. 3 of the Center for Housing and Environmental Studies, Division of Urban Studies, Cornell University, Ithaca, New York.

Fraser, Herbert W. "Simulation and the Game Approach to the Teaching of Economic Principles." St. Louis: Washington University, 1962, unpublished paper.

Inbar, Michael. "Simulation of Social Processes: The Disaster Game." Baltimore: The Johns Hopkins University, Department of Social Relations, 1965, unpublished paper.

Meier, Richard L. " 'Game' Procedure in the Simulation of Cities." In L. J. Duhl (ed.), **The Urban Condition.** New York: Basic Books, 1963, 348-354.

NOTES

1. For such a bibliography, see Hartman, John J. **Annotated Bibliography on Simulation in the Social Sciences.** Ames: Iowa State University, Agricultural and Home Economics Experimental Station, 1966, a report submitted to the U.S. Office of Civil Defense.

2. A good methodoligcal discussion of evaluation of teaching methods in general is contained in: Waller, Norman and Travers, Robert. "Analysis and Investigation of Teaching Methods." In N. L. Gage (ed.) **Handbook of Research on Teaching.** Chicago: Rand McNally, 1963, 448-505.

> *An additional source of information about new games which are being developed and the schools and other organizations which are using various games is the "Occasional Newsletter about Uses of Simulations and Games for Education and Training," put out by Hall Sprague and his associates in Project Simile, Western Behavioral Sciences Institute, 1121 Torrey Pines Road, La Jolla, California 92037.*

273

Appendix B

MAJOR CENTERS INVOLVED IN RESEARCH AND DEVELOPMENT OF GAMES WITH SIMULATED ENVIRONMENTS

Abt Associates, Inc., 55 Wheeler Street, Cambridge, Massachusetts 02138. Area Code 617, Telephone 491-8850.

This group became incorporated in February, 1965, and includes the following games designers: Clark C. Abt, president; Steven Bornstein, systems analyst; Ray Glazier, anthropologist; Martin S. Gordon, senior operations analyst; Alice J. Kaplan, historian; Holly J. Kinley, sociologist; Peter Merrill, political scientist; Peter S. Miller, systems analyst; Keith Moore, psychologist; Martha O. Rosen, economist; Richard H. Rosen, senior operations analyst; and John Blaxall, now with the World Bank in Washington, D.C.

SIMULATION GAMES
(age groups designated)

AGE GROUPS	NUMBER OF PLAYERS	HOURS NECESSARY TO PLAY
For Elementary School Level:		
Bushman Hunting	5-10	1
Seal Hunting	2-10	1
Market	20-30	2
Sierra Leone	4-30	2
Economy	12	2
For Junior High School Level:		
Adventuring (history)	3-20	1-2
Empire	10-50	2 (1+1)
For Senior High School Level:		
Manchester (economy)	8-40	1-2
Steam	6-15	2
Galapagos (evolution)	6-50	1-2
Grand Strategy (international relations) (for college students also)	20-50	2
For Graduate Students, Adults:		
Politica	50 (40-80)	3
Urbcoin (urban counter-insurgency)	20-50	3
Agile-coin	20-50	3
Adman (banking)		

Abt Associates are involved in research and development of games, primarily on a contractual basis. Basic game descriptions are available on request. Abt Associates does not manufacture or market their games, but can arrange for their quantity production.

Board of Cooperative Educational Services in Northern Westchester (BOCES), Center for Educational Services and Research, (First Supervisory District), 845 Fox Meadow Road, Yorktown Heights, New York 10598. Area Code 914, Telephone: 245-7031.

This project got underway in 1962 and was founded by Office of Education and private grants in 1963. The following people have developed games and/or are working on games at the center: Richard L. Wing, coordinator of curriculum research; Mabel Addis, teacher, Katonah Elementary School, Katonah, New York; Bruse Moncreiff, IBM Systems Development, Los Gatos, California; Jimmer Leonard, graduate student, The Johns Hopkins University, Department of Social Relations; Walter Goodman, project director of Title 3 Demonstration Project.

BOCES has focused on the development of computarized games for individual instruction (Sumeria, Sierra Leone, Free Enterprise). Some can be made available for research by special arrangement.

Carnegie Tech Management Game, Carnegie Institute of Technology, Graduate School of Industrial Administration (GSIA), Schenley Park, Pittsburgh, Pennsylvania 15213. Area Code 412, Telephone: 621-2600.

The Carnegie Tech Management Game began in 1957 as an experiment in business education; it was the first realistic management game to be developed and successfully used in a graduate business school curriculum. Instrumental in its formation in the Graduate School of Industrial Administration are: Richard M. Cyert, dean; William R. Dill, associate dean, now director of the executive program, IBM, White Plains, New York; Kalman J. Cohen, Management Game administrator and professor of economics and industrial administration; Alfred A. Kuehn, associate professor of industrial administration; Jon Heames, director of admissions, C.I.T.; also, Peter R. Winters, associate professor of business administration, Stanford University, Palo Alto, California.

The GSIA has also developed an appendix to the Management Game, the Marketing Analysis Training Exercise. Both are computer simulations which can be played by 1 to 7 people on each of 3 firms, or 3 to 21 players in total. Play may be extended over a number of months within a curriculum or can be compressed into about 24 hours time.

The Management Game can be obtained from the above address by request. Tapes include card listings for the game, initial conditions, 2 months of debug decisions and 12 months of standard history decisions.

The Johns Hopkins University, Department of Social Relations, Charles and 34th Streets, Baltimore, Maryland 21218. Area Code 301, Telephone: HO 7-3300, Ext. 800.

This project began in 1962 and has been funded by the Carnegie Foundation of New York. The games designers include James S. Coleman, professor of social relations; Sarane S. Boocock, research associate; Michael Inbar, former research assistant, now assistant professor, department of sociology, University of Michigan; Erling O. Schild, associate professor of social relations; William H. Starbuck, associate professor of social relations; Gerald Zaltman, research assistant. Project field directors: Mrs. Audrey Suhr and Mrs. Lynn Trowbridge. Several members of the project have formed a non-profit corporation (Academic Games Associates) to facilitate production and distribution of the games.

The following Hopkins Games are designed for high-school age students, although they have been played by both older and younger people:

GAME	NUMBER OF PLAYERS	HOURS NECESSARY TO PLAY
Democracy (Legislature)	6-11	½-¾
(8 independent sections)		
Life Career	6-20	6
Community Response (Disaster)	7-9	4-6
Parent-Child	4-10	¾
Consumer (credit buying)	8-16	1½
High School	6-9	1
Economic Systems	6-13	5-6
Information	6-12	1

These games are in various stages of design, development and production. The Democracy Game can be obtained from the 4-H Foundation, 7100 Connecticut Avenue, N.W., Washington, D.C. 20015. The Life Career Game can be obtained from The Simulmatics Corporation, 16 East 41st Street, New York, New York 10017, which will also be producing the Community Response and other Academic Games Associates games.

Northwestern University International Relations Program, Department of Political Science, Northwestern University, Evanston, Illinois. Area Code 312, Telephone: 492-3741.

The Inter-Nation Simulation (INS) is a product of this program. Work on the INS began in 1957-58, under the direction of the game's originators: Harold Guetzkow, professor of political science, and

Richard C. Snyder, now professor of political science, University of California, Irvine. Among those instrumental in developing the game: James Robinson, professor of political science, Ohio State University; Cleo Cherryholmes, assistant professor of political science and research associate at Social Science Teaching Institute, Michigan State University; Robert Nowell, associate professor of political science, University of California, Santa Barbara; Richard A. Brody, associate professor of political science, Stanford University; Michael Driver, associate professor of psychology, Purdue University; Charles F. Hermann, assistant professor of political science, Princeton University. Now working on the INS at Northwestern: Hiroharu Seki and Paul Smoker, both research associates.

The INS takes 15 to 30 hours and 10 to 35 players can participate. The game is now available from two sources: Science Research Associates, Inc., 259 East Erie Street, Chicago, Illinois 60611; and Western Behavioral Sciences Institute, 1121 Torrey Pines Road, La Jolla, California 92037.

Project SIMILE, Western Behavioral Sciences Institute, 1121 Torrey Pines Road, La Jolla, California 92037. Area Code 714, Telephone: 459-3811.

Project SIMILE began in July 1965 and has been financed by two Kettering Foundation grants. It has been involved in the development of games and with teacher workshops. Personnel include Hall Sprague, director; R. Garry Shirts, research associate; Lee Pratt and Margaret Kelley, research assistants.

Each of the following games has been designed for junior high through adult age levels:

GAME	NUMBER OF PLAYERS	HOURS NECESSARY TO PLAY
Plans	12-30	2-15
Inter-Nation Simulation	10-35	2-15
Business Management Game	9	2-15
Napoli	15-50	3
Crisis	8-16	1- 2

These games are available in kits for 20 or 35 students from the above address.

simulation
& games

AN INTERNATIONAL JOURNAL OF THEORY, DESIGN AND RESEARCH

Editor-in-Chief

MICHAEL INBAR

Hebrew University and Johns Hopkins University

Managing Editor

CLARICE STOLL

Center for Study of Social Organization of Schools, Johns Hopkins University

Editorial Board: Sarane S. Boocock, University of Southern California / James S. Coleman, Johns Hopkins University / Richard Duke, University of Michigan / William Gamson, University of Michigan / Peter House, Envirometrics / Allen Mazur, Stanford University / E. O. Schild, Hebrew University / James Sullivan, University of California, Santa Barbara / John Taylor, University of Sheffield / Gerald Zaltman, Northwestern University

Simulation Review Editors: Layman Allen and Fred Goodman, *University of Michigan*

Simulation and Games is intended to provide a forum for theoretical and empirical papers related to man, man-machine, and machine simulations of social processes. The journal will publish theoretical papers about simulations in research and teaching, empirical studies, and technical papers about new gaming techniques. Each issue will include book reviews, listings of newly available simulations, and short "simulation reviews."

Frequency and price: *Simulation and Games* will be published quarterly in January, April, July, and October—commencing in 1970. Subscription rates will be $15.00 annually—with a one-third discount to faculty and members of professional organizations who wish to purchase personal subscriptions, and a one-half discount to (full-time) students. Special two- and three-year rates are also available. Please add $1.00 per year additional for postage outside the U.S. and Canada.

PLEASE ASK YOUR LIBRARY TO SUBSCRIBE!

SAGE PUBLICATIONS / 275 South Beverly Drive / Beverly Hills, California 90212

EDUCATING AN
URBAN POPULATION

Edited by MARILYN GITTELL, Professor of Political Science, and Director of the Institute for Community Studies, Queens College of the City University of New York. Dr. Gittell, a consultant to the Ford Foundation, was active in the development of the innovative (and controversial) Bundy Plan and has recently completed a comparative study of institutional response in six urban school districts for the Office of Education.

CONTRIBUTORS: *Part I/Demands on School Policy: The Nature of the Problem:* Alan K. Campbell and Philip Meranto; Robert J. Havighurst; Seymour Sacks and David C. Ranney; William G. Buss, Jr.; T. Edward Hollander; Charles A. Glatt and Arliss L. Roaden; *Part II/Decision Making in the Urban School Systems: Case Studies:* Robert L. Crain and David Street; David Rogers; Alan Rosenthal; Marilyn Gittell; Louis H. Masotti; *Part III/Solutions and Goals: Achieving Change:* Werner Z. Hirsch; Richard L. Derr; Gordon J. Klopf and Garda Bowman; Thomas F. Pettigrew; David W. Minar.

Clothbound
$7.50
Paperbound
$3.95
320 pp.

METROPOLITAN AREA SCHOOLS
Resistance to District Reorganization

By BASIL G. ZIMMER, *Professor of Sociology, Brown University,* and AMOS H. HAWLEY, *Professor of Sociology, University of North Carolina (Chapel Hill)*

This volume grew out of an extensive study (funded by the U.S. Office of Education) based on lengthy interviews with hundreds of residents and public officials in six metropolitan areas. The authors analyze use of the schools, knowledge and participation in school related activities, comparative evaluation of city and suburban schools (especially in terms of parents' and officials' satisfaction levels), taxation, views on sources of school support, views on reorganization of school districts, socio-economic and political factors related to resistance to change, and attitudes of public officials toward schools and changes.

The nature of their findings led the authors to conclude that, in certain types of metropolitan areas, reorganization can be ruled out (because such measures could not be passed in any referendum). And, in those areas where reorganization is a workable alternative, the authors note that totally *different* campaigns for support of such proposals must be conducted in the suburbs (where the major effort must be focused to carry them) and the central city.

Clothbound
$7.95
320 pp.
80 Tables

METROPOLITAN AREA SCHOOLS is a fascinating and well-documented analysis of the social, economic and political factors which influence crucial policy decisions affecting the education of millions in central cities and their suburbs.

SAGE PUBLICATIONS, INC. / 275 So. Beverly Dr. / Beverly Hills, Cal. 90212

URBAN SCHOOL ADMINISTRATION

Edited by TROY V. McKELVEY and AUSTIN D. SWANSON,
Department of Educational Administration, State University
of New York at Buffalo

Administrators and supervisors of school systems com-
posing metropolitan areas, as well as university personnel who
train the professional staffs of these schools, need to understand the effects of the desegregation problem on urban school
administration. This volume presents the insights of authorities
in endeavors and disciplines related to urban school administration, in an effort to focus on the problems and potential
resolutions of this challenge.

CONTRIBUTORS: Saul Alinsky, Warren G. Bennis, David K.
Cohen, Frank J. Dressler, Mario D. Fantini, R. Oliver Gibson,
Troy V. McKelvey, Samuel Shepard, Jr., Charles E. Stewart,
Austin D. Swanson, Paul N. Ylvisaker

Clothbound
$7.50
224 pp.

AFFIRMATIVE SCHOOL INTEGRATION: Efforts to Overcome De Facto Segregation in Urban Schools

Edited by ROSCOE HILL, *Yale University,* and MALCOLM FEELEY,
New York University—with a Foreword by JAMES S. COLEMAN

A comparative analysis of eight case studies on the legal and political
problems complicating the elimination of de facto school segregation in
eight northern American cities which were originally prepared as background for *Equality of Educational Opportunity* (the "Coleman
Report"). The greater portion of the material compiled for these
studies has never been published (not even by the government!).

This volume covers for each of the eight cities (Evanston, Berkeley,
New Haven, Pasadena, St. Louis, Albany, San Francisco, and Chicago)
the following questions: (1) What specific issues arose in the context of
the particular city studied? (2) How did school boards handle the
issues? (3) When action was taken by the board, where did the proposal
originate and how was it subsequently modified? (4) What role did the
courts play? (5) Did the question of the legality and/or morality of
distributing school children by race come up? Who raised it? How was
it resolved? (6) Did the board succeed in (a) achieving significant statistical change in racial imbalance, and (b) in resolving community
conflict over the issue?

The book also contains multi-disciplinary review essays of recent
studies on race and education, and a selective bibliography on de facto
school segregation. Contributors include: William G. Buss, Jr., William
Cohen, James S. Coleman, John E. Coons, Ira Michael Heyman, Harold
Horowitz, John Kaplan, Robert Marden, Ralph Reisner, Arnold Rose,
Richard D. Schwartz, Michael Usdan, Clement Vose, and Meyer
Weinberg.

Clothbound
$6.95
192 pp.

SAGE PUBLICATIONS, INC. / 275 So. Beverly Dr. / Beverly Hills, Cal. 90212

Special Issues of
THE AMERICAN BEHAVIORAL SCIENTIST

☐ ADVANCES IN INFORMATION RETRIEVAL IN THE SOCIAL SCIENCES (in two parts). January and February, 1967. Edited by Kenneth Janda. A description of on-going activities in the field. The first issue focuses on operational information retrieval applications, the second on broader, more general, topics. $3.00 each part; $5 together.

☐ COMMUNICATION IN BEHAVIOR AND BEHAVIORAL SCIENCE. Edited by John H. Weakland. April, 1967. Focuses on the "New Communication" — actual communication as it really exists in naturally occurring human systems; and its nature, its relation to behavior, and its relation to behavioral science. $3.00.

☐ ECONOMISTS TODAY. (a survey in two parts). June and September, 1965. Contributors include de Ascarate, Dechert, de Schweinitz, Johnston, Knight, Mingay, Shils, Thimm, Wildavsky and Wilson. $3.00 each part; $5 together.

☐ ENVIRONMENT AND BEHAVIOR. Edited by Allan Blackman and the staff of The Center for Planning and Development Research, University of California (Berkeley). September, 1966. Concerned with the factors which influence human behavior. Planners and social scientists raise opportunities for continued research and analysis. $3.00.

☐ ETHICS AND SOCIAL SCIENCE RESEARCH. Edited by Leonard Reissman and Kalman H. Silvert. June, 1967. Aimed at bringing into focus some of the issues which confront social scientists today. As the editors point out, "these issues are neither of recent origin nor unique to the social sciences, even though it is doubtless true that Project Camelot in 1965 stimulated a surge of interest in the subject and equally true that some facets of these ethical problems have special application to the social sciences." $3.00.

☐ THE FEDERAL GOVERNMENT IN BEHAVIORAL SCIENCE. William W. Ellis, Study Director. May, 1964. A critical analysis of its involvements, commitments and relationships with the social and behavioral sciences ... prepared under the editorial supervision of Alfred de Grazia, Thomas F. Johnson and Evron Kirkpatrick. $3.50.

Order from: SAGE PUBLICATIONS, INC.
275 South Beverly Drive, Beverly Hills, California 90212

☐ FRONTIERS OF LEGAL RESEARCH. December, 1963. Includes articles by Layman E. Allen, Villhelm Aubert, Theodore L. Becker, Ralph S. Brown, Jr., Stuart S. Nagel and Charles Winick. $3.50.

☐ GROUP THERAPY FOR SOCIAL IMPACT: INNOVATION IN LEADERSHIP TRAINING, Edited by Wm. Fawcett Hill. September, 1967. Demonstrates that social agency personnel, other than clinical psychologists and psychiatrists, can learn to do group therapy through a brief in-service training course — analyzing a demonstration course of 50 hours given by the editor and authors to Deputy Probation Officers.

☐ INTERDISCIPLINARY RELATIONSHIPS IN POLITICAL SCIENCE. Edited by Seymour Martin Lipset. November, 1967. Includes "Anthropology and Political Science: Courtship or Marriage?" by Ronald Cohen, "The Shape of Political Theory to Come: From Political Sociology to Political Economy" by William C. Mitchell, and "Personality and Politics: Problems of Evidence, Inference, Conceptualization" by Fred I. Greenstein. $3.50.

☐ THE JUVENILE PROBATION SYSTEM: SIMULATION FOR RESEARCH AND DECISION-MAKING. Edited by A. W. McEachern. January, 1968. Based on a demonstration (including the development of a systematic technique for computer simulation of probation decisions) of a major research project in juvenile probation. $3.50.

☐ MULTINATIONAL COMPARATIVE SOCIAL RESEARCH. Edited by Alexander Szalai. December, 1966. Reports on the Time-Budget Project of the European Coordination Center for Research and Documentation in Social Sciences — and the implications of this major venture in multinational cooperation in comparative research. A separate APPENDIX of tables relating to the study data is also available. $3.00 each; $5.00 together.

☐ THE NEW EDUCATIONAL TECHNOLOGY. Introduction by Jerome Bruner. November, 1962. Articles and essays covering such varied aspects of the educational revolution as "The New Curricula," "Programmed Instruction," "Educational Publishing," "Libraries and Information Retrieval," "The Language Laboratory," "Educational Television and Films," and "Testing, Tests and Testing Service Organizations." $3.50.

Order from: SAGE PUBLICATIONS, INC.
275 South Beverly Drive, Beverly Hills, California 90212

☐ PLANNING EDUCATION FOR THE FUTURE: COMMENTS ON A PILOT STUDY. Edited by Marvin Adelson. March, 1967. Reports on a study, carried out at UCLA under a Kettering Foundation grant by a multidisciplinary group, to "generate some useful perspectives on thinkable changes in American Education." $3.00.

☐ THE POLITICS OF SCIENCE AND DR. VELIKOVSKY. Edited by Alfred de Grazia. September, 1963. A fascinating review of one of the most important and controversial cases in the history of science. $3.50.

☐ SCIENCE AND POLICY. Edited by Gerald Gordon. May, 1967. A consideration of the interaction between science and society — with particular emphasis upon policy-making and administrative decision-making considerations. Contributors include Harold Wolff, Alvin M. Weinberg, Joseph Haberer and Todd LaPorte. $3.00.

☐ SIMULATION GAMES AND LEARNING BEHAVIOR. (in two parts). Edited by James S. Coleman, Sarane S. Boocock and Erling O. Schild. October and November, 1966. In addition to analysis and description of a variety of simulation techniques currently being utilized in an educational environment, includes a selective bibliography on simulation games as learning devices and a listing of major centers involved in research and development of games with simulated environments. $3.00 each part; $5.00 together.

☐ SOCIAL RESEARCH AND LIFE INSURANCE. Edited by John W. Riley, Jr. This issue analyzes basic social research, in addition to offering studies of population, the family, and death. It includes articles by Talcott Parsons, Robert Merton, William Goode, Devereaux Josephs, and Dudley Kirk. $3.50.

☐ SOCIAL RESEARCH IN LATIN AMERICA. Edited by Frank Jay Moreno and Rodman C. Rockefeller. September, 1964. An overview of the problems, philsophical orientations, and assessments of past, present and future area research. $3.50.

Order from: SAGE PUBLICATIONS, INC.
275 South Beverly Drive, Beverly Hills, California 90212

☐ SOCIAL RESEARCH IN SOUTHEAST ASIA. Edited by Stephanie Neuman. June, 1962. Contributors include Roy C. Macridis, Frank N. Trager, Fred W. Riggs, Justus M. van der Kroef, Thomas Hovet, Jr., Samuel Seidman, Ward Morehouse, Carl H. Lande, E. H. Bryan, Jr. and Donn V. Hart. Bibliographic aides noted. $3.50.

☐ URBAN VIOLENCE AND DISORDER. Edited by Louis H. Masotti. March, 1968. The first behavioral science compendium of riot research reports. Contributors include Grimshaw, Quarentelli and Dynes, the Langs, Berkowitz, Nieburg, the Bowens, Gawiser, McCord and Howard, Tomlinson, Levy, Meier, Jenkins, Bwy and Gurr. $3.50.

☐ URBAN STUDIES. Edited by Robert Gutman and David Popenoe. February, 1963. An analysis of present trends and future prospects in this emerging academic field. Among the articles: "The Literature of Urban Studies," "Urban Studies as a Field of Research," "Education for Urban Studies," "Urban Extension," "The Scientific World of the City Planners," "Points of Attack in International Urban Studies," "Centers for Urban Studies — A Review." $3.50.

☐ THE STATE OF THE UNIVERSITY: AUTHORITY AND CHANGE. Edited by Carlos E. Kruytbosch and Sheldon L. Messinger. Contributors include Burton R. Clark, Terry F. Lunsford, Martin Trow, Troy Duster, C. Michael Otten, and the Editors. $3.50.

☐ THE VICOS CASE: PEASANT SOCIETY IN TRANSITION. Edited by Allan R. Holmberg. March, 1965. Based on the Cornell Peru Project, this study analyzes the changing values and institutions of Vicos in the context of national development. It contains a wealth of material for the study of the modernization process, including articles by Holmberg, Vasquez, Doughty, Aylers, Dobyns and Lasswell. $3.50.

The American Behavioral Scientist is published bi-monthly, and includes an annotated bibliographic supplement ("New Studies: A Guide to Recent Publications in the Social and Behavioral Sciences") in each issue. Subscription rates: $10.00 (individuals), $14.00 (institutions), $16.00 (foreign) — *special rates available on two- and three-year subscriptions.*

Order from: SAGE PUBLICATIONS, INC.
275 South Beverly Drive, Beverly Hills, California 90212